Death in Ten Minutes

Also by Fern Riddell

The Victorian Guide to Sex:
Desire and Deviance in the 19th Century

FERN RIDDELL

Death in
Ten Minutes

The Forgotten Life of
Radical Suffragette Kitty Marion

Quercus

New York • London

Quercus

New York • London

ISBN 978-1-63-506129-1

Library of Congress Cataloging-in-Publication Data is on file.

Distributed in the United States and Canada by
Hachette Book Group
1290 Avenue of the Americas
New York, NY 10104

Manufactured in the United States

10 9 8 7 6 5 4 3 2 1

www.quercus.com

Contents

London, 1913   1

Manchester, 1913   3

To Begin   7

Chapter 1: A Vindication of the Rights of Woman   15

Chapter 2: An Escape   33

Chapter 3: "What soul-satisfying exhilarations"   49

Chapter 4: Love & Lies   71

Chapter 5: "Now I was awake"   93

Chapter 6: Death in Ten Minutes   117

Chapter 7: No Surrender!   145

Chapter 8: Betrayal Takes Many Forms   175

Chapter 9: Sex: A Woman's Choice   203

Chapter 10: Kitty's Legacy—One Hundred Years Later   223

With Thanks   235

Notes   237

Index   257

Picture Acknowledgments   269

London, 1913

Imagine we have spent the day at the National Portrait Gallery, among the paintings of figures and images from history. Our clothes are heavy, our feet are tired, and we leave the airless relics of the past to step out into the crisp London air. Facing Trafalgar Square, you see a woman standing on the plinth between two lions; her voice carries on the breeze toward us, and we catch snatches of her words. Moving closer, we are caught in a crowd that pushes and pulls like a tidal wave, barely kept in check by the police officers who dart in and out of the throng, removing men and women who fight and kick, eager to hear this diminutive figure speak. A line of policemen guard her feet, holding back the crowd from the edge of where she stands, to make room for the journalists, elbow to elbow, who furiously scribble down her words on their paper pads for the next edition.

As we push our way through this vocal congregation and move along toward the bustling street of the Strand, a woman catches your eye. She is Indian, the goddaughter of Queen Victoria, and stands, ferocious, on the corner selling copies of a magazine written by the organization led by the woman on the platform. She wears a sash of purple, green, and white. Perhaps we stop and speak to her, perhaps we move quickly past, but within a few hundred feet another woman, with the same sash and the same fierce, daring stare, stands in our way. She

wears a placard over her chest announcing a new and exciting matinee just around the corner. There is a political play about the rights of
women being shown, and a queue is already forming. Suddenly, a deep
boom sounds from the direction of St. Paul's, and frightened birds fill
the air. A man struggles to keep control of his carthorse as a growing
surge of people rush past, shouting, "A bomb! A bomb! They put a
bomb in St. Paul's!"

This is 1913, and it is the time of the suffragettes.

Manchester, 1913

Here, sneaking through the Mancunian twilight, is Kitty Marion, music hall star and militant suffragette, disguising her red hair under a mill girl's shawl. She makes her way through Alexandra Park toward the glasshouse, where she leaves a pipe bomb primed to explode in the early morning. This is not her first attack, nor will it be her last, as she is a member of the Women's Social and Political Union (WSPU)—a soldier in the war raging across Britain, and the world, to give women the vote. Kitty Marion and the many women like her are part of a violently radical and dedicated branch of the suffrage movement, which conducted a nationwide campaign of terror that has never been truly acknowledged in our history before.

At half past four in the morning, on Tuesday, November 11, 1913, the cactus house in Manchester's Alexandra Park was reduced to rubble by "a stout brass tube, about three inches in diameter, and strengthened at one end by a stout brass cap, which was screwed on to it." The *Leeds Mercury* pored over every detail of the device, as police began a frantic hunt for the person or persons unknown who could carry out such violence. ". . . [T]he brass cap had been bored for the insertion of the fuse. The tube was about fifteen inches long, and in addition to a heavy charge of powder it contained a miscellaneous collection of pieces of metal, including such articles as a bed key, an iron chain, bolts, nuts and nails . . ."[1] To those picking through the debris it was clear the force of the explosion had scattered the contents of the bomb over a wide area, far from the twisted ruins of the cactus house itself.

Manchester had suffered an earlier attack by the suffragettes in April. Annie Briggs, Evelyn Manesta, and Lillian Forrester attacked numerous paintings in the Manchester Art Gallery, seizing the opportunity to smash the glass coverings of Frederic Leighton's *The Last Watch of Hero* and *Sibylla Delphica* by Edward Burne-Jones as the museum began to close at 9:00 p.m. As the attack—or "outrage," as the press often called them—took place, supporters of the women's movement had unfurled a "Votes For Women" banner in the gallery, fighting off the attendants who attempted to wrestle them into submission and tear the banner down.

The April attack was not unique. Organized in a wave of retaliation to the sentencing of the WSPU's leader—the fifty-four-year-old Moss Side native Emmeline Pankhurst—to three years in jail after she had admitted to "inciting persons unknown" to bomb the holiday cottage of the chancellor of the exchequer, David Lloyd George—numerous attacks were now taking place across the country. These "suffragette outrages" grew in violence and intensity in the years before the First World War, ranging from window-breaking, chemical attacks on mailboxes, and the cutting of telegraph and telephone wires, to the arson and bombings of churches, railway carriages and stations, MPs' homes, racecourses, golf courses, sporting pavilions, theaters, public parks, banks, newspaper offices, and museums. Anywhere you could find a woman, you could find a suffragette bomb. And yet we know so little about the women operating on this self-declared "danger duty." Why did they choose such extreme and violent action to make a political protest? What had happened to them that led to their decision to leave a bomb in a public place? Today, we find such actions morally repugnant, the tools of outsiders and organizations whose values deeply contradict our own. So how do we feel when we discover these actions in a movement we idolize? Is there room for our heroes to be flawed?

The Manchester attack, along with the many others Kitty Marion carried out on behalf of the WSPU, has long been hidden from our acknowledged history of the fight for the vote. But Kitty kept her own record, an unpublished autobiography detailing her life and actions as a suffragette and birth control activist, as she fought for respect and equality for women in all areas of their lives. Her unique story shines a light on the previously ignored actions of many involved in the women's movement, and shows us that they committed to a plan of action that violently contradicted their supposed place in society, and the rules of men.

To Begin

History is full of secrets. Untold lives that have been forgotten as the victors have decided what and, more importantly, who should be remembered. For people like me, the role of a historian is often to act as a gatekeeper; we are conduits between the past and present, supposedly maintaining an unbiased and clinical view of the facts and events that have shaped our nations and our identities. Our written history, taught in schools and universities, the basis for films and television dramas, and the answer to a question at a trivia night, is an amalgamation of facts, events, and the story historians have wanted to tell you. But a gatekeeper does more than allow stories out—they also keep stories in.

Perhaps then it would be better to call historians secret-keepers. We uncover and recover lives, feelings, and emotions of the past with the same frenzy as a child at Christmas, tearing through archives and memories in pursuit of a perfect story, for something that is always just out of reach—a complete and unequivocal historical truth. But, as many historians know, truth is a relative concept, and our history has often fallen victim to a lack of it. From the ignorance of western internment camps for Japanese Americans during the Second World War, to the existence of Britain's multicultural heritage since the Roman period, or the violent terrorism committed by the suffragettes in the run-up to the First World War, our relationship to truth and history is one still being defined by whoever is in power. Secrets and stories, and the lives of those who have challenged the powerful, lie hidden in archives and museums across the world.

For women, it is often only our leaders who have been memorialized. Queens, courtesans, spies, and revolutionaries have all found their place in history, and in our collective memory. These leaders are often idolized for what they represent, extraordinary women in power when ordinary women had none. And no women are more rightfully idolized than the leaders of the suffragettes, without whom there would have been little chance of women gaining access to the vote and without whom the society we have today would not exist. But for a long time the lives of real women, rather than solely our figureheads, have been ignored. These women—the wives, mothers, workers, writers, and activists who joined the ranks of the early women's movement—often carried out the directives and commands of those in power. But their experiences have been forgotten, left in the dust of a movement often concerned with projecting just the right image, and just the right sort of feminism. Women are no different than men when we are in power; we seek to control and manipulate our story, and in this case our history, to avoid anything that might be uncomfortable. To exclude what we cannot make conform. Because no matter how we look at it, feminism, from the nineteenth century to today, has been a club where not everyone has been welcome. It has required a conformity to the rules, a rejection of sexual identities, and an unwavering commitment to those who assumed leadership. Because of this, the women who should be at the heart of our history have been hidden, forgotten, and betrayed by those who were supposed to keep their legacy alive.

This book will challenge everything you thought you knew about the suffragettes. Beyond the marches and the women who chained themselves to railings lies another group, which operated under cover of darkness from the heart of the suffragette movement to carry out a nationwide bombing and arson campaign the likes of which Britain had never seen before—and has not experienced since. I am going to tell you two stories: first, the incredible life of Kitty Marion, taken from her own words as she spent a lifetime fighting for women's rights; and second, the story of why this life has been hidden from us. To do this, we need to go back to a time before the suffragettes, to explore the forces that set modern feminism on its path. We need to understand that those who have sought to be in control of our history of women decided to tell only one story and to exclude those voices, those women's lives, that did not conform. These are stories that need to be told.

Kitty Marion, or Katherine Marie Schäfer (1871–1944) as she was born, was a German child immigrant to the East End of London. She arrived in 1886, two years before the city was terrorized by the murders of Jack the Ripper, with his violent attacks on the women of the East End. Starting her English life in a quiet domestic bubble out toward Epping Forest, Kitty cared for the children of her aunt, while London jostled and manipulated the deaths of Mary Ann Nichols, Catherine Eddowes, Elizabeth Stride, Annie Chapman, and Mary Jane Kelly into arguments about women on the streets, in public spaces, and, of course, as sexual beings. The fact that these murders occurred among women who sometimes bolstered their economic position through sex work—a revenue stream many women in the Victorian century took advantage of—was a final nail in the coffin of public female sexual independence. Sex not only risked a woman's reputation, now it also risked her life.

At times, it seems as if we have hardly moved on from this view, and for many in our current society, sexually empowered or knowledgeable women threaten the very fabric of our world. *Sex*, it seems, is still a dirty word. Feminists have long struggled with women and sex, focusing on the manipulation men could exact rather than on the pleasure women might enjoy. But for Kitty Marion sex was at the heart of her fight for female equality. She knew, firsthand, the reality of sexual danger that many women faced, as she found herself subjected to multiple sexual assaults and attacks during her career as an actress and singer in the music halls. The expectation that a woman would be required to trade her body for employment utterly infuriated her, as she believed beyond a shadow of a doubt that a woman should have a right to work, earn money, and be independent without being subjected to sexual harassment. But she also understood the nature of love and its relationship to sex, and her desire to empower women to have control over their own bodies saw her become a leading birth control activist, the final stage in the evolution of her belief that women should be free to live whatever life they choose.

As Kitty began to fight for her right to work without fear of sexual harassment, another social revolution was taking place across British society. The campaign for women to get the vote had been gaining momentum since the mid–nineteenth century and, following Queen Victoria's death in 1901, a new radically charged wing of the suffrage movement had emerged in 1903. Formed by the previous founders of the Manchester-based Women's Franchise League—the powerful Pankhurst family—the Women's Social and Political Union maneuvered their way to center stage in the fight to give women the vote. Splitting from the National Union of Women's Suffrage Societies, the Pankhursts took to the streets and the press, encouraging the members of the WSPU to fight the government with "Deeds, Not Words": with militant action, not simply political debate. For Marion, it was a radical ideology that answered the aggressive and violent assaults she had been subjected to throughout her working life, and that offered a clear way to combat the social attitudes that dominated her world—the misogynistic belief that any man had a physical right to any woman's body, without her consent.

As a suffragette soldier, Marion traveled across the country, utilizing her music hall contacts as a network to hide herself, and her knowledge and experience of costumes to help her conduct a bombing and arson campaign in the fight for the vote. She was imprisoned multiple times, and during one single imprisonment was subjected to 232 force-feedings, which destroyed her singing voice.[1] She joined the suffragettes to fight for protection within her industry, and she sacrificed her talent for the cause. The sheer multitude of force-feedings that she endured is incredible when compared to other, better known suffragettes—Emily Wilding Davison was force-fed forty-nine times in the entirety of her suffrage activism, and the government had to deny it was or would be force-feeding WSPU leader Emmeline Pankhurst in 1913, after hysterical reports in the *Dundee Courier* that she had been force-fed once and was at the point of collapse.[2] Yet, lauded and applauded for her courage in her own time as she was, Kitty Marion's name is virtually unknown today.

The outbreak of war in 1914 forced Marion to flee England for America, after a malicious letter from an old friend accused her of being a spy for Germany.[3] The British establishment, gleeful at a chance to rid themselves of such a notoriously dangerous woman, sent her with a personal police escort to the Liverpool docks. Once in the United States, friendless and alone, Kitty discovered an opportunity to carry on the fight for female empowerment by joining Margaret Sanger's new birth control movement. She faced imprisonment, poverty, and assaults for the rest of her life, traveling between the United States and the UK to promote the campaign for sex education and female empowerment until her death in 1944. In her lifetime women not only won the right to the vote, but also saw the scientific breakthroughs that would lead to the development of the contraceptive pill. Although Kitty, and many women like her, fought hard for sex education, female freedom, and bodily empowerment, their stories have been hidden, passed over in favor of women who appear to be paragons of virtue. Feminism has not often been welcoming to the women who believe sex is something that should be enjoyed.

The battle for female emancipation raged throughout the nineteenth century. But it was governed by very strict, conservative forces, which have since dominated the suffrage movement's history. Piecing together the threads of such a movement, which has a complex relationship with women and sex, allows us to begin to understand why the lives and activism of women like Kitty Marion have so often been suppressed from our mainstream historical story. It opens up to us the world and society that Kitty Marion grew up in, which influenced her life as a feminist, as a fighter, and as a writer. We have to understand the manipulation of our history surrounding this complex and divided movement, one that has been specifically recorded to exclude some voices and legitimize others, because otherwise Marion's role feels like an aberration. While she is herself unique, she was not alone in her desires, her beliefs, or her actions. The link between sex and suffrage, between arson, anarchy, and female activism, existed for many Victorian and Edwardian women but has never before, in the history of the suffragette movement, been openly acknowledged. This story has been silenced, even denied, and the voices of women who faced the same battles we are still fighting today on consent, sexual empowerment, and sexual harassment have been left in archives and unpublished memoirs across the world.

Throughout history, the idea of feminism, of universal equality for all—of women's worth not only to society, but also to themselves—has never been defined by just one single organization. And once you begin to look at the history of feminism in this country outside of what we were taught in schools, a very different world appears. We are given a chance to reexamine the story and to challenge the identity of early feminists solely as sexless prudes who wrote pamphlets, by discovering women who advocated for your right to safe sex at the same time as they advocated for your right to vote.

Before now, to be a woman in the nineteenth century has been universally regarded as to be stuck in a life of suffering, especially where sex is concerned. For too long we have labored under the misapprehension that Victorian women knew nothing about sex, that they "lay back and thought of England," covered chair legs, and were so disconnected from their own bodies that they allowed doctors to use clunky and rudimentary devices to bring them to orgasm, simply as a cure for hysteria. None of this is true. Although influenced by the image of a

British woman on the throne, Victorian Britain is often portrayed as a time when women were little more than figures to be pitied, either facing terrible struggles due to their lack of social or economic rights, or becoming brave heroines suffering for their revolution.

After Victoria's death in 1901, the dramatic rise of a militant campaign to give women the vote has been memorialized by the sacrifices of its members; Emily Wilding Davison's death under the hooves of the king's horse at the Epsom Derby in 1913, and the traumatic imprisonments and brutal force-feedings of many other brave suffragettes. No matter where women are found in feminist history, they have been portrayed as demanding our pity. But by changing the narrative, by looking at these women not as victims, but as survivors and fighters, I want to show you a world where women pushed our world's politics and culture into the modern age. Where sex, far from being a woman's curse, became defined as her choice. Where men were held accountable for their actions, and women were not victims, but soldiers and leaders.

1

A Vindication of the
Rights of Woman

So where to begin? How do you define a movement that argued for women to be recognized in a world they had been navigating since the dawn of time? At what point do we believe women simply "woke up" and began to fight for, and demand, equality and rights protected by law? For many, the dawn of modern feminist thought begins with Mary Wollstonecraft's passionate 1792 work, *A Vindication of the Rights of Woman*. In this tiny but revelatory book Wollstonecraft argued that—much like today—the biggest problem with her society was that women were taught only to be beautiful and ornamental, and never to use their brains. She advocated a world where men and women were seen as equals, and sex was no longer used to keep one portion of society in the home and out of intellectual life. Although her name is well known, and she is now rightfully acknowledged as a beginning for the modern feminist, in the century after her death her writings were often dismissed by conservative feminists due to her sex life, her affairs with married men, and her children born out of wedlock. Fear of the Wollstonecraft "wildness," her uninhibited sexuality, drove her work out of mainstream feminism until the 1890s.[1] But soon her beliefs would reemerge as the ideological mother of the suffragettes' "wild women" bombers.

Born in London on April 27, 1759, Wollstonecraft endured abuse from an early age at the hands of an alcoholic father and a neglectful, beaten mother, an origin story she shares with Kitty Marion. One of seven children, she grew up in a household that lived beyond its means, with a father whose inability to care for and protect his family saw a teenage Mary often sleeping on the floor outside her mother's bedroom to stop her father from entering it in a drunken rage and beating his wife.[2] This early experience of married life and female subjugation defined Mary's attitudes to the place of women in the world and, more importantly, showed her how misused women were by the unfair laws and social rules of the eighteenth century.

At a time when one of England's closest neighbors, France, was caught in a violent social revolution that swept away the previous structures of power and painted powerful images of women's new place in the world, Mary Wollstonecraft began to form her own new and revolutionary belief in womankind. Much of her life had been dedicated to the teaching and education of young women, and she knew firsthand that a woman's mind was her most important asset in combating the sexism and social dismissal women often experienced. She argued that the perceived differences between men's and women's ability had only come about because women were not allowed to be educated to the same level as men: "Women everywhere are in this deplorable state; for, in order to preserve their innocence, as ignorance is courteously termed, truth is hidden from them."[3] In Wollstonecraft's mind, this truth, or knowledge of the world, was as much a right for women as it was for men.

Mary gained a sudden and unexpected celebrity when she published a reaction to Edmund Burke's anti-revolution pamphlet *Reflections on the Revolution in France*. Her *Vindication of the Rights of Men* (1790), originally published anonymously, remains one of the most powerful critiques of conservatism and traditional power structures, selling out within three weeks of its first publication. Demand for a second edition, naming the author, grew to a roar; the revelation that the author was a woman set the literary world of London alight. Not long after this, and now a household name, Mary set her mind to advocating the rights of women, and two years later published the work that has cemented her place in history. *A Vindication of the Rights of Woman* is now renowned as one of the most influential works on female enfranchisement, and Mary herself as one of the leaders in forming modern political thought. Her attitude and belief in education were shared by Kitty Marion, and by many in the suffrage movement; we can see Wollstonecraft's beliefs reemerging throughout Marion's own writings as she continued the fight against ignorance, often portrayed in Marion's time as sexual innocence, a century after Wollstonecraft began it.

With such character, ability, and wealth of empowering feminist works, you might have thought that Mary Wollstonecraft's legacy would have been claimed by the Victorian feminists who followed her only sixty years later. But sadly this was not to be. While Wollstonecraft's intellectual work has made her a figurehead of the feminist movement, her private life excluded her from much of the arguments and organization of the women's movement in the nineteenth century. Wollstonecraft's early experience of her parents' marriage led her to a rejection of traditional social rules, and she had two children by two different lovers: Fanny, whose American father, Gilbert Imlay, met Mary in Paris during the French Revolution in 1792, abandoning her there shortly after Fanny's birth in 1794; and Mary, the daughter of William Godwin, with whom Wollstonecraft appears to at last have found happiness before her death in 1797.

Godwin was an English writer and philosopher who fell in love with Wollstonecraft's writing before meeting her in person. While reading her account of traveling in Europe in 1796, which detailed her desolation at Imlay's betrayal, he wrote, "She speaks of her sorrows, in a way that fills us with melancholy, and dissolves us in tenderness, at the same time that she displays a genius which commands all our admiration."[4] Although both William and Mary had argued against the need for marriage—"As long as I seek," wrote William in 1793, "by despotic and artificial means, to maintain my possession of a woman, I am guilty of the most odious selfishness"[5]—they bent to society's wishes and married during Mary's pregnancy in 1797. However, although this legitimized the birth of their daughter, Mary Godwin, it also made clear to English society that, as Imlay still lived, Wollstonecraft had not been married when she had given birth to Fanny. Whatever joy Mary and Godwin shared was short-lived, as she died ten days after giving birth to their daughter. Godwin published a memoir of her remarkable life and beliefs the following year, 1798, which sadly only further tarnished Wollstonecraft's reputation for the Victorians, as did the posthumously published edition of her novel, *Maria: or, The Wrongs of Woman*. This novel, following the life of a woman imprisoned in an insane asylum by her husband, exposed and celebrated female desire and sexuality, even while it identified men's ability to misuse and abandon women when they exhibited a passionate nature. Wollstonecraft's sex life, and her willingness to identify women as sexual beings, led to her rejection by the Victorian feminists, for whom sex was a subject that had to be controlled at all costs. Sexual transgression had no place in the feminist movement.

But Wollstonecraft's legacy did not die with her. It had a direct and clear influence on her daughter, Mary Godwin. Raised by her father and new stepmother, Mary Jane Clairmont, alongside her half-sister, Fanny, and a brother and sister from Mary Jane's previous marriage, Charles and Claire, by the age of fifteen Mary Godwin was a force to be reckoned with. Her father, whose publishing firm was now failing, formed a connection to the poet Percy Bysshe Shelley, who found the teenage Mary captivating. They soon began to meet at Wollstonecraft's grave in St. Pancras, and in 1814 ran away to Paris with Mary's stepsister, Claire. Shelley left behind him a pregnant wife, Harriet, who, after two years of attempting to win Shelley back from both the Continent and

Mary, drowned herself in the Serpentine in Hyde Park. Shortly after this, Mary and Shelley married, and only two years later she published the work that has cemented her own place in literary history, *Frankenstein: or, The Modern Prometheus*. The themes of this Gothic horror, its combination of sex and science, of danger and manipulation as man plays God, are not that far removed from attitudes surrounding sex, women, and marriage that both Mary and her mother experienced and advocated against during their lifetimes. Written a little over twenty years after Mary's mother's passionate defense of female education, Dr. Frankenstein's corruption of science and his manipulation of human anatomy speaks as much to the emerging power of male doctors over the female body in the nineteenth century as it does to the powerlessness of women at the hands of the men who controlled the world around them.

The first edition, published anonymously in 1818, carried in its preface a quote from Milton's *Paradise Lost*, "Did I request thee, Maker, from my clay / To mould me man?" The choice of this simple set of words not only portrays the monster's final hatred of his existence, but is also redolent of Mary Shelley's own despair at the role being carved out for women in the nineteenth century. As her mother pointed out in her *Vindication*, the only justification for the perceived capabilities of men and women in the nineteenth century came from the clay they were made from—the bodies their minds inhabited. And just as Frankenstein's shattered and reassembled monster seeks to find his perfect mate, with whom he could experience every facet of marriage, from companionship to sex, the Victorians were obsessed with how their own sexual choices could impact the idea of true love. Mary Shelley's acknowledgment of this very human desire showcases that throughout the nineteenth century the search for true love, sex, and equality was a part of women's lives. This belief was shared by Kitty Marion, who knew beyond doubt that sex was both a thing of beauty and a tool of abuse.

* * *

Ever since the publication of their works, both Mary Shelley and Mary Wollstonecraft have been defined by their "unconventional" sex lives, which simply means they did not always marry their partners, or that their partners had been married to others. For much of the twentieth century, as women's lives began to be written about, those who had rejected what was defined as respectable sexual behavior—propriety, modesty, celibacy—were deemed historical oddities. Historians writing in this era, looking back on the sexual attitudes and the sex lives of our ancestors, focused on the repression and rejection of sex by both the feminist movement and the medical fraternity. How to be a woman and, more importantly, a woman who deserved equal rights with men, became intrinsically linked to the idea of sexual respectability. This attitude has stayed with us. We hold women to a far higher level of accountability than men for their sexual behavior, and a reputation for promiscuity is used to damage women in a way that it has never damaged men. Sex remains dangerous, and it is only by removing sex from a woman's character that it is possible for her to stand, unthreateningly, on the same platforms as men.

However, identifying women like Wollstonecraft and Shelley not as oddities but as the beginning of a feminist movement where the reality of sex and female sexuality is clearly acknowledged allows us to see a new pattern emerge from within our history that stretches from Wollstonecraft, through Shelley, to Kitty Marion and the suffragettes, Margaret Sanger, and the sex-positive feminist movement today.

So why did early feminists forget about sex? And why has it taken so long for us to reclaim an experience that is universally shared, and yet so often used to corrupt and manipulate women into powerless positions? To understand this, we have to turn to the women of the Victorian era, whose dedicated campaigning for both female enfranchisement and sexual safety—successfully raising the age of consent from thirteen to sixteen in 1885—clearly laid the foundations for the battles and arguments of the suffragettes. Unfortunately, it is not solely men who are to blame for the desexualization of women in pursuit of their rights, but the women themselves who chose to reject what they saw as immoral, deviant, or sensual behavior in women, as sex was the only aspect of womanhood over which they could exert control. By dividing women into those who were good or bad, wives and mothers against sexualized, sensual, unmarried women, they began to define a woman's worth not by what had been traditionally perceived as her passionate and emotional nature, but instead by her modern, calm, moral respectability.

In 1860, the *Saturday Review* remarked that society seemed "to have arrived" at a moment when the "most interesting" image of womanhood was one only concerned with its "degradation."[6] The *Review*'s acknowledgment of the extent to which prostitution—and, therefore, womanhood and its relationship to sex—had become a focus for Victorian society is not surprising. This is the decade of governmental attempts to control and regulate the sex industry, under a horrific period of legislation known as the Contagious Diseases Acts of 1864, 1866, and 1869.

These deceptively titled Acts were not—as modern audiences might assume—a defense against the tropical viruses and diseases brought back by colonial expansion, or regulations to control the spread of common epidemics, such as cholera or typhoid, that so often hit the slum areas of the big industrial cities. These Acts, enforced across cities throughout the south of England, not only introduced registers of prostitutes, but also forced many women to submit to aggressive internal examinations and dangerous treatments for sexually transmitted diseases. They had one specific purpose, and that was to establish a quarantine zone within a certain radius of specific military bases—both port and inland. Within these zones, the women with whom soldiers and sailors were known to spend time, whether that was as wives, lovers, or the mothers of their children, could be arrested, forcefully examined for signs of sexual "contagious" disease, and then placed in a "Lock Hospital" (often just a locked hospital ward) while they were treated, with little or no access to the outside world. You might think that this would be an ideal moment for some inventive Victorian to suggest that one of the many forms of birth control available at the time—from condoms to vaginal douches—would be of benefit against the rise of STDs. But sadly that was not to be.

The Contagious Diseases Acts were created to try to stem the seemingly torrential tide of syphilitic infection in the armed forces. Previous investigations into sexually transmitted diseases had unsuccessfully tried to regulate the men, but, it was recorded, this had had far too detrimental an effect on the morale of both the men and the doctors ministering to them. Men were *embarrassed* to be infected, they were *embarrassed* to seek treatment. Much like today, with the arguments surrounding male contraception, this embarrassment of men was placed far ahead of the medical needs and bodily rights of women.

Facing an STD infection rate of epidemic proportions—the *Lancet* had reported in 1860 that within the armed forces, "508 of every 1,000 men, one in every two, were venereal patients"—the government chose to implement a new Act on the recommendations of a singularly small group of doctors. These recommendations solely targeted women as the cause and transmitters of disease, rather than the male soldiers and sailors. The impact of these Acts on the communities they controlled was extreme. The Acts were passed very quickly; the women targeted—the working classes—were of little interest to respectable members of society.[7] As it was women who were believed to be the carriers of the disease, it was women, not men, who needed to be controlled. The Acts were extended to the wider population in 1869, and soon terrible stories, where women simply disappeared from their own lives, homes, and families, began to appear in the press.

In response to women's growing fear for the scope and scale of the Acts, and the abuses it allowed, the Ladies National Association for the Repeal of the Contagious Diseases Acts was founded, led by

Josephine Butler, a Northumberland woman who wrote and campaigned against the sex trade throughout her life. Writing under the guise of "An Englishwoman" in *The Daily News*, she argued against the misogyny of the Acts, saying:

> Permit me to explain, in a brief but careful way, what the danger is in which we find our country and everybody in it involved, through the ignorance and carelessness of whole classes of our countrymen, whose duty it is to know better, the apathy of legislators who have permitted the destruction of our most distinctive liberties before their eyes, and the gross prejudices and coarse habits of thought of professional men who have been treated as oracles on a subject on which they are proved mistaken at every turn.[8]

The Acts helped to create a rhetoric that saw any enjoyment of sex—any view that sex should not be restricted merely to the act of procreation—now portrayed as something bad, associated with disease and sexual immorality. In the public world, sex for its own sake was now inherently linked to prostitution. So middle- and upper-class women were forced to claim their respectability through sexual purity, and sexual knowledge became unfashionable, immoral, and to be avoided.[9] Much like the rhetoric surrounding sexual assault today, there was a belief that men were not in control of their sexual desires, and it was the responsibility of women—morally pure, and sexually passive, women—to make sure that men were not put in a situation where they might lose self-control. For the conservative Victorian feminists, this meant placing strict rules on sexual behavior and respectability; and for the conservative misogynists, an old-fashioned idea took hold, advocating that prostitutes were required by men to protect virtuous women from men's uncontrollable lusts. Men were not able to control themselves and needed access to public women—sex workers—for the safety of society. Either way, good sexual behavior was not a man's responsibility.

But not all Victorian feminists were engaged in attacks on sex. In fact, some were actively attempting to use sex to refine and refute society's control and subjugation of women. Perhaps the true heir to Wollstonecraft and Shelley's legacy is Annie Besant, the social reformer and political campaigner whose career spanned multiple continents and almost an entire century. Born in London in 1847, Annie's middle-class family found themselves penniless after her father's death, yet she managed to acquire a good education and a passionate belief in the independence of women. Married at the age of twenty to a young evangelical clergyman, she was heavily influenced by the radical writings of social reformers based in Manchester in the 1860s. But the subjects of Irish independence, poverty, social reform, and birth control quickly caused discord between the newly married pair. Worse still, her husband, Frank Besant, demanded that Annie turn over her entire income from her writing—as her husband, any money she made belonged to him.

It would be easy, perhaps, to dismiss Annie as yet another victim of the Victorian patriarchy, were it not for her whole and total rebellion against the state in which she found herself. Deciding on what many conservative Victorian feminists would have viewed as an unthinkable course of action, in the early 1870s she left her husband and arrived in London with her small daughter in tow, quickly becoming an active and forceful speaker for the National Secular Society. She formed a close relationship with Charles Bradlaugh, the society's founder, and wrote and published several pamphlets, gave lectures, and advocated a form of practical secular morality that won her as many admirers as it did detractors. But as our feminist history is so often dominated by the image of women as sexual victims, not as defenders of sexual awareness, the revolutionary actions of women like Annie are often ignored. She is now only remembered for her advocacy of the "Match Girls Strike" of 1888, where the women of the Bryant and May match factory staged a dramatic walkout to draw attention to their terrible living and working conditions.

As a journalist, Annie's commitment to documenting the hardships the women faced informed Charles Bradlaugh's parliamentary speeches on the subject, and soon the women had won the right to better and safer working conditions. Although Annie's activism on behalf of the match girls won her many admirers—and saw her begin a friendship with none other than the future leader of the suffragette movement, Emmeline Pankhurst—her name was already well known in England because of her long-held desire to educate people on birth control and safe sex. It is her legacy that belongs to Kitty Marion, and forms another link in the unacknowledged chain of female activism from the eighteenth to the twentieth century.

Although birth control was widely discussed by British society throughout the nineteenth century, the influence and power of the women's movement's condemnation of sexual knowledge promoted an increasing ignorance of birth control and sexual agency. But, outside of those conservative attitudes, discussion of contraception and sexual freedom was rampant. Just as Mary Shelley began to create Frankenstein's monster, Francis Place, arguably the father of the British birth control movement, began to make waves in 1822. His publication, *Illustrations and Proofs of the Principle of Population*, sought to reconcile the opposing views of William Godwin, Mary Shelley's father, and Thomas Malthus, who advocated the need to limit a population to its economic means, although Malthus had expressly argued against the use of birth control, instead instructing "moral restraint" in sexual relationships.

In 1823, Place began to distribute handbills of his arguments in favor of the use of birth control (specifically the vaginal sponge) entitled *The Married of Both Sexes* and *The Married of Both Sexes of the Working People*, which spread widely across London and in the heavily populated northern towns and cities. There is even a suggestion that when a seventeen-year-old John Stuart Mill (the English philosopher, and the first MP to support women's suffrage) was arrested for distributing pamphlets, it was Place's handbills he was carrying.[10]

Not long after Place's handbills caused such an uproar in England, in 1832 the Massachusetts-born Dr. Charles Knowlton quietly began to distribute his *Fruits of Philosophy: or The Private Companion of Young Married People*; and this practical little book hit British shores two years later. A well-known and highly respected doctor by his death in 1851, Knowlton chose to write a guide to the reproductive act, including ideas and methods of birth control, for his patients. His interest in sexuality and human interaction may have stemmed from his own experiences as a seventeen-year-old boy, suffering from *gonorrhea dormientium* (also known as nocturnal emissions, and for modern audiences colloquially called a "wet dream"), which he recorded in a later casebook: "[It] alarmed me exceedingly ... I do not think I ever met with one so mentally wretched as I was. I think that onanism has much to do in causing this disease ..."[11]

Knowlton's primary objective was to reduce the fear many inexperienced couples felt when first engaging in sexual relations, by providing a clear and careful guide on what these relations might entail.[12] When the text was first published in England in 1834 it yielded a yearly circulation of 700, until 1877, when it was republished to great social fanfare by Annie Besant and Charles Bradlaugh, reaching a new circulation of 125,000 in a matter of months.[13] In 1893, Besant published the story of her life, *An Autobiography*, and maintained that Knowlton's pamphlet had been sold unchallenged in the UK since the 1830s, endorsed by scholars such as John Stuart Mill.[14]

> The book was never challenged till a disreputable Bristol bookseller put some copies on sale to which he added some improper pictures, and he was prosecuted and convicted. The publisher of the National Reformer and of Mr. Bradlaugh's and my books and pamphlets had taken over a stock of Knowlton's pamphlets among other literature he had bought.[15]

Yet the influence of this text, its constant publication from the 1830s onward, and the dramatic rise in its popularity during the 1870s is never discussed by historians. Exposing this work sheds light on the unacknowledged influence of women in the birth control movement prior to Marie Stopes and Margaret Sanger, and contrasts with the desexualized history that has been guided by the attitudes of early feminist campaigners. Contraception was not a new idea to the Victorian world. Agricultural almanacs from the 1840s had included recipes for the homemade *baudruche*—a reusable condom made from the intestines of a sheep—among their healthcare and farming advice.[16] While the religious and intellectual worlds may have argued over the morality of a "checking of conception," practical aids and methods to that effect were incredibly popular throughout the nineteenth century. Even the *Illustrated Police News*, a popular early tabloid, carried multiple advertisements for condoms during the 1890s.[17] But the history of birth control in Britain is somewhat murky, even to those who were active campaigners during the many battles for its acceptance. It was only when Kitty came into contact with the American birth control movement that she learned the history of it in England:

> I learned how the Society for the Suppression of Vice and the Catholic Church were opposed to Birth Control, and there was a Neo-Malthusian movement, etc., in England where there was no law, nor ever had been, against Birth Control, that is the prevention of conception.[18]

Over twenty years earlier than Besant and Bradlaugh, in 1854 George Drysdale had published *Physical, Sexual and Natural Religion*, in which he had discussed numerous different preventative methods, suggesting the vaginal douche would be the most effective, and least disturbing, to sexual pleasure.[19] It is clear, though, whose pleasure Drysdale is most preoccupied with when he writes, "any preventative means, to be satisfactory, must be used by the woman, as it spoils the passion and impulsivity of the general act, if the man have to think of them."[20]

Yet not all sexual advice was geared toward male pleasure over female, as a long-held cultural belief maintained that a shared orgasm (with emphasis on the woman's) was the moment when conception occurred.[21] Without the female orgasm, the Victorians believed, a woman would not get pregnant. Not long after Drysdale, in 1860, the anonymous pamphlet *The Art of Begetting Handsome Children* was printed. One copy of this guide to sexual etiquette has survived, pasted into a scrapbook of pornography and erotica compiled at some point in or after the 1860s, and kept now in a museum archive. *The Art* states very clearly that it is "to be given at Marriage instead of gloves," and within its pages lies not titillation, but straightforward and practical advice for a happy sex life, although couched in Victorian language. It is utterly unique, as instead of being a sexual handbook based on medical or Malthusian ideas, its approach is social, not scientific. Held within it is advice on foreplay and female sexual pleasure that still rings true today:

> When the husband cometh into his wife's chamber, he must entertain her with all kinds of dalliance, wanton behaviour, and allurements to venery. But if he perceive her to be slow, and more cold, he must cherish, embrace and tickle her; and shall not abruptly (the nerves being suddenly distended) break into the field of nature, but rather shall creep in by little and little, intermixing more wanton kisses with wanton words and speeches, mauling her secret parts . . . so that at length the womb will strive and wax fervent with a desire of casting forth its own seed. When the woman shall perceive the efflux of seed to approach, by reason of the tinkling pleasure, she must advertise her husband thereof that at the very same instant or moment he may also yield forth his seed, that by collision, or meeting of the seeds, conception may be made.

Although printed anonymously in 1860, *The Art* is actually based on the work of sixteenth-century surgeon Ambroise Paré.[22] One of the earliest English translations of his work appears in 1709, in *An Apology for a Latin Verse in Commendation of Mr. Marten's Gonosologium Novum*, recognized today as "an anthology of erotic and pornographic passages culled from a series of medical and paramedical works."[23] It is from this translation that *The Art* appears to have been directly taken. This pamphlet, and the growing birth control movement of the nineteenth century, show that sex was not a secret. From the 1830s onward, *Fruits of Philosophy* gave its readers a complete guide to every method available in the modern world, safely suggested by a respected medical doctor, Dr. Charles Knowlton, and then verified by the radical free thinkers Besant and Bradlaugh in the 1870s.

Perhaps in an effort to counterbalance previous religious or folk-loric approaches to sex, the radical birth control movement began to join forces with the medical and scientific community at the end of the nineteenth century. Unfortunately, this community, bringing with it the memories of the Contagious Diseases Acts and entering the psychoanalytic world with Freud, was becoming increasingly pre-occupied with denying female sexual independence or reducing it to diagnosable conditions, often described by a catchall term, "hysteria." It was a culturally significant strategy that legitimized the discussion of contraception in the public world, yet also adhered to arguments surrounding respectability.

> Letters of approval and encouragement came from the most diverse quarters, including among their writers General Garibaldi, the well-known economist, Yves Guyot, the great French constitutional lawyer, Émile Acollas, together with letters literally by the hundred from poor men and women thanking and blessing us for the stand taken.[24]

Although Besant and Bradlaugh were quick to point to the support they had gained from ordinary people, they maintained that their concern was not for sexual pleasure, but to control the population. Like many birth control activists of the late nineteenth and early twentieth centuries, they connected their respectability to discussing sex within the boundaries of medical or social control, taking every opportunity to deny their detractors' claims that their work would promote sexual permissiveness. At the same time, sexual theorists like William Acton, Richard von Krafft-Ebing, and Freud were constructing women as sexually passive beings. This view, built in part on medical theories, and combined with early feminist narratives of female victimhood, has dominated our understanding of female sexual agency since the nineteenth century.

And yet, as hard as both feminist campaigners and historians have tried, you cannot disconnect the act of sex and sexual pleasure from our understanding of womanhood in the nineteenth century. The fixation on the female body, in both a sexual and a reproductive sense, dominated both the literature of the period and the feminist history that has followed it. What happened to the female body, who used it, who consumed it, has only been understood through the subjects of danger and victimhood, while the women who advocated for greater understanding of sex, female desire, and female empowerment have been written out of history as dangerous and unusual aberrations.

Against this backdrop of complex and contrasting views of female sexuality, birth control, and the fight for empowerment came the suffragettes. But for too long, our understanding of this movement has been guided by a controlled, desexualized view of the political fight to get women the vote. Sex was at the heart of the feminist movement from its conception, and yet the legacy of women like Wollstonecraft, Shelley, and Besant was co-opted into an idea of unsexed women, who, following Josephine Butler and Emmeline Pankhurst's lead, deserved the vote not because of their womanliness, but in spite of it.

Looking at sex as something not that women were scared of, but that they understood as part of themselves (and as something that could be used against them), allows us to create a new understanding of the role of sex in our society, both in the past and today. The anger of women against the abuses they suffered at the hands of men, over an act and experience that was universally shared, has not gone away. While we may have the rights Mary Wollstonecraft and Emmeline Pankhurst only dreamed of, they have not removed the abuse and assaults women across the world experience daily. Perhaps our ignorance of the history of sex within the feminist movement has held back our ability to truly counter misogyny, as we have clung to old ideas of women's sensuality as something that removes their political legitimacy. But, as Wollstonecraft and Besant prove, female sexuality belongs at the heart of feminist politics. And for the suffragettes, the centuries of male abuse could go on no longer. Rebellion, through a violent and dangerously aggressive resistance, appeared to be the only option. Women across the country, whose mothers grew up reading *Frankenstein* and hearing stories of life under the Contagious Diseases Acts, decided to use the language of war to take control of their place in society, and their rights to their own bodies. And onto this stage steps Kitty Marion, the most dangerous woman of all.

2

An Escape

London, 1888, a capital city in crisis. Over the summer months, women had marched on the streets and stood armed with weapons against a common enemy.

The radical trade union strike by the Bryant and May match girls in July had seen both the press and public flock to the banner of workers united, as the strength of the arguments put forward by the women brought to light their terrible working conditions, unfair pay, and abuses suffered at the hands of foremen. Annie Besant, a little over a decade on from publishing her birth control guide, had broken the story of the match girls' suffering in late June, causing a groundswell of support for the women and fueling their anger at work that caused serious illness and disfigurement. In retaliation, Bryant and May attempted to force the women to sign a document refuting Besant's accusations, and this, combined with the callous dismissal of one of the girls in early July, had caused a rebellion. By July 5, thirteen hundred workers from the Bryant and May match factory had walked out on strike.[1] The majority were women who had faced significant fines for the most trivial of offenses. One women even reported that she had lost a significant amount of her wage simply for fetching one drink of water on a hot summer day.

The strike raged for most of July, as the factory owners reportedly threatened to ship in workers from Scotland or relocate the factory itself to Norway, but support for the women was so great that on July 17 the strike was ended, with Bryant and May meeting a number of their demands and committing to fairer pay and a better environment for the workers. This was one of the most influential and exciting workers' rebellions to happen in Victorian London, and it was entirely led by women. But as July's unseasonable weather, full of thunderstorms and heavy rain, gave way to August's milder sun, the match girls' triumph for women workers everywhere gave way to a sense of fear and terror.

A brutal murderer was stalking the streets of London. As early as April, there had been reports of women being killed in horrifying and vicious circumstances, but on August 31, the streets of Whitechapel rang with the urgent whistles and shouts of policemen as the body of Mary Ann Nichols—wife, mother, and daughter of a Soho locksmith—was found in Buck's Row. Four more murders followed, increasing in violence and horror. Elizabeth Stride, Annie Chapman, Catherine Eddowes, and Mary Jane Kelly were killed in the following months, as both police and press identified the deaths as the work of one deranged individual. He was given the moniker "Jack the Ripper" after a series of letters were sent to the newspapers claiming ownership of the killings, but no suspect was ever caught. While the police and the government failed to protect the women of the capital, in the East End the women who walked the streets in the early hours began to arm themselves, ready to defend each other to the death, if ever needed. Refusing to be intimidated, some of the women gave interviews to the press, showing off the gigantic bowie knives they now carried.[2]

As the twin forces of violent misogyny and an early radical feminism combined to shake the foundations of the capital, out on the edges of the East End toward Epping Forest a young, argumentative, redheaded German immigrant cleared the kitchen table of her aunt's house. At the age of seventeen, Kitty Marion had been in England for two years, sent in secret by her uncle to escape the clutches of her father, whose abuse and violent temper she had suffered for many years. Her life was dull, the slow and gradual domestic monotony of a resented but useful dependent relative, caring for her aunt's five children in a well-kept but run-down house that barely contained room enough to breathe. It was an inauspicious beginning for the woman who would go on to become one of England's most famous suffragettes, and a leading figure in the founding of America's Planned Parenthood. But for now, she was just filled with a teenager's desperate sense of ennui, prone to staring out of windows, and lost in daydreams of adventures fueled by borrowing her younger cousins' American "Deadwood Dick" novels, smuggled into the house for the price of a single penny.

Kitty's mother had died when she was two years old. She had contracted tuberculosis and quickly faded as the disease took over her lungs.[3] It was a loss Kitty's father never recovered from. Gustav was an engineer "with a very mathematical mind which he thoroughly brought to bear upon my training and upbringing," Kitty recalled, "a strict disciplinarian with a fierce, violent, evidently uncontrollable temper, the full force of which I often bore the brunt."[4] Her parents' marriage had been an instant infatuation; falling in love at first sight, they were engaged within six weeks. Gustav would always regard those years as the happiest of his life.

After Kitty's mother's death, and with a small child in tow, Gustav Schäfer moved to Dortmund to marry a young Protestant woman, who became the only mother Kitty would ever truly know. Although aware of the difficulties stepmothers and their new charges often faced, Kitty found her new mother to be nothing but kind. They quarreled, as mothers and daughters often do, but she would also "scald the milk and when cold, skim off the thick, rich cream for me," and curl Kitty's red-gold hair, taking pride in her adopted daughter's striking looks.[5] Any attention to Kitty's appearance, though, was always met with disdain from her father, who believed it would only encourage her to grow into a conceited and vapid young woman. His aggressive, obsessive control of Kitty was clear. As a young girl, Kitty recalled he had brought home a puppy, supposedly as a present for her, but whose dedication to its young mistress Gustav had immediately resented:

> I used to go to the corner with Father, taking the puppy too while Mother waited at the door for my return. The puppy instead of following Father would scamper after me which infuriated him so much he beat and kicked it each time "to teach the dog who was master." Mother tried to protect it and I begged him not to beat it, but to no avail. After a few days the puppy died.[6]

At the age of five, Kitty was taken to meet her paternal grandparents for the first time, along with two of her father's sisters, Lisette and Mariechen, and an older brother, Heinrich. Lisette, prone to hysterical fainting fits if she felt she was losing an argument, contrasted against Mariechen's calm and practical approach to life's adversities. They both became immediate idols for their young niece. A winter spent in deep snow, with the jingle of bells from riding in horse-drawn sleighs and a countryside that seemed to be covered in a thick layer of sugar, became Kitty's defining memory of Germany, one she carried throughout her life. Kitty returned to Dortmund after the Christmas season had passed, and her early childhood was spent rambling through the fields and countryside that surrounded their house, set in a wealthy and friendly neighborhood of Jewish and Christian families. Little affected Kitty's day-to-day routine until, one life-changing day, she met some old friends of her stepmother:

> I entered a new, strange and magnificent world, of gorgeously dressed, lovely, kind people, who took my heart and soul by storm. There were flowers, bonbons, perfumes, the like I have never seen before, and to which I was invited to "help myself." The one thing that stood out was a huge swan, the rope attached to which I was warned not to step on or fall over, drawing a boat in which "Der Schwanenritter" arrived. The impression all this made on me is better imagined than described.

Against the background of the joy and vitality of her stepmother, Kitty's relationship with her father became increasingly abusive. One evening, as Gustav was combing her hair, a large chunk of it had fallen out of her plait. Already terrified of her father's moods, Kitty was unable to explain why this had happened, which led to the accusation that she must be lying, that someone must have cut it. Although he threatened to beat her to death if she told him a lie, Gustav was unable to drag an answer out of his child. A few days later, when Kitty confessed that she had been attempting to cut bangs—a style favored by a number of her playmates at school—"he all but did beat me to death. A favourite way with him was to strike me full in the face with the back of his hand. See stars? Yes the whole firmament in one flash, many a time!"[7] The following day her nose had a bump where it had previously been straight. Gustav had broken it. When Kitty appeared at the table for breakfast, far from showing remorse, he "jeeringly remarked that it improved my beauty and would always remind me not to tell lies."[8]

In 1877, when Kitty was six years old, her stepmother gave birth to a baby boy, but she died shortly afterward and the new baby brother followed her only a few days later. "It was all so strange and incomprehensible to me, so desolate and empty without them. I wished then and have wished many times since, that they had taken me with them."[9] Now in the sole care of her father, Kitty was briefly sent to stay with her own mother's family while her father closed up the home they had lived in in Dortmund. Staying near Cologne, Kitty found life with the prudish Catholic side of her family intensely unenjoyable, and for the first and only time in her life she was happy to see her father appearing on the doorstep. The Dortmund house having been sold, Gustav collected Kitty from her uncle and set off for the village he had grown up in.

Gustav's work required him to travel extensively, and so he was unable to care for a child as young as Kitty. So for the next two years he left her in the care of his parents. It was, perhaps, his one sole moment of true kindness to his daughter, as what followed became the happiest two years of Kitty's entire childhood, left to enjoy and explore the tiny enclosed world that was now her home. Her grandfather owned much of the village as well as being one of its leading burghers, and Kitty was quickly adopted by the villagers, who were keen to make sure she felt welcome. It was from Gustav's family that Kitty got her red hair, a trait shared with all her aunts. She soon found herself turned into their little doll, dressed in old clothes and hair curled as her father would never have allowed. Kitty especially idolized her aunt Mariechen, and took her side in the various squabbles and jealous arguments that would break out whenever one or other of the sisters received a letter from the eldest, Dora, who had immigrated to England with her husband before Kitty was born. The village itself was a mix of largely Protestant, with a few Jewish, families, and the children all attended the same village school, only being separated for religious festivals. As an adult, Kitty could still close her eyes and recall the "old world, romantic spot, surrounded by ideally beautiful, hilly, wooded country" in which the village lay.[10] It had originally been a fortress and, in the gardens of many of the residents, remains of the ancient fortifications still existed. Kitty spent as much time as she could climbing the ruins and hills and running through the fields that surrounded what, to her, seemed like paradise. "It was a great relief not to have Father storming and throwing things, and to be corrected in a kindly way when naughty and disobedient as, child-like I often was."[11]

But in 1880, death wreaked havoc on Kitty's young life once again. Her grandmother became seriously ill and, as Kitty walked home one evening, "blood-curdling howls from Uncle Heinrich's Great Dane, Pluto, met my ears."[12] Her grandmother died that night. With her Uncle Heinrich without a wife, Aunt Mariechen newly married and moved away, and Aunt Lisette hunting for a husband in Berlin, there was no one left to look after Kitty, now entirely bereft of the loving companionship that had so easily repaired the wounds her father had inflicted. But there was no choice; she had to be returned to him and, shortly after the funeral, Kitty and her father moved to the mining town of Witten, on the Ruhr.

Life here could not have been further removed from the quiet peace of the village. The town was built on the heavy industry of iron, and full of noise, mud, smoke, and metal. They stayed in a small but packed boardinghouse, and Kitty quickly became a favorite among the other lodgers. "Father evidently being delighted with the compliments he received on having such a charming little daughter who sang and recited so well . . . But gradually I felt an undercurrent of dissatisfaction with me . . . He thought I had had too much freedom and needed curbing. He gave me all sorts of instructions on my conduct."[13] If Gustav felt Kitty was receiving too much attention from the other guests he would accuse her of being a flirt, and called her a little "verfluchte Schauspielerin," or cursed actress, out of either jealousy or spite at the clear enjoyment she took from the company of anyone but him. But when he banned her from playing with the other children in the neighborhood, Kitty began to rebel. Having tasted two years of freedom and the companionship of those her own age, she would never be content with the oppressive company of a man prone to wild rages and fits of unexpected depression. Her rebellion, of course, often had only one result. "He was apt to stop any 'back-answers' with the back of his hand on my face," Kitty remembered, painfully.[14]

Daily abuse came from Gustav's regular examination of her school lessons; he corrected her homework while lecturing her about her "stupidity, carelessness, uselessness and so forth, but seldom praised and encouraged me for doing things right."[15] He had taken to smoking a long, heavy pipe, and on identifying any mistake in her work, he would beat her over the head, often with such force that a raised lump would form shortly afterward. "Naturally I would scream with pain, fear, and confusion and he would stand over me, compelling me to control my emotions and not utter a sound, but sob inwardly, wishing I could drop dead."[16]

As Kitty grew older, Gustav began to fixate on the inherent badness of women. As they moved from town to town, he regularly told Kitty she was worthless, nothing, a creature of sin, a burden that he wished had "never been born," and on at least one occasion warned her that he would break her legs if ever she behaved in an unladylike manner.[17] When Kitty confessed to a much-cherished and long-held dream of becoming an actress, he threatened to kill her.[18]

At fifteen, having left school, Kitty found brief respite from her father's abuses in a visit to her Uncle Heinrich, who had recently married. As Gustav's elder brother, and with their father's recent death, Heinrich was now head of the family. The sight of his niece, arriving pale and withdrawn, but who quickly brightened after a few days in the care of a loving family, must have preyed on his mind. Any suspicions he may have had were confirmed at Whitsuntide, 1886. The family gathered to celebrate Kitty's confirmation into the Protestant Church, but Gustav's arrival brought the festivities to a crashing halt. He demanded Kitty immediately return to him once the celebrations were over, but she refused; "there was a violent parting and much abuse for the natural daughter who deserted her father."[19] Left in Heinrich's care over the summer, Kitty received a sudden and unexpected invitation from her Aunt Dora in London. "Here was my chance to relieve Father of his 'burden' forever. I accepted aunt Dora's invitation and put the seas between us."[20] It had been decided that Gustav was not to be informed. Heinrich was undoubtedly behind Dora's sudden invitation, and he saved Kitty from the violent and abusive relationship with her father. He clearly cared greatly for his niece, and made all of the arrangements for her travel, giving her detailed instructions of hotels, trains, and the boat she would take to reach England. Putting on her first long dress, which officially marked her change from child to woman, Kitty felt incredibly grown up to be making such a long journey alone. The haste with which it was organized by the adults around her, none of whom were able to accompany Kitty, underlines the urgency with which Heinrich was attempting to get her out of the country; Gustav could return at any moment. Leaving her family behind, with all of the excitement of a child on an unknown adventure, Kitty had little thought to spare for her father. How he felt at her loss we will never know.

> On a fine, sunny, autumn morning in 1886, I arrived at Harwich, England. The language I heard around me sounded like one long word which, I felt, I could never learn to understand, much less speak. An interpreter put me on the train for Liverpool St. Station in the corner of a compartment . . . Though I had escaped unhappy conditions with Father, I felt a dread and premonition of facing new ones.[21]

The year before Kitty's arrival, Henry Vigar-Harris described Liverpool Street Station as a "centre of London vice and impurity."[22] The hub of travel from the north and east of England, the station hummed with travelers and street sellers, bringing many foreign visitors into London for the first time. "The visitor cannot pass the street without hearing the most obscene language from the vile girls who are allowed to congregate in groups there," Vigar-Harris had wailed.[23] To Kitty, the station was noisy, dirty, smoky, and smelly, and unlike anything she had ever experienced. But she quickly recognized Aunt Dora by their shared red hair, a trait that Dora had also passed on to her five children, the three girls and two boys that Kitty was now to care for.

But Kitty was in for a shock. She had grown up in mostly affluent surroundings in Germany, but Dora, struggling with five children and the little money her husband brought in, was eking out a limited existence on the allowance she now received from her parents' estate. Finding her world small and restrictive due to the language barrier, and having no one other than her immediate family to talk to, Kitty began to feel increasingly miserable and terribly homesick. This was not the grand adventure she had pictured when her journey had first begun.

Lying under the bed covers muffling the sounds of her own sobs at Christmas, Kitty realized things needed to change. To her surprise, as the months flickered by, she slowly began to learn English, often from the children's school books, a copy of the English Bible, and any newspaper she could lay her hands on. The children would often act as interpreters when she first began to accompany them into the city, but soon Kitty was able to converse with shopkeepers, travel on the trams, buses, and underground, and find her way out of the monotony of everyday life. However, not all of her self-taught lessons were an immediate success.

> Strange how one learns the "bad" parts of a language most easily. I came home one day, having taken the baby for an airing, and cheerfully hailed my aunt with "You bloody bugger!" She was shocked and horrified. Where had I heard such dreadful, etc., etc., language? I didn't know it was bad. I had passed two men in the street and one slapped the other on the shoulder, laughing, and using that expression. I thought it was something nice and friendly and as it was easy to remember, I thought Aunt would be pleased with my progress in English.[24]

Kitty oscillated between listless and unresponsive and a vibrating desperation to connect to someone, anyone who might bring with them news of the world beyond the end of her street. For the first time in her life, Kitty experienced a longing for her own mother, the woman she had never really known. "More and more I felt caged by invisible barriers which I wanted to break, not knowing how."[25] One day, answering a knock at the door, Kitty found the porch step occupied by a gypsy, who was passing down the street reading fortunes. By now her grasp of English was good enough to understand the woman, who said, " 'You have a lucky face, you will travel far and wide and make friends wherever you go.' "[26] Dora laughed at the words when Kitty relayed them, but neither of the women could have foreseen just how true they would become.

The possibility relit Kitty's sense of adventure, and this only intensified when she took her cousin to the Mile End Theatre to see *A Run of Luck*. Her childhood love of the stage instantly reawakened, and Kitty began to dream once again of a life as an actress. But for a young woman in 1889, one stage above all else was the place to be seen: the music halls.

The first purpose-built music hall was the Canterbury on Westminster Bridge Road in London. Its early performances involved vulgar songs full of sexual innuendo, while also relying heavily on opera singers such as Augustus Braham and Mrs. Henry Wallack, popularizing Offenbach's music, and giving the first British performance of *Faust*.[27] The "blithe comic and bold basso" Sam Cowell, soon to be one of the biggest music hall stars of his day, appeared as a comic singer, while the Canterbury's owner, Charles Morton, spared no expense in trying to get "first-class artists" to appear, paying up to thirty pounds a week—equivalent to more than $3,800 today—to the bigger names.[28] This early incarnation of music hall made sure to retain a connection to higher forms of entertainment, often promoting classical music or opera as its main attraction and earning the Canterbury the nickname of "the Royal Academy over the Water" when it expanded to include a picture gallery in the mid-1850s.[29]

The Canterbury's success led to an explosive rise in music halls across the metropolis and later the whole country. By the 1890s, London's premier music halls were capable of catering to a regularly attending audience of almost fourteen million each year.[30] They were an endless churning circus, looking for fresh talent and new faces, as well as a hunting ground for men who believed women owed them their bodies in return for legitimate work.

A MUSIC HALL AGENT: At Bow-street police court . . . John James Gardiner, clerk, 21, Newington-green-road, Stoke Newington, was charged with conspiring with Louis Leon Goldstein, alias Roberts, during the years 1889–91, to obtain from Lily Holton £21 and various other sums. He was further charged with indecently assaulting Lily Holton. Mr. George Lewis who said he appeared on behalf of Mr. Henry

Labouchère, MP, who, in consequence of information received, pub-lished in Truth, on Dec 10th, an article headed "The Stamford Street Road to Ruin." In this article he charged the prisoner and another man named Goldstein with carrying on an abominable traffic and commit-ting indecent assaults on girls and obtaining their money by false pre-tences. To carry out their nefarious designs they inserted the following advertisement:—"Stage, Theatres and Music Halls. Ladies and gentle-men rapidly and thoroughly prepared. Engagements procured . . . Consult here free." . . . Mr. Labouchère obtained the sworn information of many girls who had been assaulted and robbed by the prisoner and his accomplice.[31]

So opened *The Era* in 1892, with its explosive account of a pros-ecution brought against a well-known music hall agent by Henry Labouchère, Liberal MP for Northampton.[32] Labouchère was no stranger to the debating of sex in Victorian society; he had actively supported the Criminal Law Amendment Act to raise the age of consent to sixteen and outlaw sex trafficking in England. He was, unfortunately, also responsible for the "Labouchère Amendment" to the bill, which made male-to-male sexual relationships illegal in England until its repeal in 1967. This case seemed more personal, as Labouchère had for many years lived with the actress Henri-etta Hodson, with whom he had a daughter, although they did not marry until 1887.[33] Labouchère's relationship with Hodson was pub-licly acknowledged; W. S. Gilbert (of Gilbert and Sullivan) daringly referred to it when discussing a recent reviewer who was always "blowing his own strumpet."[34] The reviewer in question, of course, was Labouchère and the strumpet Hodson, to whom Gilbert had introduced the MP before they were married.[35] So Labouchère's interest in women on the stage was not wholly without personal experience. And his distaste at the men who took advantage, or believed female performers were sexually accessible, was evident in his prosecution and the women he called as witnesses.

Miss Emily Nelson, a barmaid, had paid nine guineas to Gardiner and Roberts to learn step dancing for the music hall stage and over a period of three months attended eight lessons.[36] During this period, Gardiner was "very rude to her," suggested, as he had with Lily Holton, that she "ought to wear a short dress, and suggested she should have tights for her lessons," and often kissed her and made "objectionable" conversation, to which Nelson "smacked his face and pushed him across the room to get away."[37] Gardiner had also shown Nelson a nude woman in a photograph and asked her "if I did not think it was a fine photograph."[38] Retaliating at their treatment, Nelson asked the men if this was the way they treated all their pupils and was told by Roberts, "Yes, he did as he liked with most of them."[39]

Matilda Rosalie Goure, a dairyman's wife in Notting Hill, and Miss Fanny Norris, of Richmond Gardens, Uxbridge Road, both appeared as witnesses to assaults by the men. Miss Norris reported that Roberts had asked her "if she knew any married women who got their living at night time," attempted to unbutton her dress, held her by the wrists, and used his leg to stop her from getting out of a chair.[40] On attempting to flee the room, she had been unable to do so as the door handle would not turn.[41] Roberts had later "opened it by touching it in a way that made her think it had been fastened by a spring."[42] Miss Edith Forrester, Miss Maude Cox, and Miss Millicent Anderson followed with similar accounts, and the men were convicted. Aunt Dora would be right, then, to fear for her niece's attraction to the stage. The music hall agents and their predation on the young women who flocked to their doors in search of work encapsulated everything that was wrong with Victorian society. Women seeking work were expected to trade sex in return for their independence, an expectation many men seemed to have and attempted to take advantage of without a second thought.

To Kitty, the world of the music halls meant freedom, excitement, and independence, but for many in Victorian England the halls represented only one thing: sex. Although this could often lead to abuse and mistreatment, there also existed a large community within the halls,

among the acts and artists, who acknowledged and enjoyed the opportunities the halls gave them for their own sexual freedom. *Poses plastiques* or *tableaux vivants* ("living pictures," where performers appeared
or seemed to appear nude on stage) were highly popular from 1858
onward. Strikingly, both male and female performers took part in
them, and there has been little recognition of this—nor of the connected fact that these performances were watched by an audience of
men *and* women. We need to acknowledge that women were actively
engaging in the sexual content of the stage, and were not always victimized by it.

Writing in 1869, Sarah Annie Frost argued that "there is scarcely any
way of passing a social evening more delightful and popular than that
offered by the performers of the Tableaux Vivants to the audience."[43]
And references to these performances and their multiple incarnations
appear in both Charles Dickens's and Edith Wharton's novels.[44] In
Wharton's *The House of Mirth* (1905), the character of Mrs. Fisher even
convinces "a dozen fashionable women to exhibit themselves in a
series of pictures" in which Wharton's heroine, Lily Bart, is featured.[45]

Pornography or erotica, and the sexual knowledge that could be
gained from it, was just as popular in the music halls as it was on the
streets and in bookstores across London, existing as an intricately connected web of both sexual manipulation and sexual independence, and
consumed by men and women alike. In 1874, when the empty Pim-
lico studio and home of pornographic photographer Henry Hayler
was raided, it led to the discovery of 130,248 photographs and 5,000
slides—six cartloads, according to the solicitor for the Society for
the Suppression of Vice—which were then destroyed by the police.[46]
The women who posed for such pictures were invariably drawn from
performers on the stage, who transformed their sexual independence
into economic opportunity. The diarist A. J. Munby recorded being
offered several obscene prints of ballet girls and dancers—perhaps
supplementing their stage income with a modeling fee—on the Westminster Bridge Road, which just so happened to be in the immediate

vicinity of the Canterbury Music Hall.[47] He recorded his interaction with a man who claimed to be "a theatrical agent: I can supply you Sir with girls, for ballet or poses or artists models, at an hours notice."[48] Were the models, in fact, Canterbury ballet girls? Invariably, the women who modeled for these images, just as the women who posed for the *poses plastiques* or *tableaux vivants* of the music hall stage, have been denied any form of ownership over their decisions, and portrayed simply as victims of male lust. But as sex was ever-present on and around the music hall stage, there has to be more to it than a single narrative of victimhood. Conservative feminism would have you believe that no woman on the stage, or who celebrated (and economized) her sexuality, was actually happy, but the reality of these women's lives and choices is far more complex. Kitty was about to step into a world where women were acutely aware of the power of their own sexuality, and about to begin a fight for it to be understood and defined on their own terms, not those of the men who attempted to use it for abuse.

Dora's fears of the potential dangers of the stage had little effect on Kitty, determined as she was to prove her father wrong. She knew that the stage would give her the freedom she craved, a freedom she believed every woman had a right to. With the words of the gypsy fortune teller ringing in her ears, Kitty felt the restrictions of her life more keenly with each passing day. "No prisoner in irons ever felt more shackled than I did."[49] But in the autumn of 1889 she would finally see the gypsy's words come true. Picking up the *Daily News* one day, Kitty spied an advertisement for young ladies who wanted to learn stage dancing, with the promise of a guaranteed pantomime engagement at the end of their training. At last, the stage was calling.

3
"What soul-satisfying exhilarations"

You couldn't stop Kitty Marion once she had set her mind to something. And after much argument, persuasion, and coaxing, Kitty managed to convince Aunt Dora to allow her to apply to the dancing school on Waterloo Road. Advancing her the necessary two guineas for tuition, Dora apprehensively dispatched Kitty off for her new education with detailed written instructions: which Tube, which tram, which street to take to navigate the capital successfully. For Dora, who had lived through the horrors of Jack the Ripper, the streets outside her neighborhood held untold dangers for a young, naive, immigrant girl.

For Kitty, the independence must have been thrilling. Not only was she out of the dull boundaries of the family home, but she was here! London! The great capital city full of wonder and adventure! Kitty was free to explore (though never to stray from the written instructions), free to talk to strangers (though never to a man), free to buy ginger beer, pickled whelks, sheep trotters, gherkins, currant buns (only never to admit to it) from any of the street vendors whose stalls lined the roads and alleyways between the East End and Waterloo. "I was the happiest thing on earth! What soul-satisfying exhilarations and excitement," she wrote on the first day of her new adventure.[1] Dora had given her an earnest warning not to speak to any strange men who might try to start up a conversation with her, to ignore them and keep walking, and never to look back. The warning had meant nothing to Kitty; she had no experience of the adult world and no understanding that a man might not simply want directions or to discuss the weather. Running over Dora's instructions in her mind, she decided that if a man *did* speak to her, she would simply direct him as best she could—for what was the harm in that?—or point him to the nearest policeman if she could not.

Luckily no one attempted to speak to her on that first wander through the city streets. Reaching her destination safely, Kitty quickly passed the entrance exam of step repetition and a few simple poses, and was accepted as a pupil alongside fifty other young women, all training for the Christmas entertainment season. Soon she was learning the sailor's hornpipe, highland fling, and Irish jig alongside strict ballet steps—an important part of music hall and theater culture at this time. Ballet was central to the pantomime seasons; a huge procession of dancers would take to the stage as fairies, goblins, elves, kings, and queens during the most dramatic performances. Today we might think of ballet as the reserve of the elite, but to the Victorians it was for everyone.

Having had little contact with the outside world since she arrived in England, Kitty was overwhelmed by the kindness and friendliness of her fellow pupils, "though I was shy as always, when meeting strangers and had little to say beyond answering their questions."[2] Her English, though already good for a young person who had only been in the country for three years and lived in such solitude, rapidly began to improve. The girls were training for theaters across the country, as it was the usual practice of the time to have eight to twelve dancers from London as part of any pantomime across the country. Quickly learning her steps and easily holding the poses needed to impress the dance tutors, Kitty was given her first engagement. She was to be sent to the Theatre Royal in Glasgow for an eight-week run of the pantomime *Robinson Crusoe*, with a salary of one pound ten shillings for the first seven performances, and a half-salary wage for all others, plus the first two weeks of rehearsal. The theater would pay for her fare to Glasgow, but she would need to save her money and make sure she had enough for her return.

> What a merry gathering at St. Pancras station for the midnight express to Glasgow, with reserved carriages for "theatricals" of which I was one, to think of it, though I seemed more of a quiet observer than a participant. There were a few other dancers, "old stagers" joining me, the new ones, and the chorus-show girls, usually called the big six or eight, according to their number, who "dressed the stage" garbed in gorgeous costumes, and some of whom, I learned later, looked down upon the ballet, on anyone not in their own exalted sphere.[3]

Standing there on the train platform, inside the huge wrought-iron and glass cathedral of St. Pancras station, accessed, just as one still can today, through the red-brick fairytale castle of the Midland Grand Hotel, Kitty stood apart from the others. She watched as each one hugged and laughed with the friends and family who had come to see them off. She was alone. The distance from the East End and the late departure had been too much for Dora; neither had she allowed any of the boys to accompany Kitty to make sure she arrived at the station safely. Now, clutching her bag and entering the train compartment, would have been an understandable time for Kitty's courage to fail her, "But I was perfectly content to enjoy my new experience of liberty alone, and as the express dashed through the night I wished it might do so forever without a stop."[4]

That first taste of true freedom, of what adulthood might bring, is rarely forgotten. Kitty was nineteen years old and, although she had already traveled alone, far across the Continent to meet her aunt, it had been done with the strict oversight of her family. But this, this really was freedom. The money she would earn would be hers, the friends she would make would be of her own choosing, and what happened next would be in her control and no one else's. In the dark, as the sound of the steam engine and chatter of her companions lulled her into a broken sleep, Kitty little wondered what price she might be asked to pay for such liberty and independence.

Arriving in Glasgow, one of the "old stagers," a long-time performer who had recognized just how young and naive Kitty was—having traveled all the way to the city without making any preparations for lodging, or even acquiring an understanding of how to find them—took pity on the waif standing outside the station, determined not to show how lost she was. The next morning, at eleven o'clock, Kitty arrived at the Theatre Royal for her very first day. To her, the experience was like entering church, and she crossed the threshold with the same reverence as someone entering the confessional. Here was the holy of holies, the world her father had so cruelly and arrogantly rejected. It was like entering a dream, the theater was a "strange, queer, dreary, mysterious, ghostly, gloomy" place, empty of the life and bustle that filled it in the evenings.[5] The stage was silent, the quiet echoing up to the rafters, as she tentatively made her way out onto the main stage. It was a vast space, lit by a T-shaped gas pipe, almost seven feet high, from which gas jets emitted a shaky dim light. As her eye became accustomed to the gloom around her, Kitty was able to make out a huge semicircle, the house itself, which that night would be filled with distant faces, cheers, applause, and boos. But at this moment gigantic dust sheets were draped from the gallery to the floor, covering every seat and every walkway. Apart from a table and a few chairs, the stage was empty. How long did she stand there, turning on her heel, testing with gentle pressure the wooden floor underneath her feet? Her church felt abandoned and covered in dust, not the lively, exciting world she had only been able to imagine in her dreams. But soon the doors were thrown open, and stage hands, dancers, singers, producer, and manager filled the place with their noisy greetings, as old hands and new faces of the Christmas company became acquainted. For the first time, Kitty felt she was finally home.

Sorted into sections by the stage manager and the producer, Kitty eagerly joined the ballet girls and began rehearsals. Those first two weeks building up to opening night seemed to pass at a glacial pace, but she would have felt an increasing joy at the independence she had discovered. Walking home from rehearsals at all hours of the night, Kitty often wondered what her aunt would have said if she knew; it was not the behavior she would have expected of her niece. She certainly would not have approved of Kitty's first costume: bright pink tights, pale blue trunks, a sailor's blouse, hat, and ballet shoes, to be worn to dance the hornpipe as the HMS *Grundy* carried Robinson Crusoe down the Clyde and out to sea. Kitty was delighted: "I took to them as a duck takes to water and felt perfectly at home and at ease in them," although not all of her companions felt the same: "Some of the girls were shy at first and tried to hide behind others."[6] Some, like Kitty, were unused to displaying their legs, but the reality of life on the stage meant throwing off sensibilities and the adherence to respectability that had been drummed into them since birth.

Kitty was also required to wear costumes transforming her into, among other things, a sea-swimming scaly fish and Sappho in a stately, graceful gavotte dance set in the pantomime's palace. The liberty that came with each costume, the opportunity to pretend to be something other than she was, was utterly exhilarating.

Offstage, the company quickly bonded, and Kitty found herself with a wide circle of friends and acquaintances. She'd had no friends her own age since leaving Germany, and the companionship filled the aching hole in her heart that she had been trying to ignore since leaving her country behind. It brought with it many new experiences. One Sunday, two of the girls from the ballet decided to give a dinner party, to which they invited some of the nearby students from the university. Kitty was a source of intense interest because of her German upbringing, and many of the boys were keen to try out their limited knowledge of her native language on the beautiful red-headed girl who had never been in the company of university students before.

One of the young men, Vivian Ernest Chang, was a medical student and the son of the secretary of the Chinese Legation currently in London. He taught Kitty to smoke: "They all smoked cigarettes and invited me to try 'just to be sociable' . . . [he] lit the cigarette for me and told me to smoke it very slowly, when it would not affect me, which proved correct."[7]

Kitty reveled in these new friendships and reflected: "How was it that my own family and these strangers were as opposite as the poles in their attitudes towards, and opinions of, me?"[8] In the streets, stages, and rooms of Glasgow, Kitty finally found acceptance for her ideas, attitudes, hopes, and dreams. Gone was the guilt and shame she carried, the constant questioning of her own sense of self as bad or wrong, which had come from the abuse meted out by her father. Now she had found allies and friends.

The pantomime was a great success, so much so that the run was extended for another two weeks, but after three months of "glorious freedom" Kitty was forced to return to the humdrum existence of life at Aunt Dora's. Rather than take the train, she traveled by boat from Leith back down to London. It was half the price of the railway, and gave her the opportunity to spend time with another dancer, a young widow whom she had grown close to. Conny Argus lived in Greenwich; a worldly and practical woman, she insisted Kitty have her address, "in case of emergency," an act of foresight that, shortly afterward, was to save Kitty.[9] They parted happily in London, and she dragged her feet back toward her aunt's house.

To her surprise, while Kitty was away Dora had made the acquaintance of a songwriter and his family, who had moved in nearby. His daughter was in the music hall business as a singer, and with Dora's approval, he suggested to Kitty that she should try her luck in the halls, as the salaries were much higher than in the pantomime and theater worlds. This was a definite change from Dora's initial reluctance to support Kitty; could it be that she was thinking that the music halls, the *American Idol* of their day, would transform her niece from another hungry mouth to feed into a high-earning star? The leading female performers of the halls were idolized, known across the country, and commanded huge sums of money for every performance. If Kitty could be a success there, it was unlikely that Dora and her family would ever have to want for much again.

This new family friend, so keen to aid Kitty in her career, offered to introduce her to an agent of his acquaintance. Fresh from her success at the Theatre Royal and eager to make the most of her new skills, Kitty sallied forth, armed with a letter of introduction. It was for a firm of agents on York Road, which, although heavily bombed in the Second World War, is a street Londoners still walk down today, running between Waterloo Station and the London Eye. "Poverty Corner" stood where York Road joined Waterloo Road, now home to the BFI IMAX cinema, and the place where all out-of-work performers went to try to pick up engagements from the agents who controlled so much of the theatrical industry. For the first time, Kitty felt anxious; sitting in the agents' offices among the other artists, whose reviews she had read in the papers, she realized how very new to the professional world she was. But Kitty was also determined, and this meeting could be one of the most important of her life. It had to be a success.

Not long after she had sat down, the junior partner appeared. Summoning up her courage, Kitty presented him with her letter and, after answering his questions, agreed to perform a benefit being given for an elderly comedian at the Star Music Hall in Bermondsey the following week. This was a common trick of music hall agents and managers; they would often refuse to book a new act until they had seen them perform for free, just to make sure they were good enough. Kitty agreed, but she was unaware of the hard-drinking and hard-swearing reputation of the hall; it would be a trial by fire for the shy and self-conscious, unsophisticated nineteen-year-old, especially as she was scheduled to be the first performance of the evening.

This would be a very different environment from the genteel respectability of Glasgow's Theatre Royal; arriving for her performance, Kitty discovered that the hall was packed to the rafters, and howls, hoots, and drunken laughter filled the auditorium, drowning out the orchestra as it began to play. The curtain rose.

> My future, fortune, fame, life, everything depended on this moment. Dressed in pale pink, with my hair down I tripped on to the centre of the stage and ignorant as I was, I felt the shouts and applause that greeted me were more ironic than genuine. With all the fight and defiance in me I "threw" it at them, "A Glorious Life on the Ocean!" They gradually quieted down and I finished and "took a call" to genuine applause. "Very good," said the stage manager as I rushed past him to the dressing room.[10]

This life, the music hall life, did not have the camaraderie of the pantomime. There wasn't the companionship or support of a gang of girls who were all in it together. You performed alone. Back in the dressing room, Kitty slammed the door and burst into tears, in the belief that she would never have the courage to face the stage alone again. But, pulling herself together over a small restorative glass of port and listening to the kind words of two of her neighbors, who had been in the audience, she returned home cautiously triumphant. Now it was time to return to the agency; with such a success under her belt she was sure to find work in other halls.

Securing another meeting, Kitty pushed her way through the crowded office to speak to her new agent. He had decided she needed to work some of the small, more provincial halls, to help her train her voice and also combat the stage fright that had hit her so hard at the Star. This sounded like a very reasonable suggestion, and Kitty quickly agreed. It just so happened that there was a booking available for a small resort on the east coast, not that far from London, for one week at one pound ten shillings, with the luxury of free board at the hotel the hall was attached to. What an ideal start for a young singer who craved travel and adventure; and if this went well, what further opportunities might be waiting for her now she had the support and backing of a legitimate music hall agent? There was just one flaw—the contract wasn't ready yet. Could she call back in a few days, after 5:00 p.m.?

Kitty left the office on a high. This was truly a new beginning, a way of life she had always craved. No longer would she have to cook, clean, and care for her cousins. No longer would she have to survive the suffocating domesticity of Dora's, to be told that the only fulfillment any woman was supposed to need came from her husband, marriage, and children. The days passed in a blur, until it was time to return to the hustle and bustle of York Road, with the rumble of trains overhead.

The office was empty, of course; it was after 5:00 p.m., and everyone else had gone home. But here he was. Sitting alone, at his desk, brandishing her new contract. Innocently excited, Kitty hastily signed, and he stood up, moving around the desk to give her the counterpart.

Then to my horror and disgust he threw his arms around me and insisted that I must give him a kiss, that he had fallen desperately in love with me. I was utterly taken by surprise, but being athletic and agile I wrenched myself free and protested furiously against his conduct in all the English I could think of, saying I resented such familiarity. He was between me and the door and refused to let me go unless I forgave him, he had meant no harm. He was sorry, would I forgive him? All I wanted was to get out. How dared he, a married man too, take such an unwarrantable liberty? He was surprised at me, apparently so quiet and demure, having such a temper, but I must give him a kiss before he let me go. I dared not scream for fear of publicity and struggled frantically until my head struck the edge of a desk and with an awful sensation of bells ringing and water rushing through my head, I lost consciousness.[11]

Few women forget the first time they have been assaulted. The first time someone has decided that they have the right to touch, to kiss, to take without asking. Kitty's violent rejection had caught the man she would only ever refer to as "Mr. Dreck"—Mr. Trash—off guard. He had never met someone so determined to fight back before, and "all over a harmless little kiss too."[12] He told her that most girls liked it, they wanted "to be made love to and kissed," and she would have no future in the music halls if she didn't accept and agree to this.

> My whole being revolted against even the possibility of such an outrage happening in a world in which I had been taught to trust everybody, that as I treated people so they would treat me, as I respected them and myself so they would respect me. . . . My aching heart was almost a relief compared to my outraged pride and dignity, my revolting heart and soul.[13]

How many women had heard this before, and how many women still hear it today? Why is it that certain men view their workplace as a hunting ground, where women are little more than prey, complicit in a game of sex traded for the right to work and be independent? What a false economy. How can you be free if you have to trade your very body for that freedom? The injustice of it hit Kitty as a wave of acute grief. Staggering out onto York Street, now lit by gaslight against the winter's evening gloom, she was in shock. Dreck had her told she could not break the contract now it was signed; she had to fulfill his wishes. In a daze, and concentrating on breathing in the cold evening air to dilute the smell of the sweat and cigars from the man's body pressing up against her, Kitty walked on to Waterloo Bridge. She was aiming for the Strand, from where she could catch a bus to Liverpool Street and then home to Epping Forest. Home to Dora. Dora, who believed the stage would never be a respectable place for a woman to work. Who might think Kitty had brought this on herself, and be embarrassed for the shame her niece would cause their new family friend. What could she do?

I looked over the parapet at the Thames below. Should I go over?

No, that would be cowardly and I had always wanted to be brave and courageous like a man. Like a "man," after the cowardly thing I had just escaped from? No, I would develop the courage of a "woman" and somehow, some time avenge the insult I had experienced. So I clinched my teeth, went home and kept my own counsel on the subject.[14]

Kitty never spoke about what had happened to her in Mr. Dreck's office. She only wrote about it in her unpublished autobiography, the first time she had ever committed the memory to paper or shared it with anyone. Her blinding anger, that of a young woman approaching her twentieth birthday and discovering the world was a cruel and dangerous place for women who wanted to make something of themselves, ricocheted across her entire life. Like many women subjected to such violence and violation, the experience drove her thoughts to a very dark place. But she was resilient, and for now, she had to work. There was a contract to fulfill.

On the following Monday, Kitty left for the east coast. The hall was a part of a small hotel and public house, in a seaside town full of foreign sailors, mostly from Russia and Germany. The hall itself was tiny, with a small platform at one end and just a piano for accompaniment. On her first night, with little care for her own safety, Kitty found herself in the middle of a knife fight. As her song ended, two sailors had broken out into an argument that had quickly turned violent. In a flash Kitty had pushed her way between them, grabbing the sleeve of both of the men's arms to stop the knives from striking. It was incredibly brave—and incredibly stupid.

The fight had ended and Kitty had become a darling of both the hall's proprietors and her audience, but, lying in her bed that night, had she wondered why the danger had not mattered to her? There had been an empty numbness hovering inside her lungs since the attack by Mr. Dreck, and she felt no joy in her work or the engagement. Returning to London a week later, Kitty went, feet like lumps of lead, back to the office on York Road. She had little choice; Dreck was the agent who had taken an interest in her, so where else could she go, young and inexperienced as she was at that time? Kitty made sure to appear when the office was busy and hoped that the positive and pleased reviews she had had over the last week would carry her through. But on seeing her, Mr. Dreck regretted he could do nothing further for her, as the report of her performances, he said, was not satisfactory. The cowardly lie of a man who viewed the women who came to him in search of work as easily dispensable, whether or not they submitted to his abuse.

> Life was utterly bleak, blank, volcanic and unbearable. My aunt, who had never been enthusiastic over my stage venture, now became cutting and sarcastic at my lack of ability. Even an introduction to Mr. Dreck was wasted on me. I better give up all further idea of the stage and stay with her until I found a husband to keep me.[15]

Dora's husband was even crueler. He had only ever tolerated Kitty's presence in the house, and now that she was unable to bring in any money, she was once again a burden. Worse still, Dora had written to Kitty's other aunts and uncle to tell them of her new career, and in return had received only silence or expressions of disappointment. The rejection was universal, and Kitty wondered if she was going mad. She felt crushed, suffocated by what had happened, by the roller coaster of joy and sorrow and the unbearable weight of dreams dashed beyond all hope. At the end of one particularly vicious argument, Kitty packed her bags and left, never to return. What good was a family who only thought of her as a drain on resources, a pawn to make money for them, either through talent or marriage? Who could never accept the life she wanted to live? Taking her Bible, a copy of Goethe's poems printed in 1806, and her songbooks, Kitty walked out into the night.

*   *   *

Although her experience with Mr. Dreck now forced her to seek work without an agent, the music halls were where she wanted, desperately, to be. It was a dream shared by many. Kitty came from a middle-class family, and by 1892 the *St. James Gazette* was recording that "Ladies of birth are beginning to betray a suspicious eagerness to show 'Arry their ankles," as middle- and even upper-class daughters began to see the music halls as the new home for their aspirations.[16] As the nineteenth century drew to a close, the *Nottingham Evening Post* reported that a number of children of the aristocracy had joined the ranks of the dramatic professions: the "young Earl of Yarmouth" had recently made his debut on the American stage, and in England Lord Rosslyn, the Countess Russell, the Countess of Orkney, Lady Frances Hope, and "Miss Blair of Mr. Wilson Barrett's Company" (who was also a daughter of the Dowager Duchess of Sutherland) were all appearing, or had appeared, across the theaters and music halls of the United Kingdom.[17] But the social exchange was never one way and, in contrast, the *South Wales Daily News* listed all those women who had managed to cross from the working stage into high society:

> It would be hard to tell how many actresses have of late years married into aristocratic families. Miss Dollie Tester, who sang in the chorus, married the Marquis of Ailesbury; Lord Euston allied himself to Miss Kate Cooke; Miss Nellie Leamar married the Hon. Hubert Dunscombe; a French lady well known on the London stage, Miss Carneille Dubois, married the Hon. Wyndham Stanhope; and Miss Lillie Ernest became the Lady Mansel. It seems only yesterday since Miss Belle Bilton's name was regularly in the music-hall bills; she is now, of course, Countess Clancarty.[18]

These women were rule-breakers, social transgressors, women who refused to stay in the place the patriarchal society had carved out for them. Their existence directly challenges the belief that Kitty and her contemporaries, the women of the music halls, had no power, independence, or freedom to choose. It shows us that these are women who could not be controlled, at a time when femininity was often only ever defined by men, or how men thought women should appear in public. Much like today, when conservative commentators argue that women should express themselves as "ladylike" when what they really mean is "submissive," the women surrounding Kitty in the music halls refused to obey. Their stories influenced her to carve out a place in their world, rather than ask for a man's permission to belong.

One of the most famous was Belle Bilton, known as "the much-photographed music hall artiste"; the National Gallery still holds numerous images of Belle, from both her music hall career and her later society marriage, in its catalog.[19] She was a Victorian pinup, for men and women alike. Born in Kent at some point in the mid-1860s, Isobel "Belle" Bilton first began performing in the halls when she was fourteen, and rapidly gained the attention of audiences in London's music halls, owing to her striking features.[20] Staring out of a photograph taken just after her marriage, head gently tilted to one side, Belle is both tantalizing and untouchable.

As Kitty was attending her first lessons in Waterloo Road, Belle was appearing at the "Alhambra, Oxford and other West-end halls," engaged "at a handsome salary"—reportedly between £1,000 and £1,500 a year.[21] The name "Belle Bilton" would at this time have been on everyone's lips, her position one that a young music hall ingenue like Kitty would have wanted to aspire to.

It was after a performance at the Empire Theatre that Belle first met Lord Dunlo in April 1889. Introduced at the Corinthian Club, he had soon "laid siege to the heart of the happy lady."[22] The Corinthian had close connections with the theatrical world, having been founded by journalist and theatrical impresario John Hollingshead, who referred to himself as "a licensed dealer in legs, short skirts, French adaptations, Shakespeare, taste and musical glasses."[23] It would surprise no one when, a few years after Belle and Dunlo had begun their romance there, it would be closed down for being revealed as "a disorderly house"—one where men and women could meet without fear of prying, prudish eyes.

A music hall singer like Belle, you might think, would never be taken seriously as the object of a young viscount's affections; it was therefore, perhaps, a surprising party that entered the Hampstead Registry Office a mere three months after they had first met, on July 10, 1889. The *Western Times* carried a rumor that in the few weeks prior to their marriage there had been the threat of "an impending action for 'breach' in consequence of a letter written by the young man," stoking rumors that Dunlo had simply offered to marry Belle to be able to sleep with her—promising the stars, only to try and discard her after he had gotten his way.[24] But, instead, they had arrived at the altar. Belle, "a beauty of the halls," was accompanied by her sister, Miss Flo Bilton, and the bridegroom was accompanied by his friend, Mr. Minshull Ford.[25] But there was a flaw in their plan. The viscount was only twenty years old and had yet to reach his majority, which meant he was marrying without his father's permission.[26] Dunlo would not turn twenty-one—and so be free to make his own decisions—until the twenty-ninth of December that year, and so forces were quickly moved to drive the newly married couple apart.[27] The announcement of their wedding in numerous papers carried with it the unusual statement that "The Viscount, accompanied by his tutor, will probably leave England for Australia in the course of a few days."[28] Dunlo's father, the elder Lord Clancarty, was "indignant at his son's choice of wife," having only learned of it five days later in the Carlton Club. He was determined not to have his family line sullied by a common working-class actress, whom he saw as little better than a whore.[29] Moving at lightning speed, he arranged for his son to be "sent on a prolonged tour," half a world away from the wife he had just married. There, the poor boy was "induced to become a party to divorce proceedings against his wife," as his tutor and agents from his father filled his head with grotesque sexual rumors.[30] Listed in the divorce proceedings, now issued against Belle, were the insinuations that she was conducting a torrid affair with a Mr. Wertheimer, "a name well known in the art circles," even though he had "shown the greatest friendship to the young couple."[31]

The scandal of a music hall star with a lurid sex life managing to trap a wealthy son of the aristocracy into marriage should have been resolved quickly—if we are to believe that the Victorians loathed public sexual impropriety, especially on the part of a woman. And the fact that Belle had actually married her paramour, rather than being content with only being "kept" by him, was something that shook the basis of male understanding of what casual sexual relationships meant. Kitty experienced this understanding and attitude for herself in the 1890s when, out to dinner with three young swells she had met at the stage door, she recorded the story of one of her companions, who was:

> . . . quite a nice youngster, after stopping at two or three friendly wayside inns, became reminiscent and confided to his pals that he was secretly married to a Gaiety Girl. "Good God, old chap, you're joking," they both exclaimed. But no, he told the whole story of how they had met and so forth, and the church they were married in. They seemed positively shocked at him being married to her. All right if he had merely been keeping her.[32]

Belle had achieved what some might think would have been socially impossible. She had jumped from the rough-and-ready world of the music halls to the height of respectable society. Her sexual accessibility and her potential for sexual knowledge were no longer contained within a class of women who were kept separate from decent society. If Belle was allowed to remain, and indeed was accepted by the social elites, what would this mean for the respectable women of the middle classes, women like Kitty's Aunt Dora, who defined themselves by their determined lack of sexual knowledge and anti-sensual nature? The very idea of class boundaries and sexual respectability had suddenly been challenged openly by a young female music hall star, just as they would be challenged by Kitty later on.

The trial lasted for six long summer days, ending on July 30, 1890.[33] The earl brought evidence from dismissed servants, a disgruntled music hall agent, and several hired detectives to prove the existence of adultery between Belle and Wertheimer.[34] Perhaps most shocking of all was not the accusation of adultery, but the revelation that Belle had an illegitimate child, born not long before her marriage to Lord Dunlo.[35] Belle admitted to this without any shame in the witness box. She had been involved with a man, now in prison, who had abandoned her; and she had given birth to their son, Isidore, in 1888.[36] Mr. Wertheimer had acted as her protector during the later stages of her pregnancy, furnishing a house for Belle, her sister, and her sister's husband in Maidenhead, where the baby was born. The newspapers were in raptures. On the first day of the trial, *The Northern Echo* had reported that "Belle's clear cut beautiful features and fine eyes were not concealed but further refined by the wearing of the lightest of white veils. She wore pink with white braid trimmings."[37] How she looked, how she sounded, and what she wore were of as much interest to the journalists and readers of the Victorian newspapers as the details of her sex life.

It seems highly unlikely that, even with such a fascination surrounding her, Belle could have successfully defeated the challenges to her character, especially in light of her own revelations of illegitimate pregnancy. The earl produced evidence from a number of private detectives, who stated that "after Lord Dunlo went away, Mr. Wertheimer returned and was Lady Dunlo's almost daily visitor."[38] One of them, Randle Clare, asserted he had watched "Lady Dunlo and Mr. Wertheimer together on several occasions at the Cafe Royal."[39] Marmaduke Wood, an officer in the Somerset Militia and a supposed friend to Lord Dunlo, gave a statement surrounding the circumstances in which Belle and her husband had first met, saying, "he and Lord Dunlo and Lord Albert Osbourne had tossed up to see which should have her, and the lot fell to Lord Dunlo."[40] There were also claims Wood had publicly boasted he had "been improperly intimate" with Belle, although he claimed "as an officer and a gentleman" to have no memory of saying such a thing.[41] When the earl took the stand he painted a picture of being a despairing father to a weak but mostly naive son: "he intended his son for the army, but he had failed on examination. He attempted to get him into the Hereford Militia, but he failed to turn up in time for his examination."[42]

The earl admitted that he had insisted on his son going abroad until he was twenty-one, and that he did not believe the marriage was a valid one.[43] On learning it had taken place, he had "instigated enquiries as to the lady, and had heard that his son had incurred heavy debts," but he denied promising to pay those debts if his son agreed to sign a petition to divorce his wife.[44]

This implication of parental blackmail was perhaps key to how the British public responded to "Dunlo Divorce Case." Belle was not a governess or shop girl caught out by reaching too high; as a music hall star, she dealt in fantasy, personifying romance on the stage by feeding her audience star-crossed lovers or images of virtuous domestic life. Coupled with this status as a romantic heroine in the halls was her acknowledgment of her own sexual history, which did not come with any apology, but was rather simply stated as fact. She took ownership of her sexual past.

All of this meant that the earl soon found himself cast in the role of villain. He had used private detectives in the case, and had exposed Belle's sexual history, and these looked to the public like attacks on a virtuous and honest young woman by an old-fashioned and prudish aristocrat, out of touch and heavy-handed. This attitude, and its callous delivery, was not well received at the trial, which reached a dramatic climax when Lord Dunlo unexpectedly appeared and took the stand, and immediately "protested that his affection for his wife and his belief in her were as great as ever."[45] He produced a letter from Belle, written to him during his banishment, to read from the witness box.[46] In it she declared, "Whatever people may say of me, don't believe them. I love you dearly. I wish people would leave other people's business alone."[47] Lord Dunlo's letters were equally loving, declaring "he did not believe the 'horrid, horrid things' alleged against her, and that he was dreaming of her all day and all night."[48] The letters were read at Belle's instigation.[49] It was, perhaps, her experience in the music halls that had taught her the power of words when they are performed.

The judge, Sir James Hannen, told the jury at the end of the case that "he did not think it fair to assume that every woman on the music hall stage, or every woman who had given birth to an illegitimate child, was purchasable."[50] Such a statement by a judge in an adultery trial directly challenges preconceptions of how women in the music hall, or women at large, might have been perceived by late Victorian society. Hannen was a figure of the establishment, not a radical thinker arguing for free love or female emancipation. The divorce courts existed as a form of social control, "patrolling the boundaries of acceptable marital behaviour" and identifying what was and was not acceptable.[51] Yet, when faced with a female music hall star—a class of women often publicly perceived as sexually accessible or disreputable—who admitted to previous sexual impropriety, Hannen advised caution not against Belle, but against judging her. He specifically addressed both her life as a music hall star and her illegitimate child and stated that these two factors were not indications of a woman being immoral or corruptible.

It's not as hard as you might think to find men in the nineteenth century who didn't believe that sex was their automatic right or that women were a currency to be traded between themselves. Kitty's experience of Dreck, and Belle's experience of the earl, show how clearly misogyny guided some men in their behavior, wreaking untold damage and abuse on women's lives. But it is equally clear that they were not the only kind of men alive at this time; soon, other men, those who believed women were equal, would join a fight women intended to win. The jury clearly shared Judge Hannen's position, finding no evidence of Belle's supposed adultery with Wertheimer, and the case was immediately dismissed.[52]

However, not all voices looked on the trial with favor. The *Cardiff Times* carried a scathing report of the collapse of the case, warning that the young viscount had been:

... allured by the meretricious glitter of the fast life in London, [where] this boy had his head turned by the first pretty girl he encountered, and not possessing sufficient strength of mind or determination to extricate himself from this model of life, ended up by leading to the altar a lady whose antecedents were not of that character which would be dwelt upon in any sphere of life.[53]

Describing Belle as "a few years older than her husband," and as a woman who "probably knew more of the world and mankind than ever he will do in his existence," the *Cardiff Times* represented what some might take to be the dominant opinion of women like Belle Bilton in the 1880s and 1890s.[54] Specifically focusing on lurid insinuations of her exposure "to the temptations which an unprotected girl upon the Music-hall stage encounters at the hands of every rich libertine throughout the kingdom," the paper draws a clear correlation between the status of a female music hall performer, her perceived sexual immorality, and its effect on naive young men.[55] Although Belle's salary was widely reported, it was only the *Cardiff Times* that pointed out that "perhaps he [Lord Dunlo] is to be congratulated upon the fact that his wife is clever enough to provide an income which will support them both."[56]

This acknowledgment of the earning power of female music hall stars like Belle shows just how independent and powerful these women were in their own right. These are the experiences that pushed Kitty and others like her to defend their choice to work and be independent by fighting for their rights. Not only did Belle succeed in defying public accusations of sexual immorality while at the same time revealing she had had an illegitimate child, but there were multiple reports that Lord Dunlo was now bankrupt, cut off by his father the earl in retaliation for his marriage, and it would be Belle who would be supporting them both. This she continued to do, in both music halls and pantomimes, until the earl's death in 1891.

Her place in society, as the music hall girl turned countess, was even given royal approval: the *Lancashire Evening Post* and the *Yorkshire Evening*

Post carried the same report of the great fondness Alexandra of Denmark, wife of Edward VII, had for her:

> The Queen, when Princess of Wales, took a great interest in the welfare
> of the young and beautiful countess at the time of the attempt to bring
> about a separation between her and her husband, and this interest has
> been maintained. Indeed, Lady Clancarty was especially commanded
> to meet her Majesty on the occasion of her last visit to Ireland.[57]

Belle Bilton died on December 31, 1906. Her death was reported on New Year's Day, with the papers christening her "the most beautiful woman of her time."[58] As a woman whose entire sex life and sexual history was put on public display, and yet who emerged triumphant, Belle is a fierce example of female independence in the nineteenth century. Her humanity, her acknowledgment of human nature without artifice, spoke to the British public and made her a heroine in the face of a traditional patriarchal system that was attempting to judge her.

But returning to 1890, another young woman was struggling against the negative attitudes some held toward the women of the music halls. As the door to Aunt Dora's had slammed behind her, Kitty quickly realized she was now utterly alone. Clutching a paper, likely full of the details of Belle's trial, to keep the rain from soaking her to the skin as she walked the evening streets trying to formulate a plan to keep herself safe, and also find a bed for the night, Kitty realized there was one friend who she could rely on: Conny Argus, the young widow she had met in Glasgow. In the early hours of the morning, Conny was woken by loud voices on her doorstep. Kitty hadn't wanted to wake her up and so had curled up in the porch to wait until daylight to knock on the door, but she had been discovered by a policeman who mistook her for a vagrant and was attempting to move her on. Close to tears as she was, Kitty was still steadfastly refusing. Conny flew downstairs and opened the door, hurrying Kitty inside and offering her a place to stay until she was back on her feet. An old pro, even at her young age, Conny understood how the industry worked, and also that an agent was not the be-all and end-all for finding an engagement. She advised Kitty to wait for *The Stage* to come out on the following Thursday, as it would be full of theater and music halls' calls for performers, and she would be certain to find something.

Conny was right: "Wanted at once, lady for Britannia, Theatre, French Exhibition, Earl's Court" was exactly the show Kitty needed. Having no money, she had to walk the seven miles from Greenwich to Earl's Court. Although for some this would have been the final straw after a series of awful experiences, Kitty relished being outside and seeing London. Soon Union Jacks and Tricolor flags fluttered in the sky overhead, and with each step Kitty must have felt that her run of bad luck was coming to an end. And how right she was. On reaching the theater, to her joy and relief Kitty found her old dancing tutor and several of her previous classmates from Waterloo Road. She was quickly hired, taking the central role of Britannia in the grand dramatic performance. This was followed by the renting of a room in May Street, West Kensington, and with that, Kitty's life quickly settled into the routine of Sunday visits to Conny, performances at Earl's Court, and wandering London whenever she had an afternoon to spare.

It had been a traumatic year, but as 1890 drew to a close Kitty found herself on the way to Bristol for an engagement in the pantomime *Aladdin*. Her freedom was tentatively cherished; she now understood what price might be demanded of her to keep it. But the experiences of the past months had had an unexpected effect: she was now more determined, more resolute than ever before, to have her independence, free from the power of men. Free from her abusive father, free from the abuse agents believed was their right; somewhere deep inside her a revolutionary spirit began to stir.

4
Love & Lies

"Like every normal girl I had my dreams of a wonderful ideal, hero, lover in whom all the finest qualities of the Knights of Chivalry were concentrated," Kitty recalled of her younger, naive self, "but since I was determined to remain single and self-supporting, I had transferred the love I might have given to my hero to my work."[1] Sex, other than as a definition between the genders, was an unknown element. "A mixture of something very private, personal, mysterious, sacred and nasty, not to be openly discussed," she recorded as she headed to her next engagement in Bristol.[2] The assault by Mr. Dreck was the only sexual experience Kitty had ever known, and her closeted upbringing had spared her the full knowledge of what might have occurred. But she was closeted no longer, and she found herself, as is so often the case when young women set foot in the world alone, about to receive a rapid education into the practical realities of life and love as an independent woman.

Arriving in Bristol, Kitty was quickly captivated by the rugged riverside scenery and the huge suspension bridge, towering above the Avon Gorge and linking Bristol to Somerset, that acts as the final monument to the engineering genius of Isambard Kingdom Brunel. She wandered around the city, breathless after climbing the Christmas

Steps, an ancient street that still lies in the heart of Bristol, and exploring St. Michael's Hill, where she found rooms to share with Ruby Kerr, another member of the pantomime troupe.

The estrangement from Aunt Dora and the rest of her family put out of her mind, Kitty found the Christmas season in Bristol intensely joyful, but it did bring an unexpected experience. Having only recently discovered what men thought they were owed by the girls of the stage, Kitty was about to discover the women who had every intention of both blaming and judging her for it.

After the first matinee of *Aladdin*, the ladies of the chorus and the ballet, who had formed an excited and noisy gang, were invited to tea at the theater's next-door hall. "What nice, kind people," Kitty thought.[3] She had, however, unwittingly fallen into a trap. A temperance trap, to be precise. After a round of polite tea and biscuits, the girls' hosts began to pray, and of course Kitty and the others were expected to join. "The unctuous 'rubbing in' of sin and repentance was so nauseous, I could have thrown their tea back at them," Kitty fumed.[4] This was her first experience of the rescue organizations that had grown up in a fury during Josephine Butler's campaign to repeal the Contagious Diseases Acts; they were well-meaning, but often intensely bigoted and occasionally doing more harm than good. The fertile ground of an acting company full of young men and women living together and performing, with tight costumes and tighter embraces, in full view of a paying crowd, had thrown the hall's members into an excitable religious fervor.

> We all smothered our indignation until we returned to the dressing rooms, when the storm burst in more expressive than polite language, "bloody cheek!," "what the hell do they think we are?" "You'd think they'd picked us up in the gutter." "Call that religion?" and so forth. "Impertinence" was all I could think of, my dressing room education not yet having reached a "flow of language." No more teas like that for me![5]

Unable to escape the good manners that had been drummed into her since birth, Kitty had had no ability to refuse the organization's request for her name and the address of the rooms she and Ruby had taken. A few days later, an elderly and somewhat austere lady appeared on their doorstep. What followed was an even more torturous tea than they had previously suffered, as Kitty attempted to be courteous while the matron lectured her "about the temptations girls on the stage were exposed to and men seeking their destruction."[6] On hearing these opening bars of a sales pitch on how the Good Shepherd was always looking for lost young sheep to save, Ruby left the room as fast as politeness would allow her. Never able to control herself if under attack from false accusation or unfair judgments, and without the tempering presence of Ruby to hold her to the rules of decorum, Kitty finally lost her temper: "I told her that girls on the stage were not any more exposed to temptations than in any other ways of trying to earn an honest living," and that "she ought to teach men to 'resist temptation,'" rather than leaving the defense of their virtue at the doors of young women who knew very little about what they were supposed to be defending themselves from.[7]

> What was the matter with people wanting to "save" others? Why didn't they mind their own business and save themselves? What did she mean by "men seeking their destruction"? I had never heard the expression before. I was shocked at the explanation Ruby gave me. Was it possible? And I had such a high opinion of them. Man, God's image! Was this the meaning of Mr. Dreck's conduct towards me? It was all so new and confusing to me. I couldn't broach the subject with anyone else, not feeling on safe enough ground in my English besides being shy at anything "not nice," nor did I want to display my ignorance.[8]

How confusing the world is when we first start to truly understand it. Kitty's family had done little to prepare her for a life outside of their protected and enclosed environment. She had no sisters to learn from, and had been kept by Dora as a virtual housemaid, with little connection to the world beyond the daily routine laid out for her. But now she was a free woman, with all the terrors and pitfalls freedom can offer. What had hurt her the most was not the revelation that some men could be bad, but that men could be bad at all. For the first time, Kitty began to learn how complex the adult world around her could really be, and the damage it could wreak on women's lives.

Next door to the rooms she shared with Ruby was an old-fashioned Lock Hospital, a quasi-treatment center for women suffering from STDs and a hangover from the days of the Contagious Diseases Acts. Ruby's explanation to Kitty was dramatic and mysterious; the hospital was full of women, she explained, "suffering from loathsome diseases" that they had contracted "through intercourse with men."[9] Left to picture beds full of women suffering from incurable illnesses, and slowly rotting from the inside out, Kitty made herself a promise: "No intercourse with men for me," although at the time she had absolutely no understanding of what it meant.[10] Shortly after Ruby's revelation, Kitty noticed the skin between her fingers had become blistered and sore. Hearing dressing-room talk warning of "the itch," slang for commonly contracted STD's, she tearfully confessed her fears of having contracted it to the theater doctor. His roars of laughter followed her out of the door, but he did arm her with an iron tonic and orders to rest.

Returning to London in the new year, Kitty found work in the German Exhibition, now at Earl's Court. But these gigantic exhibitions, portraying the history and culture of other countries, would pull in a grander, wider audience, and so, for the first time, Kitty adopted a stage name. It was a name she claimed as her own, chosen at this moment to make sure none of her family would recognize her in the program, should a copy of it ever fall into their hands. Katherine Marie Schäfer—abused daughter, estranged niece, undocumented immigrant—was gone, and in her place stood the soon-to-be indomitable Kitty Marion. The exhibition required a rider, and soon Kitty had learned to ride and dismount with acrobatic elegance. Her horse had been named Lady

Dunlo, a tribute, of course, to the beautiful Belle Bilton, now Countess of Clancarty. At twenty years old, Kitty was strikingly beautiful, with her red hair piled high above her shoulders and an easy manner and friendly disposition. She quickly fell in with a group of other actresses from the exhibition, and they began to regularly take tea in each other's rooms—the Victorian equivalent of accepting a Facebook friend request. One of them, two years younger than Kitty and engaged to be married, was desperate to share everything she was learning in that giddy, excitable claiming of adulthood that comes with early sexual experiences. Her brother was a doctor and she had studied his books, so was taken by the other girls as an authority on these matters. Acutely aware of her own inexperience, Kitty listened over tea and tableware with rapt attention. What she learned surprised and then angered her:

> The fact that parents, Father and Mother, not God, were the most immediately responsible for the creation of children. Their physical act, not merely the prayerful magic of the marriage service was the preliminary to human concept as well as among the "lower" animals. And this was the relationship that should be the most sacred and beautiful between man and woman which was referred to by our sanctimonious visitor in Bristol as "seeking their destruction." If "destruction" is wrong in itself how could a "marriage" license make it right? If natural and physiologically right, what need of the marriage "license"? I was thankful Father was not within my reach, for what I was now prepared to say to him would probably have led to a tragedy. How dared he, how dared any father reproach his child for being a burden and expense?[11]

It was the final straw. For her entire childhood, Kitty had carried the burden of being unwanted, a drain, an accident sent by God to torture and humiliate her father. He had caused her to think her existence was a curse, a torment he was to endure, with his great selflessness and humility. But now she knew the truth. It was not her fault. She wasn't a mystical accident, sent down as punishment or divine trial; she was the result of a simple physical act, a connection between a man and a woman—the most common side effect of love. This revelation caused Kitty to choose a path she would stick to for the rest of her life. She would never marry. No man would be worth the price of her freedom, and no man would use sex to control her.

Joining a new pantomime of *The Forty Thieves*, Kitty traveled to York, where she shared rooms with three other girls and with a landlady who was eager to acquaint her young, beautiful lodgers with the various young men she knew in the town, "in whose good conduct she had every confidence."[12] Preferring to make her own acquaintances, Kitty soon became friendly with the theater's musicians. The orchestra had been mostly drawn from "non-coms," slang for the non-commissioned officers who served in the military bands stationed in York. Riverboat parties became the main social activity for young actors and musicians, who took advantage of every opportunity to get away from the theater and enjoy themselves. And for Kitty, it brought her first tentative suitor. Corporal Billie White, a year younger than Kitty, toweringly tall and well educated, came from a good Northampton family. With an air of rakish behavior and an assumed name that, he revealed to the shocked company, he had taken on after running away from home to enlist in the Royal Dragoons, he quickly found his way to the side of the demure, intrigued, but also confused, Miss Kitty Marion. Billie escorted her to the noncoms ball and, hearing of her love of horses, took her to the Dragoons' stables. The dressing room was rife with speculation, but nothing more came of their relationship, although they shared an infrequent but friendly correspondence until he married a schoolteacher some time later.

After York, with engagements following in Manchester, Newcastle, Bristol, and London, Kitty joined a highly successful and well-respected theatrical company performing the comedy *Lady Slavery*. The company was packed with women and, surrounded by young girls either marrying or not marrying their various paramours, Kitty began to feel that she might be missing out on an important part of life. But her early experiences had left her unable to understand what it was she either wanted or needed from a man.

> So far no man had wanted to undertake the responsibility of me as wife, not receiving any encouragement in that direction though several had professed such love for me that they would "do anything for me, if I would only let them." It was easy enough to decline their love with indignation or laughter, whichever the situation required. I corresponded with half a dozen boys from different towns at the same time. They liked me, thought I was more like a boy chum than a girl, would I write just to show I thought of them sometime. No doubt, that is the story they tell all girls . . . the correspondence fizzles out when other actresses come their way or other boys your own.[13]

For Kitty, her life now was, in many ways, all she had ever desired. She was traveling across the country, meeting new friends and companions, and learning about the history and sites of interest in every town and city she arrived at. Her education was rapidly expanding, and in several towns the company found their evening performances had been preceded by the lecture tour of an American medical woman, Dr. Mary Longshore-Potts. Armed with lantern slides, and giving a series of physiology lectures "for women only," the doctor explained that she gave her lectures all over the world, except in the United States:

> where sex was not permitted in open, decent discussion. Dr. Potts ended her lectures with "procreation" and "maternity," vital subjects which, it seemed to me, should be discussed before both sexes together, since they were of the greatest, most vital and sacred importance to both, and would promote a better understanding of and respect for each other. It was certainly more elevating to listen to Dr. Potts on sex, than to the dressing room discussion thereof by those who thought they "knew all" when they knew little or nothing.[14]

But the new knowledge she had acquired inspired Kitty to try new things, and during an engagement in Edinburgh, she befriended two young veterinary students, Jack and Ernest. Accompanied by another young actress named Minnie, Kitty, Ernest, and Jack often went for "long walks in every direction outside the city the boys knew, getting home just in time for tea and the theatre."[15] Sharing rooms with two other members of the company, Kitty often found Jack and Ernest waiting for her at the stage door after a performance, and they would walk her home, coming inside for a drink and smoke while the performers had supper. Jack's gentle acquaintance quickly blossomed into affection, and Kitty confessed, "whisper it not among my own folks or to 'Mrs. Grundy,' since I don't wish to shock them, and what the mind doesn't know, the heart doesn't grieve, we kissed each other, though never likely to be engaged."[16]

That first kiss, born from affection rather than assault, would be treasured by Kitty for many years. Although she remained determined never to marry, Kitty clearly held a lot of affection for this young man, whom she wrote to long after leaving Edinburgh. It was the first time she had experienced a friendship with a man on equal terms, who saw her as she saw herself. Their connection was so powerful that, even decades later, Kitty transcribed one of Jack's early letters into her autobiography, creating a lasting record of his kiss and his understanding. It throws open a window onto Kitty, so often so careful in what she might betray, as others saw her, and as they loved her. Jack wrote:

You have a rather matter of fact temperament and inclined to take things as they come . . . very much addicted to plain-speaking which lends you at times to say things you are sorry for afterwards; very determined and fond of outdoor life and animals; capable of deep feeling which you endeavour to hide; strong in your likes and dislikes; have a hasty temper but not inclined to bear malice; self confident, vivacious, fond of company and I should say very superstitious. Have had a good deal of worry and trouble in your past life over which you sometime brood.[17]

He saw her with the clear eyes of a young lover, straight to the bone and under the skin, where Kitty kept his memory for a very long time.

But the life of a young actress has very little permanence, and soon Kitty was on her way to Nottingham, followed by Huddersfield. As the years passed she became more confident in her own sensuality, more accepting of the attention men might offer, as long as they understood the rules and did not cross her own personal boundaries. It was rather enjoyable, finding she could have a man in every town. They often conformed to a similar type: intelligent, handsome, and quick to laugh, capable of identifying a chink in her armor, just enough to get below the surface, but never enough to cause her to fall in love. Kitty remained committed to her belief that marriage was one of the quickest ways to lose her identity and her freedom, something she had no intention of ever doing. But she soon found that there were many men who had just as little intention of marrying her as she did of marrying them, and although she objected wholeheartedly to the sexual harassment and abuse of women within her workplace, in her personal life the idea of a casual intimate relationship was one that continually intrigued her.

In Huddersfield she received her first serious offer. Leaving the theater one night, loaded with parcels from her latest performance, Kitty found herself suddenly bookended by two determinedly polite and well-dressed young men.

> "... I have been admiring you every night last week at the Grand. You look so lovely in that black evening gown," said my would-be porter, still trying to take my parcel, which I relinquished rather than risk its contents being scattered. We hadn't far to go, and the situation did not warrant a "how dare you?" kind of scene. I had suffered many lectures in the dressing room and at home on "diplomacy," "spoiling sport,"

missing "opportunities" and so forth, that I became quite tolerant toward that sort of approach by men.[18]

Kitty quickly recognized the more earnest of her two suitors; he had occupied the same box every night while the show had been playing in Leeds. Now here he was in Huddersfield, determined to take her out to dinner. Allowing the two men to walk her home, Kitty received an ecstatic welcome from her landlady, who had been watching as she passed the window. "Two of the richest men in Huddersfield," she had proclaimed, recognizing Kitty's escort, only ever identified by Kitty as "J.P.C.," as the owner of the land her house was built on.[19]

Invited to supper the following night at the Wool Pack Inn, Kitty had a thoroughly enjoyable evening; dining on "Oysters, excellently cooked and served, pheasant, etc., champagne and liqueur" was a pleasant change from the careful economy with which she ran her own life.[20] The focus of the evening's conversation was monopolized by J.P.C.'s current embarrassment of being sued. When relationships broke down and women found themselves suddenly abandoned, one of the few ways they could reclaim their honor or reputation, or simply exact revenge, was to sue a former lover for "breach of promise." This made their casual sexual relationship—one outside of the confines of marriage—acceptable in Victorian eyes. It involved the woman believing, or claiming to have believed, that the man had intended to marry her, which was why she had entered a physical relationship; but, having had his way, he had refused to make good on this promise, so in retaliation many women used the courts to gain compensation. We may wonder how different the world might be if this was still an option today.

J.P.C., a young widower with one daughter, was being sued for £1,000, the sum his ex-lover believed most equal to the emotional damage his abandonment of her had caused. It's an odd approach, to use your broken promises to one woman as an attempt to attract another, but that appeared to be what J.P.C. was seeking to do to Kitty. After their dinner, which she escaped from unscathed, he invited her for a drive the next afternoon:

> . . . on the way home JPC started raving about my neck and arms again and suddenly blurted out, "I'd give you a thousand pounds to sleep with you for one night!" "I wouldn't for a million," I laughed back, "do you mean that?" "I do!" I said very empathically. He couldn't understand a woman not having her price, and such a price.[21]

A thousand pounds was a huge amount of money. It certainly caused Kitty a moment's discomfort to reject it but, although she enjoyed J.P.C.'s company, she felt no attraction to him, and so she could see no reason to enter into a physical relationship. This independence of spirit marked Kitty out among the many young women who were trying to lay claim to their independence before they won the vote. Often the complex relationship between sexual harassment and consensual sexual exchange posed too great a risk, leaving them powerless and afraid in situations they were unable to escape from. A breach of promise action was one of the few ways in which Victorian women could fight back—J.P.C. eventually settled his for £500—and they were frequently featured in the press, brought about by working women, middle-class women, schoolteachers, actresses, and music hall artists alike.

Geraldine Mary Hobbes, a music hall artist from Brighton, successfully sued a Mr. Fry, scene painter and manager of the Dover Theatre in Dover, for £100 for his breach of promise. Geraldine told the court that she had only been seventeen when she first appeared at the Dover, and Fry, promising to marry her, had repeatedly seduced her, leading to three children. When it was later revealed that Fry was already married Geraldine had left him "on account of the poor, wretched manner in which they lived" and sought compensation.[22] In stark contrast to Geraldine Hobbes's £100, in 1895 the music hall singer Catherine (sometimes Katherine) Kempshall sued Mr. Edgar

Holland, "a Liverpool gentleman of independent means," for £10,000 in damages in her breach of promise case. Unfortunately, she was not successful and, when the judge found for the defendant, Miss Kempshall launched herself across the courtroom, screaming "Beast, Beast!" in the direction of Mr. Holland. The *Western Mail* reported, almost as a side point, that later the same evening at the Old Bailey, Miss Kempshall had been acquitted of "feloniously shooting at Holland's sister."[23]

Her story didn't end there, and the following year Miss Kempshall burst into Holland's office in Liverpool and shot him three times in the chest.[24] He died shortly afterward, and she was tried for murder and sentenced to hang in 1897. But the plight of this music hall actress had caught the public sympathy, much like the case of Belle Bilton, and multiple petitions "containing several thousands of signatures" for her reprieve were sent to the home secretary.[25] The reprieve was granted and Miss Kempshall's sentence was commuted to life in Broadmoor Criminal Lunatic Asylum, where she remained until her death.[26]

The continual recurrence of breach of promise cases in the popular press demonstrates just how much of a universal female experience sex outside of marriage was known to be. Breach of promise was not a social secret; these cases were often referred to in music hall songs, not just in the lives of its performers, and Kitty would undoubtedly have heard them during an evening's performance. Leo Dryden, the popular comic singer whose affair with Charlie Chaplin's mother resulted in the breakdown of her marriage, had a song called "The Breach of Promise Case." He performed it in 1895, at the same time as Miss Kempshall's action was first receiving press attention:

> A breach of promise case there'll be 'twixt Susan Jane and me
> Because I haven't married her, exposure there must be
> Because I've been with her alone, and lingered on her face
> I now am the defendant in a breach of promise case.

Chorus: All through sitting on the sofa when the lights were low
All through being left alone, I blame her mother so
All through lingering and longering upon her female face
That's the reason of the breach, the breach of promise case.

They want five hundred pounds from me, as damages you know
I'd pay it up, if I had all the money that I owe
There's no mistake she's got me, Oh where was my common sense?
I'll tell this to the jury, when I'm asked for my defence.

The tone is comedic, laughing at the man who is being sued. There is a clear understanding of human experience, of sexual activity, and that women had the ability to hold to account the men to whom they became connected. But it wasn't only the male singers who used breach of promise cases in their material, female singers also saw them as an easy theme; the "Queen of the Music Halls," Marie Lloyd, alluded to it in a verse of her song "Wink the Other Eye":

In court, a breach of promise case,
Then they wink the other eye.
Upstairs, the maiden all forlorn
Then they wink the other eye.
She tells the judge her story
With a teardrop in her eye.
How the villain had deceived her
And she heaves a bitter sigh,
How he used to kiss and cuddle her
When nobody was nigh,
Then they wink the other eye.

Chorus: Say, boys, now is it quite the thing? Say, should we let you
have your fling? Oh! When you've got us on a string, Then you
wink the other eye.

Written in 1890, the song itself is a jolly, naughty, teasing take on Victorian life, while at the same time carrying in it an implicit warning to men about the consequences of their sexual behavior.

"Dirty dogs, that's all they think about," said Mabel, Kitty's roommate in Huddersfield, as they compared notes on that evening's gentlemen.[27] She was shocked at Kitty's refusal of J.P.C.'s £1,000 for a night with a man she might never have to see again, but equally understood her refusal to do so when she felt nothing for him. The dressing room of the theater, however, held harsher critics: "called me everything from a 'bloody prude' to a ditto idiot. I jolly-well, damn well and every other kind of bad-well, deserved to starve, refusing all that money instead of banking it."[28] Jealousy, and a shared need to survive in a world run by men, made for some unwelcome insults.

But, determined as she was to live her life free from a dependence on men, Kitty was about to meet someone who would shape the next few years of her life in an entirely unexpected way. Returning to Nottingham, she was introduced to Robert Halford, then one of the directors of the Nottingham Theatre Company. Halford was a widower, with four sons and three daughters, and he took a regular and open interest in the young ladies of his theater, although he always portrayed himself as a fatherly, caring figure. He kept a large house, Ashtree, in Nottingham, and would often invite a number of the cast to stay with him and his children while they were in town. Enjoying the company of these "fairies," as he christened the women, he believed was a privilege owed him by his older age.

Kitty rapidly became a family favorite, and it's clear that she found in the Halford home everything she had missed after her father's abuse and her estrangement from her wider family. "One of the most charming and precious experiences of my life," she wrote of the few years she was able to call Ashtree home.[29] When she was away from Nottingham, Halford would often send her gloves, or money, to help tide her over until she returned. And one Christmas, when Kitty found herself without any work for the first time in many years, to console her, Halford sent her an enormous, "delicious" Melton Mow-bray pie.[30]

However, the regard in which Halford held her seems to have had an odd tinge to it, possessive yet distant, as if she required his protection and yet he was never quite willing to claim her as his own, though he still regarded her as such. Perhaps he simply considered himself too old to be an adequate match for her, but in 1900 his attentions took a different turn. While he may not have been willing to marry Kitty himself, he had decided she would make an excellent wife for his eldest son, Bernard. "Bernard, the personification of that blond, blue-eyed, athletic, healthy British manhood you read about so much," Kitty wistfully recalled of an early meeting Halford set up between them on board Bernard's houseboat, then moored on the Trent at Atten-borough.[31] The weekend was a great success, and Kitty felt utterly at home on the water, "an ideal spot, just river, sky and country."[32] She was unaware, or determinedly unaware, of the machinations at play, but nearing thirty she would be unable to ignore the expectations Hal-ford would have for her.

As the new century got under way, Halford became tired of wait-ing for the connection to blossom between Bernard and his oblivious intended. Enjoying the late summer sunshine one day in Ashtree's conservatory, Kitty suddenly found herself beset by an unexpected proposition:

Mr. Halford entered saying, "Kitty, I hear you are going to spend the afternoon with Bernard on the houseboat." Then he placed his hands on my shoulders, looked me straight in the eyes and said, "Won't you try and 'hook him' this afternoon? I want to get him off my hands and it would give me the greatest pleasure to have you for a daughter-in-law, and on the day you marry Bernard I'll settle 1000 pounds a year on you in your own right." Who can imagine the thrill of surprise, hon-our, satisfaction, ecstasy, which I experienced! That this man for whom I had developed a reverence embracing all the finest emotions with which one human being can regard another, should want to gather me into his family as a daughter ... Dear Papa Halford. I thanked him, most inadequately I fear, placing the responsibility of the fulfilment of his hopes upon Bernard. Though I had come to regard marriage as the happiest relationship between a man and woman who loved each other, and had met several charming, congenial men, with any one of whom I felt I could be happy for the rest of my life, I still adhered to my early resolution never to marry, therefore never to encourage any man in that direction. Bernard had never paid me any particular attention, in fact, from casual remarks by his sisters I fancied he was "otherwise engaged." I fully realised all the material and social advantages I should gain from marrying him, in addition to ending my struggle for an existence, and decided should he propose I should be an utter fool not to accept him. So after lunch I set forth in high spirits for the train to Attenborough, where Bernard met and took me to the houseboat, on which my photo already graced the piano, as others did some of the rooms at "Ashtree."[33]

There was just one small flaw in the plan. Kitty, as much as she wanted to make Halford happy, was not in love with Bernard. Although, pragmatically, she knew marrying him would secure her future and return her to a happy family life, after a tea of strawberries and cream, an afternoon's rowing on the river, and a somewhat awkward goodbye kiss, she returned without an offer. Kitty had developed a deep affection for Bernard, one that they seemed to share for the rest of their lives, but she had little interest in marrying for marriage's sake, even if it would appease her favored father figure, Mr. Halford.

As 1904 dawned, bringing with it the signing of the Entente Cordiale between England and France, the birth of Graham Greene, and the opening of the London Coliseum, Kitty's time with the *Lady Slavery* company came to an end, and she began to cast around for more work. Perhaps it was time to return to the halls; she was older now and more prepared to fight for her right to work without exchanging sex in return than she had been as an inexperienced girl of nineteen. And after all, the money was always far better there than anywhere else. Setting about buying songs and costumes and finding bookings for the coming year, Kitty found herself once again in the clutches of the agents of the music halls. To her utter resignation and despair, nothing had changed since her last experience:

> . . . if I saw them in their offices, instead of talking business, they veered off to impertinent personalities, "weekends," and the old gag, "are you married?" till I felt utterly nauseated, and was glad to get out into the fresh air. They had no use for women who merely wanted legitimate work. I found that most women had to run the gauntlet in the same way. Heartsick and disgusted I wondered sometimes why life was made so difficult for women; what was the use of struggling on when the odds were all against one, why not end it all with one plunge?[34]

The disappointment Kitty felt at the abuses women regularly suffered in pursuit of their own independence was not new to her, but now it was to have a new and far more dangerous effect. After a meeting with Jack Munro of Willand's Agency, who attempted to assault her in the back of a cab at Waterloo Station, Kitty no longer felt the shame and embarrassment she had experienced in her youth. "I felt like killing the whole vile tribe," she wrote.[35] After escaping from Munro, Kitty gritted her teeth and "determined that somehow I would fight this vile, economic and sex domination over women which no man or woman should tolerate."[36]

But her bad luck was not at an end. Three weeks later she met with Mr. Sam Bury, who offered her an engagement at the Pavilion Glasgow, followed by the Pavilion Newcastle, for the next two weeks. Relieved that she had finally found a booking, Kitty called at the office for her contract but, to her horror, found that Bury was determined to replicate the advances of Mr. Dreck. He demanded a kiss.

I told him not to be silly and tried to "chaff him off," as I had been advised by other artists as a better way of handling such a situation, instead of becoming indignant. I said I'd kiss him when I returned from the north. Much as I wanted the work, I walked towards the door, not waiting for the counterpart of my contract, when he followed me and threw his arms around me, refusing to let me go until I kissed him. "All right" I said, and gave him what he called a peck on the cheek and dashed out. Some time later while discussing him and others of his ilk, as we often did in the dressing room, one of a sister turn told me she had "got used to it," that when first she resented this same Sam Bury's overtures, he laughed at her and said "I've had your sister, why shouldn't I have you?"[37]

So much had changed in Kitty now, she was so worn down by the violence women were faced with every time they tried to find legitimate work, that she was beginning to lose hope that there was any way to fight against such a corrupt system. "I felt sick, nauseated. How dared men take such brutal advantage of their economic power over women!" she furiously recalled.[38] In September, Kitty managed to secure a booking on the same bill as Houdini at the Regent in Salford, followed by a short engagement in Newcastle, but with little other work on the horizon, and with no interest in attempting to secure a proposal from Bernard, circumstances were becoming dire. But a sudden meeting in Newcastle brought with it the opportunity for a lifetime of security.

Misunderstood, henpecked, and dissatisfied Freddy, the son of a wealthy shipowner and alderman, had been compelled to marry a woman older than himself by his father, in the hopes that it would have a suitably calming effect on the wayward and passionate young man. It had, of course, only resulted in him becoming wilder and, looking for nightly refuge away from the domestic cage that his family had built for him, Freddy spent his nights in the music halls. One evening when Kitty took to the stage, her voice and bright red hair captivating the audience, Freddy found he had fallen utterly in love. Pursuing her relentlessly, he offered Kitty the chance of being what she had always dreaded most, a "kept woman." But by now, knowing what she did, and having only ever experienced abuse and assault in pursuit of her work and her freedom, what other option did she really have?

> I was becoming more and more disgusted with the struggle for exis-
> tence on commercial terms of sex, and seriously considered the pref-
> erence of living with a man who professed to love me, to being at the
> mercy of so many who hinted, expected, even demanded sex submis-
> sion, as well as coin of the Realm in commission, as an inducement to
> procure work for one.[39]

Kitty was not alone in considering a life that would give her some form of freedom and security in exchange for being a man's mistress, rather than the captivity of marriage. The history of the music halls contains many women who manipulated their sexuality for social or economic gain. Bessie Bellwood, known off stage by her married name, Mrs. Kate Nicholson,[40] was a well-known singer in the 1870s and 1880s. She had become so popular that the 1882 Hunmanby Hare Coursing competition had been won by a dog bearing her name.[41] Bessie left no room for innocence in her performances, reveling in the heavily sexualized and erotic image of a working-class woman. As one reviewer proclaimed:

> We think it must be said that Miss Bellwood sails as close to the wind
> as possible in the way of suggestiveness; but nobody seems to find
> fault with her, and the "faster" she becomes the more she appears to
> be appreciated.[42]

Bessie's "fast" nature on the stage soon began to appear after the curtain came down; Lord Mandeville, Duke of Manchester, had become so enamored with her that he left his wife and lived with her openly in a "scandalous public relationship . . . ostracised from London drawing rooms."[43] Determined to have her husband returned to her, the

Duchess sent Bessie a message saying that if she would "permit the Duke of Manchester to return to his own home, the Duchess will pay all his debts and will allow him £20 a week"; the Duchess received a quick retort, in a note that read, "Miss Bellwood presents her compliments to the Duchess of Manchester, and begs to state that she is now working the Pavilion, the Met, and the South London, at £20 a turn, so she can allow the Duke £30 a week, and he is better off as he is."[44] This was the world Kitty stepped into, where women like Bessie and Belle Bilton fought for their freedom with a defiance and a refusal to submit. Bessie's career continued, and she even won success in America—something others were unable to achieve—after she sued Mandeville for abandoning her in 1892.[45]

So why didn't Bessie's sexual behavior—the married woman who seduced, and then sued, the Duke of Manchester—result in her rejection by Victorian society? Was it her profession, working on the music hall stage, that acted as armor, making acceptable an active sexual female identity? Or is it that her case, just like Belle Bilton's, demonstrates that much of what we think we know about sex and the Victorians does not accurately reflect the reality of the sex lives our ancestors were living? Kitty was well aware of the opposing forces at work in the halls, of the existence of positive sexual experiences against the abuse and assaults (or prudish ignorance) that she and so many women like her suffered. And she had grown to resent the double standard whereby men could do as they wished, and yet women were punished for it, partly because, to her, there was clearly so little difference between men and women at all.

Mr. Halford, for so long her idolized father figure, had been of little help. He seemed instead to rather enjoy her "heroic struggle," the battle to find work when no man would willingly employ a woman unless in exchange for sex.[46] It suited him to receive Kitty's increasingly desperate letters, to comfort himself that there was at least one good and respectable (by his standards) young woman on the stage, to dispense some vague advice about the terrors of men and carry on with his own life, little aware—or preferring to remain ignorant—of the reality Kitty truly faced. In an attempt to shock him into action, and in a particularly despondent moment, Kitty impetuously wrote to Halford to tell him that she saw no other choice left open to her other than accepting the lovelorn and unhappily married Freddy's offer to keep her. She would become what she had always feared for the sake of security, if only to maintain some form of independence in her life that marriage would not bring.

Posting her letter in Nottingham before she left for North Shields, Kitty hoped that when she arrived it would be to a telegram from the man she saw as an adopted father, "dragging me back from the abyss over which I appeared to be going."[47] None arrived. Like many who attempt a game of emotional manipulation with little skill or aptitude, who have a good nature rather than Machiavellian instincts, Kitty found the silence unbearable. Meeting Freddy at the theater, she refused his offer in no uncertain terms. Bereft now of both her mentor and her would-be provider, Kitty traveled to her next engagement in Newcastle, hoping against hope that the silence would be broken.

> Next morning came a letter from Mr. Halford, the most cruel letter, it seemed to me, ever written. He not only expressed his opinion of the man, but of the woman, which was much worse, who would live together under such circumstances, and forbade me all further association with any member of his family and household. I have not kept the letter, so cannot quote from it, but I answered immediately, resenting the eagerness with which he cast the first stone at me for a sin which so far I had not committed. He ought to have known me better. For once in my life I had no tears. I felt too stunned.[48]

How easy it is, for those who want for little, to decide what is right and good for those who are in need of much. At Halford's, Kitty had always been able to ignore the problems within their relationship because he had reminded her so much of the comfortable, well-to-do sanctuary of her grandparents' home; it was this blindness of nostalgia that had stopped Kitty from seeing the reality of his own double standards. After all, he had attempted to buy her for his son, offering her an income all of her very own if she should marry Bernard. Taking comfort in the advice of the other actresses in her company, many of whom knew Halford—and had been on the receiving end of his "kindness" themselves—Kitty slowly began to adjust to the certainty that she was alone once more. Ethel, one of the more clear-sighted and practical actresses of Kitty's acquaintance, "always said I ought to marry him, never mind Bernard . . . 'he's jealous, that's all, evidently hasn't the courage to ask you himself and is angry at someone else wanting you,'" Ethel had surmised.[49]

Righteously angry at the world she and so many women found themselves in, Kitty wrote to *The Era*, a well-known newspaper for the acting community, to complain about the abuses within her industry. "It is most disheartening. Sometimes you cannot get a return because your manager does not like you, and sometimes you cannot accept the offer because he likes you too well."[50] Now in her mid-thirties, Kitty found herself in the middle of a personal crisis. How could she, or any woman, survive in a world where they had to exchange their bodies in return for legitimate work? Why was every woman required to prostitute herself for a chance of freedom and independence? Finding herself once more in the back of a four-wheeled cab and fighting off a supposed agent for the very last time, in 1908 Kitty made a decision. No more violent attacks, no more threats to call the police—who did little but shame her for being alone with a man. It was time to force a change. Women deserved the right to be safe in their working environments, and to have their independence without having to sacrifice their bodies to get it. If the men around her wouldn't listen to reason, then by God she would have to do whatever was necessary to finally make her voice heard.

5

"Now I was awake"

Banners fluttered in the wind. It was an achingly warm summer day in June 1908, the twenty-first to be precise, when, according to the *Denbighshire Free Press*, 300,000 men and women descended on Hyde Park to demonstrate their support for women's rights.[1] This was the "Woman's Sunday" march, one of the largest gatherings the WSPU had ever organized to try to persuade the British government that women deserved the right to vote, and an equal place in British society. Since 1867, when John Stuart Mill had first presented a bill for female suffrage, the campaign to award women a voice in government had grown in strength and support. Previous to this, in 1832, a woman named Mary Smith had attempted to petition for unmarried, tax-paying women to be given the right to vote; but her request, taken before Parliament by the MP Henry Hunt, had only been laughed at.[2] Although many suffrage societies had been formed across the country since the 1860s, it was the Women's Social and Political Union, created in 1903, that became one of the most influential—and controversial—organizations in the fight for universal franchise.

The WSPU, founded in Manchester and led by the powerful oratory of Emmeline Pankhurst and her family, with the careful counsel of Frederick and Emmeline Pethick-Lawrence, believed that a new and more aggressive campaign was needed to force the government to agree. Beginning by disrupting political meetings and sending deputations to Parliament, they adopted the motto of "Deeds, Not Words," a clear and constant reminder that the language of politics had unfairly limited women. When words had failed to persuade the government after decades of campaigning, it would be the deeds of women that would finally make them equal with men. The *Daily Mail* soon christened these women "suffragettes," a sneering attempt to belittle them and demonstrate how separate and different they were from the rest of the women's movement.[3] It backfired. Although the WSPU was rapidly gaining a reputation for hooliganism, violent rhetoric, and unladylike behavior, the idea of "the suffragette," the female rebel, began to take hold. Under the direction of Emmeline's daughter, Christabel Pankhurst, there was an increasing shift toward using the papers and press to create a clear suffragette identity. In 1908, the Union, under the direction of Emmeline Pethick-Lawrence, selected the colors of purple, white, and green, and branded them on every possible element of their organization, from ticket stubs to medals, ribbons, pins, and banners. "Purple is the royal colour," argued Emmeline Pethick-Lawrence, "it stands for the royal blood that flows through the veins of every suffragette, the instinct of freedom and dignity . . . white stands for purity in public and private life . . . green is the colour of hope."[4] The suffragettes had embraced the *Daily Mail*'s distaste for their actions, and used it as reason to bring more women to their cause; for Kitty, it became "a title of honour which I was proud to share and live up to."[5]

The Women's Sunday March, on June 21, was to be the first time the colors of the WSPU were used in mass procession, as women from across the country arrived in London to hear lectures and march in the hope that their strength of numbers would force the government to pay attention. Since the election of the Liberal government in 1906, attempts had been made to bring a bill for female enfranchisement before the Houses of Parliament; in March 1907, Mr. W. H. Dickinson proposed that the vote should be extended to women, and during the debate in Parliament, the prime minister, Sir Henry Campbell-Bannerman, said he "considered that there were many legislative questions on which a woman's opinion was quite as valuable as a man's, if not more so," and that "the exclusion of women from the franchise was neither justifiable, nor expedient, nor politically right."[6] But the debate went on for so long that no vote was taken, and the opportunity was lost. Even though there seemed to be widespread support in Parliament for extending the franchise to women, a largely conservative and powerful element continually fought against such measures. At this point, not even all men could vote, and to some the thought of enfranchising any woman before a working man caused serious issues. But for women like Kitty, who worked and could be elected to positions within their industry unions, there was simply no reason that could justify withholding their political rights in a modern and civilized world. It was this frustration, built on the support and then the confusing rejection of female enfranchisement by the government, that the WSPU began to tap into to draw women to their noble "cause." The government could not be trusted, and if they could not be trusted, they did not have to be obeyed.

Miss Edith Walton-Evans, the daughter of an archdeacon, packed her banner onto a hot and crowded excursion train. It featured a huge, flaming Welsh dragon flanked by a leek on a bright blue background, and during the procession she would proudly explain to a young female journalist, "We came from the wild hills of Wales, and we're longing to get back there, and the language on our banner is Welsh, and reads 'Votes For Women,' 'Wales for Ever.'"[7] Another banner, this time the bright red of the Socialists, led by Keir Hardie, followed behind her as bands played and ballads and songs filled the air.

In the middle of all of this noise and color and excitement, we find Kitty. Not yet a committed suffragette, she had not wanted to join the actresses' contingent, which marched from the Chelsea Embankment to Hyde Park, but had grudgingly accepted a place after being teased by her friends; although she insisted she would have nothing to do with the "hooligans" of the WSPU, who she had read about in the newspapers, as they fought with police and disrupted society. But as she marched along Oakley Street, the King's Road, Sloane Street, and Knightsbridge to Hyde Park, the "Women's Marseillaise"—the anthem of the suffragettes—played ahead of her. A swell of voices sang the words, set to the music of the French national anthem:

> Arise! Ye daughters of a land
> That vaunts its liberty!
> May restless rulers understand
> That women must be free
> That women will be free.
> Hark! Hark! The trumpet's calling!
> Who'd be a laggard in the fight?
> With vict'ry even now in sight
> And stubborn foemen backward falling
>
> To Freedom's cause till death
> We swear our fealty.
> March on! March on! Face to the dawn
> The dawn of liberty.
> March on! March on! Face to the dawn
> The dawn of liberty.

The original, "La Marseillaise," had been written in 1792, during the French Revolution's Reign of Terror, and as Mary Wollstonecraft published *A Vindication of the Rights of Woman*. How fitting that its essence was now repurposed by the suffragettes, who were fighting their own revolution and civil war, and whose members would indeed swear their loyalty until death for the great cause. For Kitty, a woman who had faced so much abuse in her working life, and who had to suffer the abuses and assaults of men who believed they had a right to her body simply because she wanted to work, the march led to a sudden and total revelation. For so long she had felt completely alone, fighting against the forces in her industry that cared little for a woman's point of view. She had tried every route, every option available to her, and nothing had changed the deep-seated sexism and inherent misogyny that she experienced every day of her working life. But now, suddenly she found herself surrounded by women who felt just as she did, who wanted change, dramatic and consistent social change, to make the world a safer place for everyone around them.

Reaching Hyde Park, Kitty felt as if she had entered a new utopia:

> I heard my own ideas expressed much better than I could ever express them. I heard of the injustice to women in being deprived of a voice in the government to which they were subservient; of having to pay taxes in the expenditure of which they had no voice, in inequality between the sexes before the law regarding divorces, the ownership of legitimate and so-called illegitimate children, the difference between the sexes regarding conditions and payment in the labour market, the differences in punishment for similar crimes committed, and so forth. The scales were falling from my eyes and I recognised the other "mad women," the women who had actually been demanding change in conditions of which I had practically only been "talking in my dreams." Well, now I was awake. I was one of them and would do all I could to help and make our dreams of a better world come true.[8]

How many other women had the same epiphany that day in June? How many others, as Kitty did, immediately committed themselves to the suffragette cause right then and there? If we think of the WSPU as a cult, then Kitty had become a full-time, committed, and unwavering member. It would alter the path of her life forever. On October 13, 1908, she had her first opportunity to take part in a serious protest against the government. On the third anniversary of committing the WSPU to its new militant campaign, Christabel Pankhurst organized an evening rush on the House of Commons, taking over the duties from her mother, who was in hiding from the police.[9] At Caxton Hall, Kitty volunteered to join a deputation led by twelve women, chosen by Mrs. Pethick-Lawrence, to attempt to reach the prime minister. The rush had been well advertised and, in retaliation, almost 5,000 police officers had been tasked to guard the Houses of Parliament, to keep what was now an ever-growing crowd in Parliament Square away.[10] More than thirty people were arrested as the square grew increasingly violent during the police's attempts to try to keep the suffragettes back. Escaping arrest and returning to her lodging, Kitty found her "arms and shoulders black, blue and painful, as were every woman's who had taken part."[11] She was "aching in body and soul," but "though frightfully mauled," the police attacks had had little effect on dampening her spirits.[12] If anything, the violence at the hands of the state made her more convinced that the cause was just.

Returning to WSPU headquarters soon after, Kitty made clear her commitment to the organization by becoming a newspaper seller for *Votes for Women*, the magazine edited and compiled by the Pethick-Lawrences to persuade the general public to support female enfranchisement. It was an acid test, one all new recruits to the WSPU who were eager to prove their use were subjected to. Newspaper-selling was one of the most difficult and soul-crushing jobs the members could do. For some, it became the reason for their militancy; faced with daily insults and comments from both men and women, who would whisper or shout graphic sexual slurs, generic sexist comments, or even threats of physical harm, a newspaper seller like Kitty developed a uniquely hard perspective on the fight they had just joined. Kitty's beat was the island in Piccadilly Circus, near the flower sellers. Here, standing in one of the central hubs of London, she would sell papers, carry sandwich boards, or pass out advertisements for meetings and important events. Her music hall training would have stood her in good stead—she could lift her voice and shout "Votes for women!" above the noise and chatter of the Circus's daily life.

My friends all reacted differently to my interest in Votes for Women. Some always thought I was crazy, now they were sure. Some had always credited me with more sense, while others were converted, since it must be right if I, with all my common sense, believed in it. Some just dropped me. Minnie Hayden, whom I happened to meet doing the rounds of the agents one day told me she was too disgusted ever to speak to me again.[13]

The life of a suffragette seemed to push and pull Kitty in all directions. But with every insult, every cost she was made to pay for her support of the WSPU, she became even more determined. When she wasn't working for the Union, Kitty would still wear the WSPU's colors at every opportunity. Meeting a music hall agent who had previously failed to find her work, Kitty reminded him that once women like her were in charge, men like him would have little opportunity to wield their own power over women by forcing them to trade sex in return for work. Attempting to mollify her, he offered to see that she was booked up for life, promising her leading roles and first-class tours if only she would take off the colors and renounce the suffragettes. Kitty refused.

Her rage, for so long bubbling under the surface, growing with every dressing room discussion and horrifying attack that she and so many of her friends and colleagues suffered, was fed by the anti-harassment language she found at many of the WSPU meetings. Why did women suffer in silence? Why were men allowed to carry out these attacks and face no punishment? Why had she suffered so much abuse, simply because she wanted to work and be independent? Kitty was determined be silent no longer.

Sitting in a meeting of the Variety Artists Federation (VAF), her own trade union, not long after she joined the suffragettes, Kitty listened to a list of complaints and issues in the industry from its members with a growing resentment. Something was not right, something was being ignored. Unable to accept the silence that so many deemed necessary on the abuses faced by women in the industry, Kitty got to her feet.

Interrupting another speaker, she let her loud, clear voice echo around the hall: ". . . they won't give me work because I won't kiss them!"[14] A shocked silence, followed by applause and shouts of "Bravo," ensued, and men and women came forward to support her claim. It was as if she had opened the floodgates and reports of years of abuse from agents and managers poured through, not only from her, but from many in the audience. After the uproar had subsided, the chairman for the evening, a Mr. Clemart, making himself heard over the excited and rebellious mutterings, called out to Kitty, asking her to give a written statement to the London County Council (LCC) so that these abuses would become known and those who had committed them could be held accountable.

How did Kitty feel, returning to her lodgings that night? Did she hang up the colors of the WSPU and quietly marvel at her own bravery, to take on, without a second thought, the might of those who ran the industry she worked in? Did she feel trepidation or fear at what she might be risking? The reaction to her statement was quick; agents no longer answered her calls and work that had been promised suddenly disappeared. She had attempted to shine a very bright light on the deeds men do in secret and yet rely on public complicity to carry out; but exposing them had only resulted in damaging her reputation, and while she became a figurehead for the fight against sexual harassment in the entertainment industry, she would now find the struggle to survive even harder in her working life.

There was little more she could do other than commit herself full-time to the cause; at least by fighting for women in every corner of British society she would be able to fight for the others who had suffered, who were still suffering, just as she had. The WSPU held an exhibition at the Prince's Skating Rink, Knightsbridge, in 1909, and it was here that Kitty first met Mrs. Flora Drummond, "The General," who led so many of the grand processions on horseback. Given the task of answering the telephones—which she hated—Kitty quickly learned the intricate networks of the WSPU branches and offices that had spread out across the country. She immersed herself in the daily life of the WSPU, attending meetings, organizing deputations, and writing to Herbert Asquith, formerly chancellor of the exchequer, who had become prime minister after a series of heart attacks forced Campbell-Bannerman's resignation. He had a wildly different, unfavorable view from his predecessor on the question of female suffrage. Writing to Asquith on June 25, 1909, days before she joined another deputation to Parliament, Kitty made her feelings clear: "One of the strongest arguments in favour of Woman's Suffrage is that it would enable us to put an end to the pressure that is brought to bear, which sometimes forces a helpless woman to a course of absolute immorality, against herself."[15]

Her own struggle for work, to be free of sexual harassment and simply be able to survive were at the forefront of her mind. On June 29, Kitty joined the latest "Raid on Parliament." This time, more than a hundred women were arrested, while the crowd began to throw stones at the building and attack MPs who were foolish enough to let themselves be seen on the streets. Kitty was arrested, along with Emmeline Pankhurst, who had smacked a police inspector in the face when he had attempted to detain her.[16] Although the charges were dropped, news of a new violation at the hands of the government suddenly spread through the WSPU's ranks. Just before the latest deputation, a forty-four-year-old suffragette named Marion Wallace Dunlop had managed to access St. Stephen's Hall in the House of Commons and graffitied a "Bill of Rights" onto one of the walls. She had been arrested, but once in prison had adopted a new and surprising tactic—she had gone on hunger strike. Taken by surprise, and far too nervous about the death of a suffragette at government hands, the authorities released Marion after a few days. This became the new tactic of the suffragettes, as Mary Leigh, Emily Wilding Davison, and many others who were arrested in the next few weeks found themselves quickly released if they adopted the same practice. But by October, the government decided this reaction could not continue. The suffragettes were becoming increasingly

violent in the damage they would do to buildings during their demonstrations. Windows were smashed, roof tiles were pulled off and
thrown to the ground, and MPs were at risk of being seized by angry
and outraged women who demanded that they should be allowed to
speak.

At the end of the year, Winson Green Prison, Birmingham, which
was then holding eight suffragette prisoners—Patricia Woodlock,
Ellen Barwell, Hilda Burkitt, Leslie Hall, Mabel Capper, Mary Edwards,
Mary Leigh, and Charlotte Marsh—decided they would attempt to
force-feed the women.[17] The method was torturous, the result was
excruciating, and the reaction among the WSPU was shock, disgust,
and utter, total rage. To its members, the WSPU existed to promote the
legal right of women to make their voices heard, and demonstrate—as
was their right to do—over any problems and issues they had with the
government. In retaliation, the government had arrested and imprisoned them, and now had resorted to state-sanctioned abuse. Reading
of this outrage on the part of the government drove Kitty to Clem-
ent's Inn, the headquarters of the WSPU—it "incited me to violence"—
and she offered herself not only as a newspaper seller, but as a soldier
in the feminist revolution.[18] Receiving her orders, Kitty had her first
opportunity to make a protest with "Deeds, Not Words" by throwing
a stone through a window of the post office in Newcastle upon Tyne
on October 9, 1909. She was joined by Dorothy Pethick, the sister of
Mrs. Pethick-Lawrence, as Christabel Pankhurst orchestrated a widespread attack on several sites in the city. The militants were ordered to
wait for 7:00 p.m.:

> With two stones in my muff, feeling deadly sick and nervous, I made
> my way to the GPO which I knew so well. Without "recognising" Miss
> Pethick, I joined her as she was entering, to see that no one was near the
> windows to get hurt by falling glass. Luckily, the coast was clear and we
> strolled out, separately in opposite direction, waiting for the stroke of
> the clock, which seemed as if it would never strike again.[19]

The glass shattered as the clock bells rang out, and Kitty and Dorothy were immediately arrested and taken to the police station; a large crowd began to gather outside, chanting "Votes for women" while skirmishes broke out among the opposing factions of police, suffragettes, and anti-suffragists. This was Kitty's first attack on the government, and as she waited in her cell, hearing the shouting and scuffles of the crowd outside, the enormity of her actions slowly took hold. But she had not undertaken the task lightly, and had spent some time examining her own conscience and the world she found herself in to be able to believe that violence was an acceptable action for the WSPU. Setting it out in her mind, Kitty justified her actions as being part of a wider British heritage of political protest:

> Destruction of government property, such as post offices or other government office windows, is a time-honoured British argument on the part of the people when the government fails to listen to verbal argument and reason, which certainly it had failed to do in the case of Woman's Suffrage since 1832, and to make matters worse had resorted to force against the women, which is symbolic of a savage beating a female into submission. Were self-respecting, civilised women, worthy of the term, going to submit to that? No! From King John signing the Magna Carta at the point of the Barons' swords down to recently keeping an old gun in the place where the people wanted it, they have resorted to militancy from window smashing to arson, such as the burning of the bishop's palace, prison, mansion house, custom-house, excursive office and other public buildings at Bristol in 1832.[20]

These words would echo back to her time and time again over the coming years, but her reasoning never faltered. Violence had been a man's weapon to secure his rights; why should it not be a woman's too? If the government refused to listen to reason, it would have to be forced into accepting women's suffrage—which was only ever a simple argument for sovereignty and independence of the individual, as should be the right of any British citizen. At her trial, Kitty used her time under examination to make the case for "the great cause of women's freedom" and argued that the WSPU's methods were only what the new chancellor of the exchequer, David Lloyd George, had advocated in a recent Sunday paper. "Revolt is the only weapon to carry on a cause," he had said. "The realm of politics is like the Kingdom of Heaven, it suffereth violence and it is the violent that take it by storm."[21]

There was little holding back the suffragettes now, as violence became the new doctrine. The press recorded the attacks as "suffragette outrages," a term that soon began to appear with increasing frequency in papers across the country. One of the earliest recorded "outrages" was in the *Morpeth Herald*, November 20, 1909, when Theresa Garnett attacked a young Winston Churchill with a horsewhip on the platform of Bristol railway station.[22] In the same month, Selina Martin and Leslie Hall disguised themselves as orange sellers and, armed with a catapult and missiles, attacked Prime Minister Asquith's car in Liverpool.[23] All across the country, the militant members of the WSPU began to marshal their forces. No longer content with just marching for their rights, and reading of the suffering of their members, many of the women began to feel that there was no turning back from further violent action.

Imprisoned in Newcastle alongside Emily Wilding Davison and Constance Lytton, Kitty fought against the traditional procedures of stripping, bathing, and prison dress. Once led to her cell she immediately barricaded herself in, so successfully that it took the guards twenty-four hours to regain access, which then only came once they chiseled off the door hinges. Like a true suffragette, she adopted the role of a hunger striker, and refused to dress or leave her cell. After three days, it was decided that she would be force-fed:

> In the evening two wardresses asked me to come with them, I refused and, struggling all the time, they managed to put some clothes on me and drag me to the top of the stairs where I shook them off, preferring

to walk down myself for at the bottom there were several more. They
surrounded me and took me to the doctor's room, where three doctors, two in operating aprons, awaited me. One asked me to drink some
milk. I refused and was seized and overpowered by several wardresses,
forced into an arm chair, covered by a sheet, each arm held to the arms
of the chair by a wardress, two others holding my shoulders back, two
more holding my knees down, a doctor holding my head back. I struggled and screamed all the time. Not knowing the procedure of forcible
feeding and thinking it was done though the mouth, I clenched my
teeth when they had me in position and helpless, when suddenly I felt
something penetrate my right nostril which seemed to cause my head
to burst and eyes to bulge. Choking and retching as the tube was forced
down to my stomach and the liquid food poured in, most of which was
vomited back especially when the tube was withdrawn. There are no
words to describe the horrible revolting sensations. I must have lost
consciousness for I found myself flat on the floor, not knowing how
I got there.[24]

As they dragged her back to her cell, Kitty, disoriented and numb
from what she had just experienced, screamed and shouted her disgust at a government and a medical profession that would sanction
such horrific treatment of women. As she was pulled up the stairs,
Kitty came face-to-face with one of the prison's doctors, and "with all
the force and venom I cried, 'You brute! If you had an ounce of manli-
ness in you, you would protest against doing this.'"[25] She struck him
across the face with the back of her hand, shouting "Votes for women"
and "Down with tyranny!" until they managed to throw her back in
her cell. Collapsing on the bed, the rage and mental agony she felt at
such a physical violation was overwhelming. But within moments,
she heard screams echo along the corridor, the terror of another suffragette being subjected to the same ordeal. Desperate, and without
thinking, Kitty grabbed the chair from her cell and hurled it at the
window, high up above her. The glass shattered and the cold night

swept in, bringing with it snatches of voices calling "Votes for women" and singing suffragette songs. During their members' incarcerations, groups of supporters would gather outside the walls of prisons holding suffragettes to yell support and try to keep their spirits up, but this time the noise drowned out Kitty's screams. Standing on the chair, wretchedly shouting to try to make them aware of what was happening, the noise of the band they had brought with them drowned her out, and Kitty could only listen with a crushing despair as their voices faded into the night.

Soon after, Constance Lytton and a number of the other suffragettes were released, leaving Kitty in prison and at the mercy of the doctors. Deciding she had to make a serious protest, anything to try to force her release and stop the torture, Kitty waited until the early hours of one morning to set fire to her cell. Breaking the glass surrounding the gaslight, she used coconut fiber from her pillows and bedding to create the base of her fire, and lit it using pages torn from the Bible in her cell. The blaze was instant and, of course, was between her and the door. The fumes had quickly filled her cell and, unable to breathe, Kitty collapsed on the floor. The smoke spilling through the door soon raised the alarm; prison staff fought their way in, doused the flames, and pulled her out into the corridor. Lying on the cold stone of the corridor, Kitty watched as they attempted to put out the fire on the wooden cell floor. Unable to offer any protest, she was half dragged, half pushed to a padded cell directly underneath the one she had just set fire to and thrust, unceremoniously, inside. This punishment, as she lay on the floor listening to the gentle drip of water from the burned and smoking cell above her, had only one effect—she was proud. "What a mistake the authorities make in forcing women into such ugly reflections of their own minds which help to make a prisoner merely unrepentant and vengeful."[26]

Later, having been moved back to a normal cell, Kitty found she had been placed on suicide watch. A wardress would sit outside her cell through the night and regularly check on her, not only to make sure she hadn't started another fire, but also to see that she hadn't attempted to hurt herself. Surprisingly, one night her old life came back to haunt her. The woman on duty was an avid fan of the music halls and could remember seeing Kitty perform at the Manchester Hippodrome. Another time, another life. Lying there listening to the other woman telling how she had been enraptured by the costumes, the lights, the dazzle of the stage, Kitty must have felt a sense of both loss and renewed purpose. So much had happened in her life to bring her to this point. The child who had fled an abusive father, the young woman who had set out to make her own way on the stage, the newly committed activist who wanted nothing more than to make the world a safer place for other women so they never had to experience what she had. That encounter convinced Kitty to break the hunger strike. Going against WSPU policy to maintain a strike no matter what, Kitty realized it would leave her too weak to work; winter had arrived and she had no engagements booked in the theaters or music halls. She would only be able to fight on if she was strong.

A month after her release, Kitty found herself at the Royal Albert Hall, where a grand mass meeting had been organized to welcome Emmeline Pankhurst back from a recent trip to foster support in America, and also to award those who had suffered force-feeding a medal for their endurance and strength. The medal, engraved at the top with the words "For Valour," was set on a ribbon of the WSPU's colors. A pendant underneath bore the words "Hunger Strike," and for those who suffered multiple incarcerations a new metal bar, with the date of each event engraved on it, was added to their ribbon. These became treasured emblems of their suffering. Filmed at Caxton Hall in 1955, a reunion of the suffragettes recorded Mary Richardson, famous for slashing the *Rokeby Venus*, still proudly wearing hers, complete with a myriad of bars on her ribbon.[27] At the Royal Albert Hall in 1908, walking behind Constance Lytton in a procession of all those who had fought against the government that year, Kitty felt an overwhelming sense of pride:

It was a glorious reunion and a great triumph, honour and privilege to
walk in that file of splendid fighters for Women's Emancipation, from
the boxes at the back of that great crowded hall, down the centre aisle,
onto the platform, to meet Mrs. Pankhurst who made the presenta-
tions, to the cheers of that enthusiastic throng, while the organ pealed
forth the "Women's Marseillaise," "To Freedom's Cause till death, we
swear our fealty."[28]

Having managed to secure three weeks' worth of bookings in the
Christmas pantomime season, Kitty learned that, while she had been
busy fighting for women's rights, her earlier bravery at the meeting of the VAF, when she had stood up and exposed the behavior of
so many men in the industry, was to go unrewarded. The London
County Council felt there was no need to launch any serious investigation into the agents and managers who used sexual harassment in the
theaters and music halls as their work ethic. As the new year came in,
Kitty decided to take a leaf out of the suffragette handbook. Knowing
that if she was arrested her statement would most likely be printed
in the newspapers—as was common practice then—she decided she
would draw national attention to the sexual abuse within her industry
through a violent protest. Armed with half a brick, Kitty arrived, late
in the evening, at the offices of Moss Empires in Cranbourn Street,
Covent Garden. Here she would strike a blow at the most famous and
influential music hall syndicate. Readying her brick, Kitty suddenly
found a hand clamped around her arm. Two young policemen, constables on the beat, stopped her before she had a chance to do any
damage. What followed was somewhat surprising, as the constables
attempt to persuade her to simply go home. "What you say is true, we
know, but why make a martyr of yourself?" they attempted to reason
with her; how many have heard the same, when they attempted to
bring to light the sufferings and abuses they had personally experienced or witnessed?[29]

I told them there was no martyrdom in this, but in the insults women received when they asked for work, etc., and if they did not arrest me now, I would have to make another attempt, so, like good sports, they took my intention for the deed, picked up the incriminating evidence and escorted me to Vine Street police station.[30]

Kitty got her wish for the press to take an interest in her case, but sadly it was not in the way she had intended. Too fond of victim-blaming, too quick to see actresses and female music hall stars as women who were "asking for it" by choosing to work in the entertainment industries, even the *Performer*, the VAF's own weekly paper, made fun of her attempt. She didn't have enough star power to be seen as another Belle Bilton or Bessie Bellwood, and almost twenty years after their heyday—and in an attempt to reduce the influence of the suffragettes—society was determinedly clamping down on any woman's freedom of expression, especially when it advocated her independence. The failure of the LCC to implement any change in the way the industry was run, or to protect those who were the most at risk within it, had given the predators and misogynists a renewed sense of confidence. The *Performer* even attempted to portray Kitty's views as moral judgments on the women themselves, insinuating that she saw them as to blame for the general immorality of the stage. Her frustration was acute.

It has become a characteristic of our modern society to try to understand how a person can become radicalized and commit acts that endanger, or even kill, other people. Kitty's journey toward violent serial offender began in these moments of defeat. She knew how necessary it was to protect women in her industry, to protect women everywhere, but at every turn her desperate efforts were frustrated and denied.

For the suffragettes as a whole, 1910 would bring one of the greatest governmental betrayals; the final straw that pushed many women to abandon the rule of law for the rule of rebellion. There had been multiple attempts by individual MPs to bring a suffrage bill into being, and in January 1910 support for such an action forced the formation of a committee to bring about cross-party consensus on the issue. Made up of fifty-four MPs from all political parties, and chaired by Constance Lytton's brother, the Earl of Lytton, the Conciliation Committee was the strongest opportunity yet for female enfranchisement.

As the debates and compromises began, the WSPU declared a truce: no militancy would be undertaken while the committee did its work. But by November, the committee's strength was being questioned as the prime minister made it clear that he would offer no opportunity to discuss any suffrage bill at that time. In retaliation, the WSPU sent three hundred women to march on Parliament. Carrying banners with the words "Asquith vetoed our Bill" and "Where there's a Bill there's a way," the women made their way from Caxton Hall toward the seat of government.[31] The resulting violence became known as "Black Friday." Winston Churchill, then home secretary, had sent in the mounted police.

Police horses, breath misting the air, hooves striking the dust of the streets, surrounded Parliament, forming a barrier against the women marching, unwavering, toward them. What followed was a scene of absolute carnage. Photos from that day show women being pushed and pulled, attacked and abused. Many reported aggressive sexual assaults at the hands of the police. In one of the most famous images, a suffragette lies prone on the ground, clutching her face and attempting to curl up into a fetal position. She is surrounded by police officers and a man in a top hat; it is not clear if this man is attempting to restrain the officers or if he is about to be pulled away. A teenage boy smiles as he looks down on her. For many members of the WSPU, their brutal experiences on this day shaped the rest of their lives as activists, but Kitty makes little mention of it. For her, violent sexual assault was not a new experience.

Throughout the following year, while a shaky truce between the government and the WSPU held, Kitty scrabbled to find work, either for the Union or for herself. Appearing at the Colchester Liberal Union- ists Association, she found her notoriety had preceded her and she was billed in the evening's program as "Music Hall Artist and Militant Suf- fragette." Her performance was met with rapturous applause and con- fident reviews, yet she was unable to find any other agents or managers willing to employ even a popular turn if she identified as a suffragette.

By the end of the year, the government's lack of commitment to the Conciliation Committee's bill became clear. Asquith, with the backing of Lloyd George, declared that the question was no longer one of women's suffrage; it was manhood suffrage—extending the vote to all men—that should be the question. If that could pass in Parliament, the enfranchise- ment of women could simply be taken care of with a later amendment, if it was still deemed necessary. So the bill would never pass, and on November 24, 1911, Asquith gave a speech in Bath where he bragged of having "torpedoed" the Conciliation Bill.[32] Perhaps full of his own bril- liance, or simply unaware of the intelligence and ability of the women who were now focused with razor-sharp precision on his every word, Asquith reminisced that "When power was withheld from democracy, when they had no voice in the Government, when they were oppressed, and when they had no means of securing redress except by violence— then property has many times been swept away."[33]

Property was exactly where the suffragettes would set their sights next. Gone was any thought of a truce, gone was any belief in concili- ation or compromise. The WSPU and the women of its membership would have female enfranchisement at any cost. In retaliation, Kitty broke a window at the Home Office and was sentenced to twenty-one days. She used the time to hone her hatred of the government, which valued property "above the bodies and souls of men, women and chil- dren."[34] From now on, the suffragettes were finished with believing the broken promises of the men in power, and the war of "Deed, Not Words" began in earnest.

On St. David's Day, March 1, in 1912, Christabel Pankhurst and the suffrage leadership organized a new form of attack.[35] "Danger duty" required volunteers for a secret mass window-smashing campaign in the shopping and leisure districts of London. Unlike with the raids on Parliament, there was no forewarning to the government, and at 5:45 p.m., Kitty and more than a hundred other women smashed windows on Regent Street, Oxford Street, Bond Street, the Strand, and Piccadilly. Earlier they had each been armed with a hammer and given their individual orders. Kitty's were to break the windows of the Silversmiths Association and Sainsbury's at 134 Regent Street. She was, of course, immediately arrested. The twilight smash caused serious damage to businesses and shops across London, and many of the women were remanded in Holloway Prison, where they continued to break windows and cause riots whenever possible. Kitty was bailed out after a week, and began to prepare for her trial. Standing in the dock, she was resolute and unrepentant:

> From time to time members of the Government have taunted the women with not being as militant nor doing as much damage as the men did when they fought for the vote, thereby inciting the women to further and stronger militancy. If the Government must have damage as a token that women want the vote, damage they shall have.[36]

Sentenced to six months' hard labor and transferred to Birmingham's Winson Green Prison, Kitty witnessed firsthand the impact the suffragette campaign was having—in a surprising way. Overseen by Dr. Ahern, the wardens and doctors dealing with the suffragettes were unable to cope with the toll of force-feeding multiple women, many of whom were far from hardened criminals used to the prison system. Taking part in a hunger strike, Kitty prepared herself to be force-fed. As her door opened, she was greeted by an unexpected sight. The wardresses were in tears. They had already performed more than twenty force-feedings that day, and each woman had fought and screamed against the horror of the operation. Taken aback by the emotions of those who felt they had been forced to inflict this violence on the bodies of the women in their care, for the first time Kitty offered no resistance. Trying not to struggle, in the hope it would make the experience pass more quickly, Kitty closed her eyes. But something was horribly wrong.

> I was suffocating and in my involuntary struggle for breath, I raised myself up to my feet and gasped, "take the tube out" in spite of which they poured food down which mostly came back up. When the tube was withdrawn, I collapsed into a chair and could only breathe and talk in short, sharp, painful gasps. Trying to take a deep breath caused the most excruciating agony. They supported me back to my cell where I lay on my plank bed, gradually growing worse. From the waist up I experienced every pain imaginable. What food had remained down, I coughed and vomited back now. I grew icy cold and, when soon after a wardress came to see me she went at once for a hot water bottle to place at my feet.[37]

While Kitty was undergoing the violence of force-feeding, the suffragettes who had escaped or simply not taken part in the grand window-smashing campaign were formulating their new methods of attack. One of the most aggressive moments of this new militancy occurred in Dublin, in July 1912.[38] Traveling from England in pursuit of Asquith, Mary Leigh, Gladys Evans, Jennie Baines (using the alias of Lizzie Baker), and Mabel Capper attempted to set fire to the Theatre Royal during a packed lunchtime matinee while the prime minister was in attendance.[39] They left a canister of gunpowder close to the stage and hurled gasoline and lit matches into the projection booth, which contained highly combustible film reels.[40] Earlier in the day, Mary Leigh had hurled a hatchet toward Asquith; it narrowly missed him and instead cut the Irish MP John Edward Redmond on the ear.[41] Redmond's focus on the campaign for Home Rule had seen his refusal to insert a clause giving women the vote, and had assured his status as a target for the women.[42] In the following months, Glasgow Art Gallery had its glass cases destroyed, while bank and post office windows were smashed from Kew to Gateshead.[43]

After release, rest, and recuperation, Kitty was sent to Wrexham, where Lloyd George was speaking at the Welsh National Eisteddfod. This cultural festival drew an audience from across Wales and brought together hundreds of people in excited celebration. It was the perfect place for a suffragette disturbance. And this would be Kitty's first attempt at a direct attack on a cabinet minister. As Lloyd George swayed along to the audience singing "Land of My Fathers," Kitty seized her moment. "How dare you have political prisoners fed by force!" she shouted, and rushed toward the platform where he was standing as pandemonium broke out.[44] The stewards and policemen attempted to reach Kitty before the crowd, dominated by anti-suffragists, could get hold of her. But they didn't get there soon enough. A howling mob tore off Kitty's hat and pulled her hair loose, raining down blows on her from all sides. Interviewed in *Votes for Women* shortly after, Kitty said, "My clothes were ripped back and front, my very undergarments torn to shreds. Being thrown to wild beasts is nothing to being thrown to an infuriated human mob. The former might tear you to pieces but draw the line at indecent assaults."[45]

One of the most incredible photographs of Kitty in existence was taken at this exact moment. Escorted by policemen holding both of her arms outstretched, as if she were on the cross, Kitty strides through a baying crowd, her hair wild and free in the wind, with a triumphant smile across the entirety of her face. A woman, her face contorted in rage, screams abuse as Kitty is marched by: Kitty records that she was shouting, "A disgrace to your sex!"[46] On the way back to London the next day, Kitty stopped to see friends in Maidenhead on Thames. Getting out at the station, she discovered that the photograph had gone the Edwardian equivalent of viral. Taken by a press photographer, it had quickly become a poster that was pasted outside every news dealer, across the town and the country.

The year 1912 proved to be an escalation point in the violence of the militant suffragettes. While Kitty was visiting Wrexham, twenty-three trunk posts, a huge network point for telegraph wires, were cut on the London road at Potters Bar, and on November 28 simultaneous attacks on mailboxes occurred across the entire country.[47] By the end of the year, 240 people had been sent to prison for militant suffragette activities.[48] The newspapers began to carry weekly roundups of the attacks, and reports of suffragette violence were clearly evident across the country, with the *Gloucester Journal* and *Liverpool Echo* both running dedicated columns to report on the latest outrages.[49] But little could have prepared them for what would happen next, or what the suffragettes themselves would be asked to do.

6

Death in Ten Minutes

"What can we do now," asked Emmeline Pankhurst, "but carry on this fight ourselves?" She was speaking to a crowded meeting of the WSPU in Hampstead Town Hall, a leader reaffirming her soldiers' commitment to war. "I want you not to see these as isolated acts of hysterical women, but to see that it is being carried out with a definite intention and purpose. It can only be stopped in one way: that is by giving us the vote!"[1] Powerful words, at a time when the glorious cause had become a "guerrilla war," fought in the dark with weapons women were not supposed to have. In the years since Kitty had suffered attacks at the hands of the police, endured abuse selling suffrage propaganda, disrupted political meetings, hounded the prime minister, and suffered through horrendous force-feedings while on hunger strike, the WSPU had moved from being a war of words to a war of weapons.

We think of this as a period of window-smashing, women chaining themselves to railings, and the rushes on Parliament, but the reality was far more extreme. Guns, bombs, and arson attacks became second nature to the women involved, radicalized by a combination of the revolutionary leadership of the WSPU and the physical violence they experienced at the hands of anti-suffragists, the police, and the prison system. As the government repeatedly betrayed and discounted the suffragettes, the rage felt by the women who only wanted to be seen as equal and have ownership over their own destinies rather than leave them to the decisions of men drove the organization to commit highly aggressive acts that have since been erased from our history. The violence of the suffragettes has been sanitized, downplayed, and, in some cases, simply denied—a final injustice to those brave women who made impossible choices in the hope that the ends could somehow justify the means.

From 1912 to 1914, Christabel Pankhurst orchestrated a nationwide bombing and arson campaign the likes of which Britain had never seen before and hasn't experienced since. Hundreds of attacks by either bombs or fire, carried out by women using code names and aliases, destroyed timber yards, cotton mills, railway stations, MPs' homes, mansions, racecourses, sporting pavilions, churches, glasshouses, even Edinburgh's Royal Observatory. Chemical attacks on mail carriers, mailboxes, golfing greens, and even the prime minister—whenever a suffragette could get close enough—left victims with terrible burns and sorely irritated eyes and throats, and destroyed precious correspondence.

Imagine the Internet suddenly becoming inaccessible all the way from London to Glasgow, and all phone communication suddenly ceasing. That was the impact of the suffragettes cutting the huge trunk telegram and telephone posts across the country, on numerous occasions taking out communications for the government, police, and ordinary people. Bombs were left outside banks and newspaper offices and could also be sent in the mail—one discovered at the South Eastern London District Post Office, made of nitroglycerin and gunpowder, was so large that if it had gone off it would have destroyed the entire building, killing all two hundred people inside.[2]

At the site of one of the most daring attacks, on the St. Leonards home of the MP Arthur Du Cros in April 1913, the immediate aftermath of the destruction was caught on film. The newsreels were a growing business, and Pathé's camera arrived while the ruins were still smoldering. As it pans along the shell of the house, figures fill the frame: men trying to salvage roof tiles, women observing the wreckage, and a young schoolgirl, standing on the lawn, staring directly into the camera. She turns, looking up at the remnants behind her, while all the other figures hurry across the frame. What did she think of the arson executed in her name, to secure her a future in a utopia of political equality? The dull thud as the workmen's hammers hit the charred wood was not recorded, but even without sound the power of the arson attack is clear, a century later. Kitty was the author of this destruction. Did she watch Pathé's newsreel of the attack's aftermath, wearing her suffragette colors as the images flickered across the screen?

Du Cros had consistently voted against the enfranchisement of women, which was why he had been chosen as a target, and the razing of his house to the ground was part of the growing "Reign of Terror" that Christabel Pankhurst organized from her Parisian hideaway.[3] She had fled the country after the grand window-smashing campaign and taken up residence in France. Her commitment, and her commitment of the WSPU, to this radical aggressive action caused a deep schism within the leadership. The Pethick-Lawrences, who had for so long stood beside the Pankhursts and whose newspaper, *Votes For Women*, Kitty sold on the streets, were ousted by Christabel and her mother for their opposition to the growing violence at the end of 1912. Determined to exercise full and total control over every aspect of the WSPU, Christabel created a new weekly newspaper for the Union, *The Suffragette*, priced at a single penny, to carry forward both her edicts and the reports of the actions of other members. Kitty was devoted to the new paper: "*The* Suffragette became more and more daring and defiant and was continually being raided, everybody, including the printers, being arrested, but never missing an issue since secret reserves were always ready to 'carry on.'"[4] Many of her fellow suffragettes had now been tasked with carrying out destructive and dangerous attacks. As words had not worked, the WSPU issued a new manifesto warning of a "fiercer spirit of revolt" that was awakened and was "impossible

to control."[5] Emmeline Pankhurst made her directives clear in a now
legendary speech:

> Be militant each in your own way . . . Those of you who can break
> windows—break them. Those of you who can still further attack the
> secret idol of property, so as to make the Government realise that
> property is as greatly endangered by women's suffrage as it was by
> the Chartists of old—do so. And my last word is to the Government: I
> incite this meeting to rebellion.[6]

On the platform, Kitty rose to cheer wildly.[7] She was committed to the
new violence with a radical and burning passion. The women involved
were given many different names in the press, from "wreckers" to "wild
women" or the individual "professional petroleuse," language that
conjures up images of these women as the daughters of the French
Revolution—a rejected social group bent on political representation,
brandishing the colors of the WSPU and shouting out an anglicized
war cry reminiscent of "Liberté, Unité, Égalité."[8] Christabel lost no time
in linking the cause to a Francophile revolutionary spirit; she appro-
priated the image of Joan of Arc, a female martyr who gave her life for
what she believed in and was the equal of any man and, under the head-
ings of "Reign of Terror," "Guerrilla Warfare," and "Fire and Bombs!,"
devoted double-page spreads in *The Suffragette* to reporting the bomb
and arson attacks that were now occurring around the country.[9] Following photographs and articles of suffragettes still suffering after
force-feeding would come the photographs of burned-out buildings
and railway stations and parks wrecked by bombs or chemical attacks.

Reported in the ordinary press as the "suffragette outrages," 1913
rapidly became one of the most violent years in suffragette history. Sylvia Pankhurst, Christabel's long-suffering sister and fellow suffragette,
recorded broken street lamps, "Votes For Women" graffiti in public
parks, railway carriages having their seats slashed, and flower beds and
golfing greens destroyed by acid. Hoax calls were made to the Army

Reserves, and elderly ladies began to apply for gun licenses, just to "terrify the authorities."[10] But underneath these general annoyances ran a far more violent and radical campaign.

On January 29, 1913, letters addressed to "Mr. George" and "Mr. Asquith" exploded into flames as they were lifted out of mailboxes.[11] The envelopes contained fragile glass tubes full of a chemical liquid that, when broken and exposed to the air, immediately caught fire. In the following weeks, further attacks on letters and mailboxes came in Coventry, London, Edinburgh, Northampton, and York.

The first bomb attack, and one of the most spectacular in its daring, came on February 19, when Emily Wilding Davison and her companions succeeded in blowing up David Lloyd George's new holiday cottage at Walton-on-the-Hill, near Epsom.[12] The *Pall Mall Gazette* reported the attack under the headline "SUFFRAGETTE TERRORISM," and that "the perpetrators of the outrage appear to have used a motor-car, and they got away, leaving only two broken hatpins as clues."[13]

In July 1912, an abortive arson attack on the Nuneham home of Lewis Harcourt, by Helen Craggs and Ethel Smyth, had demonstrated the lengths the suffragettes were now willing to go to. After they had refined their methods, the arson campaign kicked off in earnest on February 20, 1913, when Lilian Lenton and Joyce Locke successfully burned down Kew Gardens' tea pavilion.

In March, fires raged at railway stations and private homes across Surrey, and telegram and telephone trunk masts and railway signal wires were cut in Glasgow, Kilmarnock, and Llantarnam. Watching the escalating violence, Sylvia Pankhurst recalled, "Telegraph and telephone wires were severed with long handed clippers; fuse boxes were blown up, communication between London and Glasgow being cut off for some hours."[14]

April brought with it a full-scale war on the railways: carriages at Davenport Junction, Stockport, exploded after devices were placed underneath the seats.[15] Oxted railway station was decimated by a bomb left in the lavatory.[16] A traveling basket was found, containing a clock

timed to go off at 3:00 a.m., while the fuse had been laid with gunpowder. On April 9, two bombs were left on the Waterloo to Kingston line,
placed on trains going in opposite directions. One bomb was found at
Battersea on the train coming from Kingston. In a previously crowded
third-class carriage, the railway porter had seen smoke slowly creep-
ing from under a seat. He discovered a white wooden box containing
a tin canister, measuring about eight inches by four, in which sixteen
live gun cartridges, wired together and joined up with a small double
battery, had been attached to a tube of explosive.[17] Packed in among the
cartridges were lumps of jagged metal, bullets, and scraps of lead. Four
hours later, as a train from Waterloo pulled into Kingston, the third-
class carriage exploded and was quickly consumed by fire. Although
it was empty, the rest of the carriages were full of passengers, and the
risk to their lives was considerable.[18]

Throughout the month, bomb and arson attacks occurred in Aber-
corn, Portsmouth, Sheffield, Bath, Aberdeen, Tunbridge Wells, Plymouth Hoe, York, Thanet, Birmingham, Newcastle, Cardiff, Preston,
London, and Manchester. There was even an attempt to bomb the Bank
of England, using a device containing about two ounces of gunpowder,
a quantity of hairpins, and a small electric battery attached by wire to a
small chronometer watch, set to explode the bomb at eleven o'clock.[19]

At many of the attacks, copies of The Suffragette were found scattered,
or postcards scrawled with messages such as "Votes For Women!,"
"More To Come / Give Us The Vote," "Votes for women, and damn the
consequences," "In honour of Mrs. Pankhurst," "Burning for the Vote!,"
"Beware of the bomb, run for your lives!" or "Votes For Women R.I.P."[20]

A bomb discovered at the Lyceum Theatre, Taunton, was revealed
in the press to have the words "Votes For Women," "Judges Beware,"
"Martyrs of the law," and "Release our Sisters" painted along its side.[21]
At Smeaton's Tower, an old lighthouse on Plymouth Hoe, a bomb—a
circular tin canister containing explosive material and a lit but defused
wick—had been painted with the words "Votes For Women. Death In
Ten Minutes."[22] Every attack was reprinted in detail in The Suffragette;

Christabel was determined to use the paper to heighten the passion and commitment of those instructed to carry out these attacks.

Although the violence of the campaign had intensified after the betrayal of the Conciliation Bill, the idea of adopting such violent revolutionary methods had been part of the women's movement for a long time. As the language surrounding female suffrage became increasingly dismissive and patronizing, it pushed suffrage supporters to locate targets in government who were responsible for holding back women's political rights. Lewis Harcourt, the Oxfordshire-based Liberal MP for Rossendale, was an ardent anti-suffragist. He appeared to have feared attacks from those he opposed long before there was any evidence that the WSPU had decided to use bombs. On February 23, 1907, he recorded an unpleasant discovery in his diary:

NUNEHAM 23.2.07

In cutting down a tree near the boat house here today a bomb fell out of the hole in the trunk! It was a very heavy iron or steel bottle of this shape with a fuse hole for a percussion cap at the top and surrounded with a hand cement of five clay or dynamite filled with slugs and swanshot, I did not fancy opening it myself so I sent it in by sale to the Oxford police to do what they liked with. Perhaps it is a delicate attention to me from the female suffragists.[23]

Harcourt became a deliberate target for the suffragettes from 1910 onward, when he assumed the post of secretary of state for the colonies in the cabinet; and later in 1912, Helen Craggs would be discovered in the grounds of his Nuneham home, armed with enough material to burn it to a cinder, but she was caught before any damage could be done. So perhaps Harcourt's 1907 discovery was indeed an early attack; the suffragettes certainly began to threaten publicly that they would start to use bombs for the first time in the following year. Having been arrested for breaking windows at 10 Downing Street in 1908, Mary Leigh—who would go on to be a member of the Theatre Royal attack on Asquith in Dublin in 1912—had stated to her arresting officer, "It will be bombs next time." Brought before the magistrate at Bow Street, she and her companion, Miss New, were questioned further:

> MR. MARSHAM: One of you said "It will be bombs next time." That means something very different to stones. Bomb-throwing is an offence punishable by hanging. Do you repudiate any idea of the kind?
>
> MISS NEW: I cannot say what will happen in the future. It will depend upon whether justice is done to the women of this country.
>
> MR. MARSHAM TO MRS. LEIGH: It is stated that you said something as to throwing bombs.
>
> MRS. LEIGH: I admit to saying that it might mean bombs next time.
>
> MR. MARSHAM: You see it is a very serious matter.
>
> MRS. LEIGH: We quite realise that it is a very serious position, and we hope the Government will also realise the serious position of affairs.
>
> MR. MARSHAM: You are not likely to attain your object by conduct of this kind. When women want to obtain anything from men they are more likely to obtain it by gentle means than they are by any other method. Men appreciate gentleness on the part of a woman.[24]

The argument that men could be persuaded by kindness, rather than conflict, fell on deaf ears. For the suffragettes, little had been gained by women's kindness to men. To many, like Kitty, it was the betrayal they had experienced in their relationships with men that had begun their radicalization. But the threat of hanging certainly seems to have had some effect on the planned use of bombs by the WSPU. They would need to discover a way that would not result in the deaths of their members.

A variety of methods were attempted over the next two years. Attending a meeting of the cabinet at 10 Downing Street, on

September 15, 1909, Herbert Gladstone, the home secretary, brought with him a cylindrical piece of black wood, eighteen inches long and about an inch in diameter, inscribed in white letters with the word "Bomb." It had been thrown through the window while he had been taking a meeting, potentially, Gladstone believed, by a suffragette.[25] Two months later, speakers at a suffragette meeting in Bristol attended by Annie Kenney argued that if the present government was "a statesmanlike one it would take warning from India, where bombs had been thrown at the Viceroy."[26]

It wasn't only the WSPU that was starting to make plans for aggressive action; in 1909, the police were also informed of a suffragist plot to assassinate Prime Minister Asquith.[27] Mrs. Moore of the Women's Freedom League reported five of her members "who had given expression to their intentions to commit acts of violence," two of whom had been seen practicing with a Browning pistol at the same range where another assassin, Madan Lal Dhingra, had trained before shooting Sir William Curzon Wyllie, aide-de-camp to the secretary of state for India.[28] Dhingra was fighting for Indian independence from British rule, and his assassination of Wyllie on the steps of the Imperial Institute, Kensington, was another example of how far a disenfranchised people would be willing to go to secure their rights.

Just as Irish—also fighting for their country's independence—and Indian activists sought to force the British government to finally grant political rights to their citizens, the suffragettes too created a group within their organization to carry out radical and dangerous acts. A gang of devout, radicalized young women who carried out a large number of bomb and arson attacks on Christabel's direct instruction would become the most dangerous suffragettes of all.

Founded in 1907 by Jessie Kenney and Adela Pankhurst, the younger sisters of the suffragette leadership, an internal organization, existing secretly within the WSPU, had been formed to bind together the younger women who were drawn to the suffragette cause. They called themselves "The Young Hot Bloods." Born out of the violent rhetoric

of bombs and revolution, and pledged to undertake "danger duty"—
the suffragette code for extreme militant action—they were the most
radical and the most aggressive of all of the suffragettes. Even today
their total membership remains a secret.

The *Yorkshire Evening Post* uncovered the root of the name in 1913;
it "was derived from a taunt thrown at Mrs. Pankhurst by one of the
newspapers, which ran: 'Mrs. Pankhurst will, of course, be followed
blindly by a number of the younger and more hot-blooded members
of the Union.' This secret society formed the nucleus of young suffragettes who were willing to support the Committee of the Wom-
en's Union in any militant action. No married women were eligible
for membership."[29] The qualification for the Young Hot Bloods to
be unmarried women is a criterion met by so many of those who were
arrested and charged with the arson and bomb attacks. Kitty, Mary
Richardson, Clara Giveen, Lilian Lenton, Joyce Locke, Olive Hockin—
were all potentially members.

The existence of the group remained a closely guarded secret until
May 1913, when it was uncovered by the conspiracy trial of eight members of the suffragette leadership: Flora Drummond, Annie Kenney,
Harriet Kerr, Agnes Lake, Rachel Barrett, Laura Lennox, Beatrice Sanders, and Edwy Godwin Clayton, a scientific chemist. As always, the
suffragettes took to the stand with a determination to encourage those
who would read the transcripts of their cases in the papers to continue
in the fight. Rachel Barrett, who also helped publish *The Suffragette*,
encouraged active rebellion: "When we hear of a bomb being thrown
we say 'Thank God for that.' If we have any qualms of conscience, it is
not because of things that happen, but because of things that have been
left undone."[30] She was unshakable in her commitment to this course
of action, and it would have echoed throughout the organization, run
now by multiple survivors of governmental violence, who had either
fully committed to the cause without question or had seen their reser-
vations blown away after the abuse and torture of so many members
of the WSPU displayed in their pamphlets and newspapers.

The methods the WSPU used to organize the Young Hot Bloods and other women like them were recorded by Sylvia Pankhurst:

> . . . when the policy was fully under way, certain officials of the Union were given, as their main work, the task of advising incendiaries, and arranging for the supply of such inflammable material, house-breaking tools and other matters as they might require. Women, most of them very young toiled through the night across unfamiliar country, carrying heavy cases of petrol and paraffin.[31]

The threat these women posed, and the devastation they could wreak across the country at any given moment, was clear. Capitalizing on the growing public concern surrounding the actions of the militants, and in a blatant attempt to pressure the government for an increase in funds, a "distinguished member of the London Police force, whose special duty is to deal with the suffragettes," gave a long and detailed interview to the *London Telegraph.* Arguing that the WSPU was operating as an anarchist crime organization, the policeman pointed out that, if a well-known anarchist set foot in England, he would be shadowed for his every waking moment, thereby significantly reducing any opportunity for crime or social disruption. He believed the current "crime mania" of the suffragettes would only be curtailed by similar procedures, saying, "It would be comparatively easy to do so if we had sufficient men, and also, I may add, a liberal scale of expenses. It is practically impossible to do so as things are."[32]

So how did the police deal with the problem of suffragette terrorism? What methods did they have for attempting to deal with the devices turning up in public spaces and threatening the security of society at this time? The Metropolitan Police had spent much of 1911 assessing and reassessing their ability to investigate and examine organizations that might see fit to use bombs against the British public. A hangover from the Victorian threats of anarchist plots, a bomb disposal unit had been built on Duck Island, in St. James's Park. The "Duck

Island Magazine" was "fitted up with the apparatus for the purpose of opening infernal machines without danger to the operator," but by 1911 no clear or up-to-date plans for it existed. Major Cooper Key, His Majesty's chief inspector of explosives, had surveyed the magazine on Duck Island in April, at the request of his counterpart in India, who was facing a serious bomb campaign from Indian revolutionaries. The decision had been reached that the British were woefully under-prepared for the disposal and investigation of bombs, and so Cooper Key decided to visit France, with the agreement of Winston Churchill, as the Municipal Laboratory in Paris was renowned for dealing with hundreds of different devices. Here, Cooper Key discovered a hydraulic press for the destruction of bombs, and also the use of a special car that had been built specifically to carefully transport bombs from their location to the laboratory without risk of explosion.[33] But here is where our records stop.

One of the most frustrating parts of trying to understand this area of our history is that so much remains hidden. Police records, which would undoubtedly showcase the first active counterterrorism investigations, remain missing, and intimate accounts of the bombers and their dealings with the police can only slowly be pieced together from the records Kitty and a few of her companions left behind.

One of the most eye-opening accounts of suffragette methods comes from Mary Richardson, sent to bomb a railway station in Birmingham. After receiving direct instructions for a "protest of the utmost importance," Mary transported a primed and ticking bomb—or "Black Jenny" as she called them—from London to a house near to the site of her next attack.[34] Given the delicate nature of these devices, the timers the suffragettes used made an increasingly loud ticking and spluttering noise to show they were getting close to exploding. This alerted Mary and her companion to the fact that their bomb, which they had hidden in the wardrobe of the house they were staying in, was drawing close to detonation.[35] Packing it into a bag—gently, given its temperamental nature—they gingerly made their way through the midnight streets to the railway station (possibly Hagley Road Station) and left the bomb, constructed from a marmalade tin, in the ticket office. Marmalade tins then were far larger than today's jars, and easily housed the contents of the devices behind the WSPU's attacks.

Hoping to defuse any potential public admiration of or attraction to the cause and the actions of these young suffragettes, the police attempted to portray them as little more than disruptive teenagers when speaking to the press:

> Several of them have a habit of sleeping here or there, with friends or otherwise, and of securing food in the same way. Curiously enough, these "young hot-bloods" are not the women who would get the vote in Parliament if either of the recent bills had gone through. They own no property, and are not married women: I don't think some of them are ever likely to be.[36]

Can you picture the newspaper being thrown across the room in jocular disdain, and landing, rumpled, near the fireplace as the members of the YHBs toast muffins, pour tea, and plan their next attack in the rooms and flats of their co-conspirators?

By now, the attacks were drawing more women to the suffragette cause. A letter recovered by the police during a raid on suffragette property, sent to Emmeline Pankhurst by Marianne Cunningham, a supporter of the suffrage cause, made her growing commitment clear:

> I applaud your courage, and I believe in militancy ... What is done now ought to be SOMETHING BIG—SOMETHING BIG by members— some careful night attack where all the women could get off scot free if possible. Why not a gigantic raid on pillar boxes filled with staining acids such as sulphurated hydrogen. I am a volunteer for that personally.[37]

Kitty viewed the attacks as the only way that the government could be convinced to listen to women. They were proof of how serious the

WSPU was in its pursuit of the vote. She and many of the suffragettes, who were educated, intelligent women, didn't need to look far to find other groups fighting for their rights with exactly the same, if not even more violent, methods. Across the water in Ireland, Sir Edward Carson was opposing Home Rule and incited his followers to armed rebellion, but unlike Mrs. Pankhurst and the rest of the suffragette leadership, he was not arrested. The government's brutal treatment of suffragette prisoners compared with their "cringing, fawning attitude toward Sir Edward Carson and his men" was, for Kitty, just another example of the hypocrisy and cowardliness of men.[38] The WSPU seized on this anger, as Mrs. Pankhurst challenged the government: "You have not dared to take the leaders of Ulster for their incitement to rebellion. Take me if you dare and if you do I tell you this, that so long as those who incite to armed rebellion and destruction of human life in Ulster are at liberty, you will not keep me in prison."[39]

Emmeline Pankhurst defined the violent militancy as "continued, destructive, guerrilla warfare against the Government through injury to private property," which had one sole aim: "to make England and every department of English life insecure and unsafe."[40] The suffragettes were proving to be exceptionally successful in the scope and scale of their attacks, made easier by the Prisoners (Temporary Discharge for Ill Health) Act 1913, better known as the "Cat and Mouse Act," which allowed the prisons to quickly release any hunger-striking suffragettes, supposedly stopping the need to force-feed them. Prisoners were allowed to recuperate at a suffragette nursing home, and then they were supposed to return to prison. It was utterly unenforceable. By the middle of 1913, the government found itself dealing with a large, highly radicalized, and organized group of women, committed to extreme violence against the government. The leadership made clear that the aims of the attacks were to cause serious terror and fear among the British population. The scale, a nationwide bombing and arson campaign, caused such extreme damage that museums, parks, churches, and public attractions were forced to either close or take out specific suffragette insurance.

But for some reason this violence has been forgotten. We seem unable to leave behind a gendered politics of revolution; inherent in our society is a belief that women cannot commit the same acts of violence or destruction as men. This has created a paradox in how we view terrorism: we allow for men to be terrorists, while thinking women cannot be. But if the action is the same, if a person leaves a bomb to explode in a public space as a political message, why does their gender alter our perceptions of the act itself? It only takes a single act of terror to cause significant social distress in modern society.

Taking one look at the reality of suffrage violence, it's clear that many of the actions of the militants can be viewed as acts of terror.[41] They were specifically designed to influence the government and public to change their opinions on women's suffrage, not by choice but by threats of violence. This was never something that either the leadership of the WSPU or the soldiers of the Union shied away from. The sole purpose of the attacks was to cause terror. "The result," wrote Emmeline Pankhurst, "was exactly as we anticipated. The public were thrown into a state of emotion of insecurity and frightened expectancy."[42] They achieved their aim. Looking back on the public and expert reaction to the violence of the previous six months, it is clear that there were few illusions about the aggression of the suffragettes. "The militant campaign of terrorism, ranging from arson and bombs to window-breaking and chemicals in letter boxes, was a carefully planned and organised conspiracy," reported the *Illustrated Police News*. "The leaders of the movement had at their command an army of some hundreds of women who carried out faithfully the instructions given to them."[43] Experts and commentators alike tried to unpick why women would be drawn to the violent actions of the WSPU:

> You can well imagine how incendiarism or destruction by means of bombs appeals to young women, who may be placed as belonging to one of two classes:—1) Those whose lives as ordinary honest workers,

shop assistants, typists, etc., would necessarily be humdrum and ill paid; and 2) Those of a better class, who, although not in want of money, feel, nevertheless, for various reasons, the lack of social excitement and opportunity.[44]

There was little room in the conservative pundits' minds for the idea of female agency, that women might feel driven to such horrifying acts simply because they felt their legal and political rights were being denied. For Kitty, this was the final option left open to her, having spent so long trying to persuade the people around her of a woman's worth, her right to work, and the dangers and risks that came with the acceptance of sexual harassment. She had been radicalized by the government's treatment of her, and the powerful speeches and protests made by the women around her. Her commitment to the WSPU, and to the militancy orchestrated by Christabel Pankhurst, was absolute.

But what was the cost for the women Christabel committed to these violent and aggressive campaigns? She seems to have had little care for the effect of such actions on the lives of those she was repeatedly placing in danger; little understanding that such events could tear a family apart. It fell to her sister, Sylvia, to understand the damage Christabel's cause could wreak on her soldiers. She didn't forget, as Christabel and Emmeline appear to have, the cost of the militant campaign. Included in her 1931 memoir, *The Suffragette Movement—An Intimate Account of Persons and Ideals*, is a brief mention of Miriam Pratt, whose photo sits alongside Kitty's in the police surveillance records.[45] Although Miriam was only fleetingly referred to, Sylvia is clearly trying to address the serious imbalance between her mother and sister's public record of the WSPU—one which lauded their own triumphs—and the lives and courage of the women she had known firsthand, who have since been forgotten.

A young Norwich schoolteacher in her early twenties, Miriam Pratt became a notorious figure for her commitment to the suffragette war. But her actions came at great personal cost. On the night of the

Newmarket by-election, May 17, 1913, she had set a fire at an empty building attached to the Balfour Biological Laboratory for Women, in Storey's Way, Cambridge. Endangering the laboratory was, perhaps, an unusual decision for the suffragettes, as it had been opened in 1884 to instruct the women of Girton and Newnham Colleges in scientific study.[46] Here, among the huge windows and open galleries, women learned about anatomy, dissection, microbiology, zoology, chemical compounds, and physics, in a state-of-the-art laboratory that had been built solely for their use. Botany, biology, and marine studies, the intimate examination of the physical world, all took place at Balfour, memorialized in photographs that show desks covered in microscopes, animal skeletons, and pages of students' notes.

But what good was a university laboratory, and a university education, if women were refused the right to be awarded their degrees? Although universities permitted women to attend courses and take exams, they were not allowed to graduate, and there was little opportunity for them to use the knowledge they acquired in the world outside the protected college atmosphere. Perhaps it was the unbearable unfairness of this inequality that removed any qualms Miriam and her companions might have felt that night, as they broke in and set a fire that consumed a considerable amount of the adjoining building before the alarm was raised. The university had been the target of a failed bomb attack a week earlier, when a device was discovered in the football pavilion—the fuse had failed to ignite, but the suffragette threat was clear, and Cambridge's borough police force was now on high alert.

Madingley Road was surrounded by fields and farmland. In the early hours of that May morning, PC Alfred Smith and his companion, PC Brooks, dressed in plain clothes and pushing their bikes along beside them, saw flames against the sky in the direction of Huntingdon Road.[47] Cycling at breakneck speed, they followed the fire to Storey's Way and discovered not one, but two buildings burning. In the aftermath, a bloody windowpane was found and, nearby, a woman's gold watch, among the scattered suffrage literature that was often left at the site of an attack.[48] It was the gold watch that would lead to Miriam's downfall.

For some time she had been living with her uncle, Sergeant William Ward of the Norwich City Police, at 9 Turner Road, near St. Paul's school, where she was teaching. The family had been close, and when Miriam had left to study at St. Gabriel's College, London, five years earlier, her uncle had given her a gold watch to commemorate the occasion.[49] Since returning home she had worked and paid rent, and was well known as a suffragette newspaper seller throughout the city. How had the conversations around the dinner table gone, with Miriam the suffragette and William the policeman? Had he supported women's rights, but not the violence? Miriam's membership in the organization was no secret, and yet he placed no limit on her activities.

On the week of the Cambridge fire she had told him she would be going to the city—although only, she said, to sell newspapers—and he had not stopped her. But Miriam had also been in Cambridge a week earlier, at the same time as the bomb was found in the football pavilion—was it this that started to make him suspicious? Reading a report of the fire in the *Norwich Evening News*, what had he thought when his niece returned home the next evening, smiling secretly to herself? Certainly it played on his mind enough for him to ask his wife to check if Miriam's gold watch was in her bedroom. It was not.

Confronted, Miriam begged him not to tell anyone the watch was hers. The betrayal must have been shocking for a man who had spent his life working to enforce the law; to discover that his niece, educated and hardworking, had committed such a dangerous crime. Miriam claimed she had nothing to do with the fire itself, but William had read about the broken windowpane, the blood found at the scene. He examined her hands. The cuts were clear.

What happened next, what accusations were flung, what family ties were broken and torn apart that night we may never know. But shortly after William confronted her, Miriam was arrested at their home by the chief constables of Norwich and Cambridge. She was taken by mail train back to the scene of the crime. Crowds gathered outside the police court to hear the evidence against her, jostling to get a look at the "tall, pretty girl," who was "dressed in a light blue corduroy coat, a blue cloth skirt, and black velvet toque trimmed with light blue ribbon."[50] Sitting in the court were the WSPU organizers for both Cambridge and Norwich, Olive Bartels and Margaret West, who quite possibly had intimate knowledge of the attack. After the evidence was heard, the case went forward to the Cambridge Assizes in October, where Miriam found herself one of six cases, including one of murder. At twenty-three, and in front of a grand jury of doctors, colonels, and army majors, Miriam chose to represent herself. Confidently, she cross-examined landladies and taxicab drivers, and accused policemen of altering their statements to support the evidence. When her uncle took the stand, the toll Miriam's commitment to the suffragettes had taken on the family was clear. Her anger, and her uncle's sadness, all come through in the transcripts of the case:

MIRIAM PRATT: Is it legal for the witness to give evidence of a statement he alleges to have obtained from me not having first cautioned me, he being a police officer?

HIS LORDSHIP: That does not disqualify him. He was not acting as a police officer: Were you acting as a police officer or were you making inquiries as being her uncle?

WITNESS: As her uncle.

MP: When you had made up your mind about the watch you knew I should be arrested?

W: Yes.

MP: And yet you went on questioning me?

W: I did.

MP: Don't you think it was your duty as a police officer to caution me?

W: Yes, it was my duty, but I was speaking to you as a father would do, and I omitted to caution you.[51]

Although she denied having anything to do with the fire, and spent considerable time calling into question her uncle's ability as a policeman as well as the rest of the evidence in the case, Miriam sealed her fate with her closing statement. Like so many of the suffragettes who were prosecuted for violence, she used her final words as a defense of militancy:

> I ask you to look again at what has been done and see in it not wilful and malicious damage, but a protest against a callous Government, indifferent to reasoned argument and the best interests of the country. A protest carried to extreme because no other means would avail . . . show by your verdict to-day that to fight in the cause of human freedom and human betterment is to do no wrong.[52]

Sentenced to eighteen months' hard labor, Miriam was nonetheless released within a week; she had begun a hunger strike the moment she entered Holloway Prison. Never one to miss an opportunity to capitalize on emotion, *The Suffragette* ran a story—unknowingly, on the day of her release—stating, "Lord, help and save Miriam Pratt and all those being tortured in prison for conscience sake."[53] Perhaps Christabel had not expected her to be released so soon, but the damage force-feeding had inflicted on Miriam was swift and brutal. Her doctors ordered three months' bed rest due to the serious effect the hunger strike had had on her heart, perhaps, with the loss of her family, broken in more ways than one.[54]

Christabel's need for sacrifice, for commitment to the cause above all things, left no room for the reality of human relationships. "I regarded this new policy with grief and regret," wrote her sister, Sylvia, "believing it wholly mistaken and unnecessary, deeply deploring the life of furtive destruction it would impose upon the participators, and the harsh punishment it was preparing for them; for these unknown girls there would be no international telegrams."[55]

In March, Kitty had received her orders and attacked two railway stations: at Saunderton the building was completely destroyed, and placards reading "Votes For Women" and "Burning For the Vote" were left nearby;[56] Croxley station near Watford suffered an identical fate, although the attack was not attributed to militants until a copy of *The Suffragette* was delivered to the stationmaster with the scribbled inscription "Afraid copy left got burnt."[57] In the same month, a plot to kidnap the home secretary, Reginald McKenna, was discussed both in the press and the House of Commons; the suffragettes were reported to be contemplating kidnapping one or more cabinet ministers and subjecting them to force-feeding.[58] The threat was taken so seriously that, for their own protection, private detectives began to shadow the ministers.[59] April brought Kitty further orders, and she attacked a train left standing between Hampton Wick and Teddington. It was almost totally destroyed by fire in the early hours of Saturday morning on April 26:

> The train was afterwards driven into Teddington Station, where an examination resulted in the discovery of inflammable materials in almost every set of coaches. Among the articles found in the train were partly-burnt candles, four cans of petroleum, three of which had been emptied of their contents, a lady's dressing case containing a quantity of cotton wool, and packages of literature dealing with the woman suffrage movement. Newspaper cuttings of recent suffragette outrages were also found scattered about the train ... The method adopted was very simple. First the cushions were saturated with petroleum, and then small pieces of candle were lighted immediately under the seats.[60]

Many suffragette arsonists and bombers took their secrets with them to their graves, but Kitty seems to have been unable to leave behind the habits of her old life, even if they could result in her own imprisonment; just as she did with the tours and reviews of her music hall life, she kept a detailed personal scrapbook of the press reports on all the attacks she carried out as a suffragette solider, cutting and pasting in these new reviews and annotating them by hand.[61] Her sense of pride in these violent and controversial actions is clear. Her cross-country knowledge, gathered from her life as a young touring music hall artist, allowed her to easily escape down side roads and back alleys in towns she knew well.

Desperately attempting to bring the violence under control, the WSPU was banned from open-air meetings, as police raids on head-quarters and private houses attempted to find the bomb-makers' arsenal. The militants hit back, and a number of prominent society members who opposed suffrage saw their homes destroyed by fire and incendiary devices.[62] The bombs became more complicated, and more deadly. Reporting on an attack on the Royal Astronomical Observa-tory on Blackford Hill, Edinburgh, the *Western Gazette* read:

> The scheme had been well thought-out. On gaining an entrance the perpetrators had taken the bomb to the top of the spiral stairway under the dome and carried a fuse thirty feet long down into the chronograph-room, where it was fired by means of a lighted candle, the remains of which were found. The quantity of gunpowder used must have been considerable, as fragments of the earthen jar which held it were embedded in the wall and woodwork, and the glass of two windows was blown out and carried a considerable distance. A bag, some biscuits, and Suffragette literature were left behind.[63]

Adding to the danger of bombs themselves, the suffragettes also began to issue death threats, aimed at the wider British public. In May 1913, at her trial for attempting to blow up the Empire Palace in Dublin, evidence against Marcella Gertrude McGuirk included leaf-lets with the text "Votes For Women—No Property or Life Safe Until We Get It," and—although she denied any link to the bomb or the suffragette movement—the threats left by the perpetrators were very clear.[64]

Two months later, Liverpool was rocked by the trial of a Mrs. Edith Rigby, who had planted a bomb in the town hall and told the magistrate "that she wanted to show how easy it was to get explosives and put them in public places."[65]

After Emily Wilding Davison's bombing of David Lloyd George's cottage, Emmeline Pankhurst had quickly claimed "the moral responsibility for it as one of the leaders who are preaching the suffrage war." Christabel, from the safety of Paris, gave interviews proclaiming:

> Perhaps the Government will realise now that we mean to fight to the bitter end . . . If men use explosives and bombs for their own purpose they call it war, and the throwing of a bomb that destroys other people is then described as a glorious and heroic deed. Why should a woman not make use of the same weapons as men. It is not only war we have declared. We are fighting for a revolution.[66]

Reading Christabel's words, it is difficult to understand *why* it is that the suffragettes' power and influence has been downplayed or ignored. If the speaker had been male, and all the events described previously had been solely male-authored, would history have hesitated to describe the militants as terrorists? Or brave freedom fighters?

The historian C. J. Bearman first highlighted the WSPU's use of warlike language in its public speech to expose the connection between suffragette militancy and terrorism. He played on the use of imagery and rhetoric—from the uniforms adopted by the WSPU to the language used to discuss militancy—as demonstrations that the women fully understood and recognized that their actions were illegal, dangerous, and life-threatening in pursuit of political change. This is clearly evident from the formation in 1913 of what became known as "Mrs. Pankhurst's Army."

> A meeting was held at Bow, London, last night, for the purposes of inaugurating the projected suffragette "army," to be known as the People's Training Corps. About 300 persons assembled, mostly young girls and women . . . Miss Emerson, in an address, said that their intention was

to train the corps that they could proceed in force to Downing Street, and there imprison Ministers until they conceded women's suffrage. They had all heard of bloody Sidney Street, but the bloody scenes that might be expected at Downing Street would be worse.[67]

But the self-identification of the women as warriors or soldiers engaged in domestic warfare was not a new one. Since the early 1900s, Mrs. Flora Drummond had been known to the press, and within the WSPU, as "the General," and on one occasion was seen riding on horseback at the head of a suffragette procession of more than two thousand suffragists, while the "Women's Marseillaise" played behind her.[68] The WSPU was a beacon of militancy, with a clearly defined brand of female empowerment. They used a language that invaded masculine public space, with images of what had previously been viewed as male-dominated arenas of war and danger. Women had been seen as a threat to men before, but only in the context of sexual impropriety—the immoral woman of the night, sex workers, or the colonial female "savage" of the Empire. The sexist and racist language used to control and disregard the women who fell into these categories is still endemic in our culture today. But the violent women of the militant suffragette movement occupied the same space as men; they demanded equality and used actions, words, and political protest that they believed were the only methods men would understand. Clearly evident in the trials of the suffragettes, as well as in the messages left at attack sites across the country, is a committed language of political resistance. And as Kitty made clear, the suffragettes who took part in the hunger strike campaign justified the actions that had led to their imprisonment by the violence they suffered at the hands of the government.

One of the main modern arguments against the severity of suffragette violence focuses on a misguided belief that the suffragettes did not cause harm to anyone with their attacks. However, there is clear evidence that this is not true—many mail carriers suffered horrific burns from the chemicals found in mailboxes—and, although rarely, in some

instances causing harm *was* the intention. While some militant suffragettes maintained that they did not wish to cause harm to anyone, but
rather only wished to demonstrate the lengths that they *could* go to, the
destruction and fear that these acts provoked in society far outweighs
any protestations of innocence—of which few actually exist.[69] Most
women when convicted seem to have remained defiant and devoted
to their cause.

As the bombing and arson campaign continued to escalate, the
police launched an all-out attack on the WSPU leadership. Emmeline
Pankhurst's proud admission that she had incited others, additional to
Emily Wilding Davison, to conspire in the bombing of Lloyd George's
cottage had led to her arrest and sentencing to three years' penal servitude. She had been removed to Holloway Prison on April 3, although
she was released shortly afterward, having immediately gone on hunger strike. After raiding the headquarters of the WSPU, the police had
found enough evidence to arrest and charge Flora Drummond, Annie
Kenney, Harriet Kerr, Agnes Lake, Rachel Barrett, Laura Lennox, Beatrice Sanders, and Edwy Godwin Clayton with conspiracy. Clayton was
suspected of being responsible for the chemicals and possibly even the
explosives used by the older suffragettes and the Young Hot Bloods in
their attacks on the government. The suffragettes retaliated; Emmeline
Pankhurst's April arrest and the raids on the WSPU were followed by
some of the most violent and dangerous months in British history.

In May 1913, there were fifty-two attacks, including twenty-
nine bombs and fifteen arson attempts on churches, railway stations, and post offices. A bomb was even sent to Bow Street Police
Court, addressed to Mr. Curtis Bennett, the magistrate hearing the
charges against the WSPU leadership. The small package, wrapped
in brown paper and marked "Immediate," consisted of a tobacco tin
filled with gunpowder, a live cartridge, and a nail.[70] The delivery had
been timed to occur just as the leadership appeared. "Deadly," was
the police assessment.

Kitty, following the success of her attack on Arthur Du Cros, was responsible for the burning of a large private house called The Highlands, in Coolinge, near Folkestone, Kent. The detailed newspaper report, proudly pasted into her militant scrapbook, announces that "the outrage was the work of a well-educated person, who had apparently gone to considerable trouble to gather, from the works of some of the great writers, quotations applicable to the motive which underlay the action."[71] Two small white postcards addressed to "The Right Dishonourable Prime Minister" and "The Right Dishonourable Reginald McKenna" were discovered at the scene; they were covered in quotes from Tennyson, Carlyle, Milton, Shakespeare, and Charlotte Brontë: "People hate to be reminded of ills they are unable or unwilling to remedy," ran the quote from *Shirley*, Brontë's 1849 novel about an independent and willful young woman, the equal of any man around her.[72] Hardly a surprising heroine for a suffragette arsonist to choose.

Access to The Highlands had been via a side window at the front entrance where, ingeniously, brown paper had been smeared with treacle and plastered over the pane to keep the pieces together and deaden the sound of breaking glass.[73] Once inside, Kitty had set the fire underneath the staircase, so that it would quickly spread through the entire heart of the house. The attack went undiscovered until midnight, when Captain Jacob and Lieutenant Clark of the Sandgate Fire Brigade were roused by reports of smoke from the constable on duty near Coolinge Lane. Arriving on board a fire engine carrying seven more men, they quickly entered the house to find the staircase caved in and the fire rapidly spreading through the entirety of the house. Desperately attempting to salvage what was left, the brigade took four hours to bring the blaze under control.

Kitty's violence may have been against an empty house, but many of the attacks carried with them a significant and increasing risk to life. At Kingston on May 14, as a packed passenger train arrived from Waterloo, three bombs were discovered in the third-class carriage, rigged to a timer. Two were tin canisters measuring three inches high and one and a half inches in diameter, filled with what appeared to be nitroglycerin; the third was a square box, six inches by four inches and wrapped in brown paper, connected by wire to "three accumulators and clockwork mechanism."[74] The tins had been wrapped in suffrage literature and the colors of the WSPU, with labels reading, "Raided—Votes for women. Give us our votes and we will give you peace," "Mr. Lloyd George is a crone and Mr. Asquith is a liar," and "Lloyd George ran away in police-man's clothes. Coward! Cad! Asquith is a rotter and funks. Give us the vote, and we will give you peace. Life and property not safe till we get the vote."[75]

Death, it seemed, was inching ever closer.

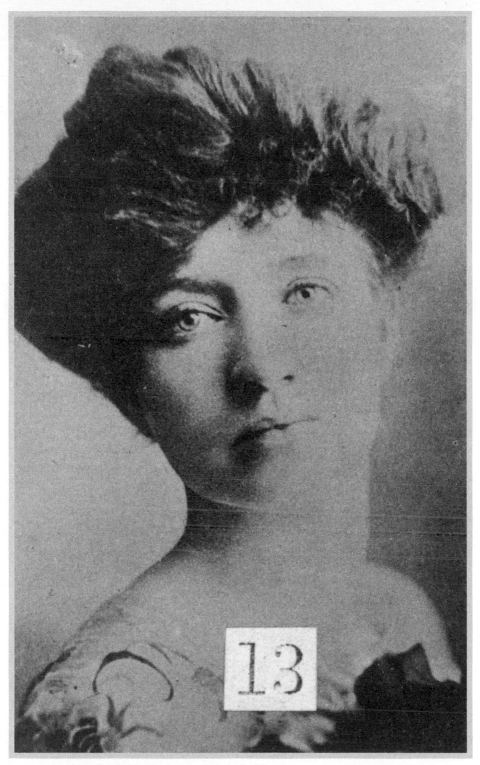

Kitty Marion. Taken from a famous set of surveillance photographs showing twenty of the most dangerous suffragettes operating in England, this image of Kitty—her performer's calling card—was included by the police in 1914.

Sylvia Pankhurst addressing a crowd outside the headquarters of the East London Federation of Suffragettes, Old Ford Road, Bow, 1912.

A game entitled "Elusive Christabel," satirizing police failure to find and arrest Christabel Pankhurst. Sold as a penny novelty by street traders as the police attempt to stop Christabel's escape to France in 1912.

Emmeline Pankhurst arrested while trying to present a petition to the King at Buckingham Palace, May 21, 1914. Carried past a group of reporters, Emmeline called out, "Arrested at the gates of the Palace. Tell the King."

1912 Suffragette Hunger Strike medal in silver with green, white, and purple striped ribbon. Inscribed "For Valour, Hunger Strike," with the name of the suffragette and the dates of her incarcerations.

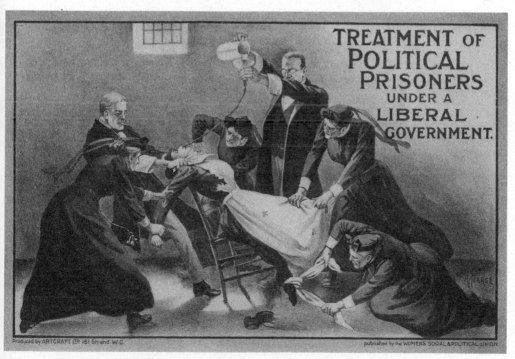

Famous poster used by the suffragettes to show the torture of force-feeding women in prison. Front cover of *The Suffragette*, February 6, 1914.

Kitty Marion arrested for heckling David Lloyd George at the Royal National Eisteddfod, Wrexham, Wales, Thursday September 5, 1912. Kitty Marion gained admission to the meeting with the sole aim of heckling Lloyd George.

A suffragette struggling with a policeman on "Black Friday," November 18, 1910. The government attempted to have the photographs of the attacks and abuse the women suffered destroyed. Their publication led to a serious scandal for the home secretary, Winston Churchill.

" DEATH IN TEN MINUTES."

SUFFRAGIST ATTEMPT TO BLOW UP AN OLD LIGHTHOUSE.

An attempt was made on Friday night, presumably by Suffragists, to blow up Smeaton Tower, on Plymouth Hoe. While passing the tower about eight o'clock on Saturday morning a man named William Chubb found in a doorway a circular tin canister, six inches long, containing explosive matter. In the cover was a wick saturated with oil. It had evidently been lighted, but had been blown out by the wind.

Painted in crude letters on the tin were the words: "Votes for women. Death in ten minutes." The canister was handed over to the police, who are endeavouring to trace the culprits.

Smeaton Tower is the old lighthouse which for one hundred and fifty years stood on the Eddystone reef, but was taken down and erected on Plymouth Hoe, when the present Eddystone lighthouse was built, about thirty years ago.

No. 14,917

BOMB OUTRAGE.

EXPLOSION AT MR. LLOYD GEORGE'S NEW HOUSE.

SERIOUS DAMAGE.

SUFFRAGETTE TERRORISM

HAT-PIN CLUE.

The Suffragettes to-day took a new and grave departure in their dastardly campaign of violence and terrorism.

Two bombs were placed in the house which Mr. Lloyd George has had built at Walton-on-the-Hill, near Epsom.

One of these exploded in a bedroom and created great havoc. The second did not go off, as the plans of the miscreants slightly miscarried.

There was no one in the house, which is not yet quite ready for occupation.

Mr. Lloyd George is at present travelling on the Continent in company with Sir Rufus Isaacs and Mr. T. P. O'Connor.

The perpetrators of the outrage appear to have used a motor-car, and they got away, leaving only two broken hatpins as clues.

THE DISCOVERY.

LATEST DETAILS OF THE OUTRAGE.

The Daily Mirror

THE MORNING JOURNAL WITH THE SECOND LARGEST NET SALE.

| No. 2,910. | Registered at the G.P.O. as a Newspaper | THURSDAY, FEBRUARY 20, 1913. | One Halfpenny. |

THE LATEST POLITICAL ARGUMENT: MR. LLOYD GEORGE'S NEW COUNTRY HOUSE WRECKED BY A BOMB.

Aftermath of Kitty's attack on a railway train carriage at Teddington, Middlesex, April 1913. Fire burned out three compartments of the train which was parked in sidings overnight. She left suffragette literature and incendiary materials at the scene.

The aftermath of Kitty's attack on Levetleigh, St. Leonards, Sussex, the home of Arthur Du Cros, Conservative MP for Hastings, April, 1913.

Emily Wilding Davison's funeral procession, June 1913. Fresh from her arrest for burning down Hurst Park's Grandstand in Emily's name, Kitty marched with her companions.

Margaret Sanger, 1879–1966. Founder of the American Birth Control League in 1921, which is now known as Planned Parenthood.

Suffragette Ruthless Rhymes of Martial Militants, book of satirical cartoons written and illustrated by Nelson Harding, first published in the *Brooklyn Daily Eagle,* 1913–1914.

Kitty Marion selling *Birth Control Review*, New York.
Kitty first began to sell *Birth Control Review* on New York's streets in
1917, and continued to do so until 1930. She was a well-known sight
in Times Square and outside Macy's department store.

7

No Surrender!

All movements have their martyrs. Leaders or soldiers who give their lives for their ideals, the ultimate argument to demonstrate their cause is just. It remains one of the most pointless actions in human culture. To glory in death is to glory in failure, a futile attempt to hide the fact that you have not managed to achieve your aims. We might think of martyrs as being purely religious figures—the Catholic Guy Fawkes and his Gunpowder Plot in 1605, or the Protestant poet Anne Askew, burned at the stake in 1546—but religious martyrs have always been, in some way, political. Martyrdom at its core has only ever been about one thing: power. You die because you are convinced that your beliefs demand sacrifice; to show those who oppose your ideas, your system of living, that their power does not control you. You die because you love something outside of yourself with such force and passion that your own life becomes meaningless. The cause, whatever it may be, demands a blood sacrifice.

Women have died for their beliefs throughout the centuries. Politics, religion, and war have all claimed female martyrs, either through choice or action. The Greek philosopher and mathematician Hypatia was head of one of the most important schools in fifth-century Alexandria. A famous center of knowledge and teaching in the ancient world, Alexandria lay on the Egyptian coast, home to a great library and several of the Wonders of the World. By the fifth century ad, it was a thriving metropolis of Jewish, Christian, and pagan ideologies, each jostling for power and legitimacy in the face of shifting cultural sands. As Christianity sought to cement its growing power across the continents, the old world order of the classical Greeks and Romans, and their emphasis on an intellectual life, began to fall. And so a blood sacrifice was demanded. In 415, the cultural warfare between rival Jewish and Christian factions turned deadly and the city's Roman governor, Orestes, set out harsh penalties for his citizens, publicly torturing a troublesome Christian leader, Hierax, to make his point clear.[1] In retaliation to this and further attacks on his community, Cyril, the bishop of Alexandria, ordered his followers to violently expel any Jews living within the walls of the city. Rumors were spread that Orestes had sought advice from Hypatia, a renowned non-Christian teacher, on how to maintain order in the city, and that she had advised him to rebuff any peaceful overtures Cyril might offer. The religious and secular leaders had found a scapegoat. Hypatia was ambushed in her chariot as she returned from teaching and dragged to the Caesareum. Cleopatra had ordered this ancient temple to be built in the memory of her lover Mark Antony, but now it had been converted to a Christian church and was Cyril's stronghold. Here, Hypatia was stripped naked and hacked to pieces. Her only crime was to be a powerful woman whose advice was sought by powerful men. Her death and mutilation at the hands of an angry Christian mob is one of the earliest recorded instances of a woman dying because of her role in politics.

The Martyrologium Hieronymianum (or Martyrologium sancti Hieronymi, as it is sometimes known) is a list of Christian martyrs, written at some point during the fourth and fifth centuries AD. Held within it are references to the martyrdom of Saint Euphemia, a woman who died in the Roman arena at Chalcedon, the remains of which now lie deeply buried underneath modern-day Istanbul. Her life and death are almost as closely woven into the history of the early Christian church as that of either Mary; mother or whore. Euphemia's tomb, now held in Istanbul's Patriarchal Church of St. George, was responsible for the "Miracle of the Council of Chalcedon." Attempting to bring consensus among the many and varied factions of the early church, its leaders met in 451 ad to decide, once and for all, on the nature of Jesus Christ. Was he God, was he merely a man, or was he both? Each definition was written on a scroll, and these were placed on Euphemia's breast, within her tomb. Three days later, when the tomb was reopened, held in Euphemia's hand was the scroll defining Christ as being both divine and human.

And so the body of a woman, a martyr, defined and continues to define our understanding of God. But the importance of Euphemia, the details of her life, her death, or her miracles—even this one—has been largely forgotten, restricted and controlled by the Christian Church. These early martyrs died because they refused to conform or agree with powerful men. Whether Christian or pagan, living or dead, these women came to represent a deeply feminine belief in self-sacrifice and death that has continually reoccurred throughout the centuries. Wherever we find female martyrs, we also find men scrabbling to maintain their pride, dignity, and power over the changing world around them.

In 1640, when Ann Hibbins found herself excommunicated from the Puritan First Church of Boston, Massachusetts, it was because she had dared to challenge male ineptitude. Disagreeing with the carpenters she had hired to work on her house, Ann had publicly accused them of attempting to overcharge her, bringing in other workmen to assess what had been done and recommend a fairer payment. You might think that Ann's actions were simply that of an individual refusing to be taken for a fool, but in the new Puritan colonies of America, women were not expected to be independent of either their husbands or any other man. Ann's self-confidence was seen as an attempt to undermine male sovereignty, "and that is transgressing the rule of the apostle in usurping authority over him whom God hath made her head and husband . . . as if she were able to manage it better than her husband, which is a plain breach of the rule of Christ."[2] It was clear that the rule of law was God, and God saw independent women as dangerous. It was no small twist of fate that, not long after her new husband's death, Ann was publicly accused of witchcraft, and hung on the Boston Common in 1656.

But as civilization moved forward and the Enlightenment began to shine its bright and utopian gleam across the European world, women continued to demand, increasingly, their universal right and place in the world. While Mary Wollstonecraft's ideas and arguments for female emancipation and education were being spread through the publication of *A Vindication of the Rights of Woman*, the French revolution was sweeping on, offering women the tantalizing opportunity of a social freedom and independence like none before. Petitions for equal education and equal representation circulated from 1789; women marched on Versailles, formed political clubs, and sought an active and loud voice in the National Assembly. As France fought its battle between royalist and republican, prominent movements identified their leaders and took up immovable positions.

Just as with all revolutions, tyrants emerged, and in 1793, after the brutal massacre of more than a thousand political prisoners and the execution of King Louis XVI, Maximilien Robespierre became a prominent leader of the new republic. He initiated the original "Reign of Terror"—the murder of more than sixteen thousand men and women who were seen as disagreeing with the revolution and its aims. This violent and bloody attack on the very fabric of French society created one of our first purely political female martyrs—Charlotte Corday. In her, we see one of the earliest examples of the rebellious and determined political spirit that drove so many of the suffragettes to commit violent and dangerous acts for their belief in the cause.

Charlotte Corday, or Marie-Anne Charlotte de Corday d'Armont as she was born, would surely have been adopted as a suffragette. Born in 1768, the daughter of a well-to-do family in Normandy, Charlotte was educated at the Abbaye aux Dames in Caen.[3] Here, her mind was fed by philosophical works and texts on the nature of society and humanity, while around her France began its brutal and transformative revolution. Horrified by the deaths orchestrated by the Republic's new leaders and bayed for with animalistic greed by the inflammatory and aggressive writings of the journalist Jean-Paul Marat, Charlotte decided to strike a blow to the hearts of those she held responsible.

She obtained a meeting with Marat in Paris, while he was in the bath—this was where Marat took most of his meetings because he suffered from a bad skin condition.[4] Charlotte waited until they were alone and killed him with a single stab wound to the heart. Immediately arrested and taken before the Revolutionary Tribunal, Charlotte was given the opportunity to defend her grave crimes against the Republic.

She had not come unprepared. With her was a manuscript entitled *Adresse aux Français, amis des lois et de la paix*: to her "friends in law and peace."[5] Charlotte had written out her motivations for the assassination, which were a defining manifesto for peace in the Republic. But, unsurprisingly, the court was unable to see her as an independently minded revolutionary woman. The movement from the rule of men toward universal equality had swung back again, and the women of the revolution were finding their clubs and meetings were being outlawed. Charlotte was not seen as a defender of the Republic but as another example of women's interference in government—and a threat that needed to be eradicated.

Examined for three days following Marat's death, Charlotte remained stoic. There was no denying what she had done; her commitment to her act and her justification for it were now widely known. But she found no allies, and instead was sentenced to die a traitor's death underneath the guillotine's blade. Charlotte requested that her portrait be painted in the hours before her execution.[6] In it her face is turned toward the viewer, and there is little to indicate that this is an image of a woman about to die. She seems sorrowful, but for herself or for the Republic we will never know.

For much of history the deaths and lives of women like Charlotte Corday, and her many predecessors, have been written about as aberrations; they are portrayed as women who behaved like men. To give your life for a political cause has often been thought of as the domain of men, of soldiers on the battlefield. But to the suffragettes, martyrdom was not a distant dream but an ever-present end point. A sacrifice that some had decided would have to be made before the government finally agreed to their demands.

Members of the WSPU often made threats of death. A month before her attack on Lewis Harcourt's Nuneham Park home in 1912, Helen Craggs had been arrested at Llandaff Cathedral. Only twenty-three years old and "handsomely dressed," she had climbed a three-foot fence and appeared in front of the king and queen, who were arriving at the cathedral in the company of the home secretary, Reginald McKenna. Appealing to the queen in the name of "woman's suffrage," Helen had rushed forward and seized Mr. McKenna's arm, shouting, "We will die for the women suffering in Holloway."[7] What more could be asked of the women who put their bodies and lives on the line in the name of women's suffrage? Who could blame those who committed themselves, physically and mentally, to the fight for the vote for taking that belief to its logical conclusion? Those suffragettes, radicalized by both their leadership and the violence of the government's attempts to control them, were prepared to do anything, *anything*, in pursuit of their final goal.

Directing and manipulating the complex machinations of the WSPU from Paris, Christabel Pankhurst was every inch the radical revolutionary leader. She demanded absolute loyalty and inspired a religious devotion among the many women who read her words or heard stories of this great suffragette. But her hold over the actions of certain members of the organization was slipping, and she was soon to learn exactly how great a cost she had asked of those who committed themselves, body and soul, to the suffragettes' own holy war. There had to be a price for threatening violence, for adopting and using aggression as your designated political language; and it is a price rarely paid by leaders, but often paid by their soldiers.

For months, Christabel had organized a complex network of suffragette bombers and arsonists, relaying her instructions to her followers through Annie Kenney. Annie arrived in Paris each weekend, having traveled from London in disguise, to receive her instructions and update the absent leader of the success and failures of the women she had left behind. Christabel had demanded violent and aggressive actions from women who were now convinced that this was the only option open to them, the only way to win the civil war that they found themselves fighting in. Safe in Paris, she felt little of the impact of the new reality her orders created. The horrors of carrying bombs and setting fires, the danger and risk to life, the terror of arrest, and the utter violation and pain—terrible, lasting pain—caused by force-feeding were not experiences she had to contend with. What she asked of others, what women were daily convinced to do in her name, in the name of the cause, she had no actual hand in. There should be a word for those who ask more of others than they are willing to commit to themselves, especially when it includes serious risk to life. Christabel had created a highly emotional and radicalized environment within her organization, women who were ready for the ultimate sacrifice, for martyrdom; and on June 4, 1913, that is exactly what happened.

Born in Greenwich, London, to a Northumberland-bred merchant family, Emily Wilding Davison was the third child of her parents, Charles Davison and Margaret Caisley. Her father had been married before, to Sarah Seaton Chisholm, and it is from her family that the "Wilding" in Emily's name is taken.[8]

By the age of thirteen, Emily had lived in London, Hertfordshire, and France, the product of a home education, with a growing curiosity about the world. She was clearly intelligent, winning a bursary to study literature at Royal Holloway College in 1891. Here, on a tree-lined campus, among the turrets and quads of the red-brick Founder's Building, Emily discovered an enclave created solely for the education of women. But in 1893, her happiness was shattered when her father's death ended her study; with twelve children and a widow to support, there was little left over from the estate to provide Emily with the money for her twenty-pound-per-term fees.

Much to her mother's sorrow, Emily was forced to abandon her love of words for the world of work, and the reality of the precariousness of women's lives quickly became all too apparent to her. Over the next few years, working in various positions as a governess or teacher, Emily quietly saved enough money to enroll at St. Hugh's College, University of Oxford, to finish her final term and take her exams. She achieved first-class honors in literature but, as a woman, was barred from graduating and receiving her degree. How frustratingly pointless the whole exercise must have seemed, to know she was more than equal to the male students around her but would never have her intelligence legitimized simply because of her sex. How maddening, to achieve such high marks and then read, only two years later, of a baying mob of male students at Oxford's rival university, Cambridge, who hanged and burned the effigy of a woman on a bicycle as retaliation for the university offering a vote to its student body on whether women *should* be allowed to be awarded their degrees. The vote failed, 1,713 to 662.[9] Later, the remnants of the burned and battered lady cyclist effigy were stuffed through the gates of Newnham, one of Cambridge's all-female colleges. The press dismissed this violent episode as mere "horseplay."[10] For women like Emily, highly educated and intelligent, whose ability was wasted thanks solely to the curse of their sex, a change was long overdue. And that change would come with the suffragettes.

Emily joined the WSPU in 1906 and soon became a full-time salaried campaigner. Like many of the militants, she became increasingly violent following her arrests at processions and parliamentary demonstrations. She burned letter boxes, bombed, and marched with many of the women who would go on to become violent militant soldiers: Kitty, Mary Leigh, and many of the Young Hot Bloods. One of her most famous and earliest insults to the government was to hide in a cupboard on the night of the 1911 census. It was no ordinary hiding place, but the cupboard of St. Mary Undercroft in the Houses of Parliament. The heart of government occupied throughout the night by one determined suffragette. She was discovered the next morning and added to the House of Commons census, and her daring was later immortalized by a plaque placed where she had once hidden by the MP Tony Benn.

Kitty first met Emily while they were both imprisoned in Newcastle, after the window-smashing campaign of 1909. They appear to have found in each other kindred spirits, and met to plan suffragette attacks right up to the night before Emily went under the hooves of the king's horse at the Epsom Derby. Her total commitment to the cause, at the risk of her own life, was something Kitty remembered very clearly:

> Emily Davison had always expressed great faith in the dramatic death of a woman arousing public opinion sufficiently to compel the Government to pass the necessary franchise bill to stop further militancy. How that faith was rewarded we all know, and we could only mourn and honour her all the more.[11]

It was Emily's refusal to compromise, or to be content with the WSPU's approach—empty threats of violence and death—that saw her paid membership of the WSPU terminated. She was too uncontrollable, too radical, too inclined to seek violence without official sanction.

But even being abandoned by Christabel did nothing to change her commitment to the suffragette cause. Having experienced the horrors of force-feeding, Emily decided it was a punishment no other woman should be forced to endure. Imprisoned and force-fed on a six-month sentence for carrying out arson attacks on mailboxes on Fleet Street, she threw herself from a balcony of the prison. The events of that night were published in Emily's own words by the *Daily Herald* on July 4, 1912:

At ten o'clock on the Saturday night a regular siege took place in Holloway. On all sides one heard crowbars, blocks and wedges being used; men battering on doors with all their might. The barricading was always followed by the sounds of human struggle, the chair of torture being pushed about, suppressed cries of the victim, groans; other horrible sounds. My turn came, and my door was forced open with crowbars. I protested loudly that I would not be fed by the junior doctor, and tried to dart out into the passage. Then I was seized by about five wardresses, bound into the chair, still protesting; and they accomplished their purpose. In my mind was the thought that some desperate protest must be made to put a stop to the hideous torture. As soon as I could get out I climbed onto the railing and threw myself out on to the wire netting, a distance of between 20 ft and 30 ft. The idea in my mind was that one big tragedy might save many others; but the netting prevented any severe injury. When a good moment came, quite deliberately I walked upstairs, and threw myself from the top on to the iron staircase. If I had been successful I should have undoubtedly been killed.[12]

As Emily attempted suicide, the suffragettes around her cried out "No surrender" and other suffrage mantras. On sending a copy of her statement to *The Suffragette*, to show just how far the prisoners were being pushed, Emily found her sacrifice was unwanted—Christabel refused to print it, unlike the *Daily Herald*. Was it a step too far, even for her? Sylvia Pankhurst remembered that there had been "a general desire at Lincoln's Inn House to discourage her [Emily] in such tendencies . . . she was condemned and ostracised as a self willed person who persisted in acting upon her own initiative without waiting for official instructions."[13]

Was that the problem—not the violence itself, but the fact it was not done under orders? Christabel's need to control and dominate the actions of her soldiers, even from another country, was clear. She was prepared to ask them to risk their lives on a daily basis, but only with her instruction. The arrogance of a leader who risks little and yet demands total obedience. But the moment when a leader cannot protect her soldiers is often the moment when lieutenants step forward and take control. In the months after her suicide attempt, hearing of the suffering of Mary Leigh and others during force-feeding attempts, Emily lost no time in reminding both the British public and the leaders of the suffragettes just what great a cost they were asking women to pay when they underwent this government-sanctioned torture. Writing to the *Pall Mall Gazette* in September 1912, she made her feelings abundantly clear:

> I speak as one who does know, as I have faced death several times in this cause, and faced it quite recently in the way that they are doing now. When I attempted to commit suicide in Holloway Prison on June 22 I did it deliberately and with all my power, because I felt that by nothing but the sacrifice of human life would the nation be brought to realise the horrible torture our women face! If I had succeeded I am sure that forcible feeding could not in all conscience have been resorted to again.[14]

Although abandoned by the leadership, Emily remained close to the other violent and dangerous suffragettes. Now in her mid-thirties, she had lost none of her commitment or dedication to the cause; in fact, in June 1913, she chose to make her most aggressive attacks on those who opposed women's rights and saw fit to torture those who would fight for them. There has always been a great deal of circumspection and argument around Emily's choice to go to the Epsom Derby, and whether she meant to die on that day. But piecing together her last hours from those who knew her best reveals secrets that have never been acknowledged before.

On the night before the derby, Emily, Mary Leigh, Kitty Marion, and friends had visited the Empress Rooms in Kensington, where a WSPU bazaar was being held to inform the British public about female enfranchisement and earn money for the suffrage cause. There, under-neath a plaster statue of Joan of Arc, Emily had laid a wreath and read aloud the words "Fight on, and God will give the Victory."[15] The martyr-dom of Joan of Arc, a noble female warrior brought down by the inad-equacies of men, had long been part of the militant identity. Christabel Pankhurst had called her "the patron saint of suffragettes," and it is not difficult to understand why her language of sacrifice and dedication appealed so strongly to Emily in this moment.[16]

Three versions of that final night exist: accounts by Kitty Marion, Sylvia Pankhurst, and Mary Richardson. Only Kitty claims to have been present, and it is her account that sheds an utterly unique light on Emily Wilding Davison, one that has never before been heard. Although all three women agree that Emily broached the prospect of making a protest at the derby, both Sylvia and Kitty claim that no final conclusion was reached during the evening. Mary claims, having been told secondhand by Alice Green (one of Emily's closest confidantes), that in fact Emily had made it very clear to her companions that she was willing to die in the protest. Although we can never be sure of the entirety of that conversation, as the evening was drawing to a close Kitty and Emily said their last goodbyes, and it is in this moment that Emily's central role in the most extreme, and the most aggressive, acts of suffragette violence becomes clear: "Before we parted that night, Emily gave me a tiny green chamois purse containing a sovereign for 'munitions I might need soon.'"[17]

This tiny single sentence tears apart the carefully constructed image Christabel enforced after Emily's death. Here was not a hysterical, emotional, or irrational woman who made desperate choices in dark moments, but a committed, careful, clear-sighted suffragette soldier, providing means and ammunition to those around her. The real Emily Wilding Davison is almost more mysterious than her martyred memory: Sylvia Pankhurst names her as responsible for the Lloyd George bomb; Kitty outs her as a clear link in the chain providing money and instruc-tion for further attacks. So why is it that we know so little about her real life and death—has her memory suffered, as do the memories of so many martyrs, from being used to fulfill a purpose rather than an honest truth?

The clearest account of Emily's death comes not from the official sources, but the memoir of the only other suffragette who was there. Mary Richardson, controversial, confident, and as committed as any other soldier at the heart of the WSPU, had been sent to the derby by Christabel Pankhurst to sell copies of *The Suffragette*.[18] She recalled, in vivid detail, the final moments of Emily's suffragette militancy:

> Just as the first race began I summoned up all my courage and took out a copy of *The Suffragette* from my bag and waved it in the air. It was not until the end of the third race that I saw Emily Davison. We had met several times and from the talks we had had I had formed the opinion that she was a very serious-minded person. That was why I was so surprised to see her. She was not the sort of woman to spend an afternoon at the races. I smiled at her, and from a distance she seemed to be smiling faintly back at me. She stood alone there, close to the white painted rails where the course bends round at Tattenham Corner; she looked absorbed and yet far away from everybody else and seemed to have no interest in what was going on around her. I had a sudden premonition about her and found my heart was beating excitedly, I shall always remember how beautifully calm her face was. But at that very moment—as I was told afterwards by her closest friend—she knew she was about to die her life for the cause. . . . I was unable to keep my eyes off her as I stood holding *The Suffragette* up in my clenched hand . . . And suddenly she slipped under the rail and ran out into the middle of the race course. It was all over so quickly. Emily was under the hooves of one of the horses and seemed to be hurled for some distance across the grass. The horse stumbled sideways and its jockey thrown from its back. She lay very still.[19]

Chased by an angry mob back to Epsom Downs Station, Mary was hidden by a porter until the arrival of a fast train back to Waterloo.

Although Christabel Pankhurst did not make use of Mary's account at the time, there is evidence to corroborate her story. The *Morning Post* carried a report of a suffragette newspaper seller who was seen outside Epsom Downs Station at 5:00 p.m., the same time as a "Pullman-Limited" nonstop train was due to leave for Victoria Station.[20] Could this have been Mary Richardson? It would certainly support her story of hiding in the station before catching the fast train back to London.[21] Doubt appears to stem from a tenuous argument that because her recollection of the event did not appear in *The Suffragette*, it simply could not have happened. But Mary makes it very clear that when her report was asked for by headquarters she was unable to add anything to the official account. When a WSPU messenger from Christabel, a stranger, arrived at her flat, Mary was in tears, only just off the train and still unable to fully absorb what she had witnessed: "'I have to get back,' she said. 'Is there anything to report to Christabel?' 'No,' I said. 'I just saw her dash out and fall. There was nothing more.'"[22]

There are many reasons why Christabel would choose to omit Mary from the reports of the time. Far away across the Channel in her Parisian hideaway, Christabel knew Emily Davison's death placed the WSPU on a knife-edge. The threat of martyrdom had been an important pressure for her suffragettes to keep exerting on the government; it was the fear of a woman dying on hunger strike that drove the absurd Cat and Mouse Act into existence and allowed so many suffragettes to abscond from prison while they were out on license, "recovering." But now that threat had been realized in a violent and aggressive act.

Emily Wilding Davison was not a weak woman whose slow death could be played out for weeks to garner sympathy and public disgust at the government's treatment of the imprisoned WSPU; she had committed a deadly and graphic attack on the monarchy, or at least on the monarchy's horse, at a moment of public celebration. For Christabel, these were the worst possible circumstances for a suffragette martyrdom, and the least likely to find support or sympathy from the British public. Little could be gained from drawing attention to the presence of another suffragette at the derby; it would only have added to the idea that this inexplicable act might have been preplanned—or worse, fully supported—by the leadership of the WSPU. Publicly, at least, they still clung to the claim that, even with the bombs, arson attacks, physical attacks on ministers, and threats of death or violence, the WSPU did not intend to go as far as murder. For a suffragette to be seen to willingly attempt to take a life, either her own or someone else's, ran contrary to the leadership's supposed directive. The next few days would need to be handled with extreme precision. At the moment of her death, Emily had moved from being her own independent agent to being an idea, an image, even a myth to be manipulated by all those around her. There was no need for a suffragette witness to the event when it was being played out, frame by frame, on one of Pathé's latest newsreels in cinemas across the country, and the world.

Kitty read of Emily's protest in the evening papers, and of the terrible cost it had exacted from her. For the next four days, Emily remained unconscious, slowly succumbing to her terrible injuries. Kitty immortalized this in her autobiography with a defiant "Deeds, Not Words!" and quoted Emily's own justification for such actions: "The glorious and inscrutable Spirit of Liberty has but one further penalty within its poor, the surrender of Life itself. It is the supreme consummation of sacrifice, than which none can be higher or greater. To lay down life for friends, that is glorious, selfless, inspiring!"[23]

In honor of Emily's "daring deed," Kitty and Clara "Betty" Giveen (another probable member of the Young Hot Bloods) decided to make "good use of the 'munitions' Emily had paid for."[24] Clara was ten years younger than Kitty, a "beautiful blonde" of "good family and independent means."[25] It is not unusual to find the pairing of a woman in her mid-thirties with a younger, early-twenties woman among the militant suffragettes who caused such damage at this time. The bonds between these women, working in pairs, became unbreakable. It would be Kitty's fifth fire for the suffragettes, and in retaliation for the injuries done to Emily at Epsom, they chose the grandstand at Hurst Park racecourse near Hampton Court Palace. An edict from Christabel had recently been issued to "do all the damage possible without being caught," but for Kitty, this protest would prove to be an unlucky one.[26]

In the days before Emily's death, Kitty and Clara scouted the racecourse for a place that would provide them with easy access late at night. They found no entrance apart from over a tall fence with a spiked top that neither of them could reach, above which were a further two rows of barbed wire. Kitty was staying with her indefatigably stalwart theatrical landlady, Ma Mac, who had clearly adopted this wayward and irrepressible woman as a surrogate daughter. Returning from her scouting mission with Clara, Kitty put their problem before Ma Mac, who suggested that they use a piece of carpet, of which she had a ready supply in the shed, to help them climb over both the spikes and the barbed wire. Kitty selected a piece and, rolling it up, strapped it into a neat and tidy shape. Preparing for the attack, she packed a wicker suitcase with a gallon of oil and firelighters, and waited for Clara to call. Unbeknownst to Kitty and Clara, as they boarded the evening train sometime after 9:00 p.m., Emily succumbed to her injuries and died. Their protest was no longer in unity with their fallen comrade, but in her memory.

Kitty and Clara walked toward the racecourse, cutting across an adjoining cricket ground. Using a tool shed that backed onto the course to aid their scramble over the fence, they threw the carpet over the barbed wire and managed to climb over. How difficult it must have been to conquer what the press later called an "unclimbable fence" in the long skirts, corsets, and large unwieldy hats that Edwardian women were forced to wear. Landing on long grass, wet with late spring dew that soaked their skirts and made them even heavier, Kitty and Clara carried their munitions toward the grandstand. It was nearing midnight when they finally found an open door leading into the pavilion, their footsteps echoing around the empty wooden building that, on race days, was filled with excitement and trepidation. Spreading their flammable materials around the pavilion, they soaked everything they could in the oil Kitty had brought with her, leaving suffragette literature to identify who was responsible for the attack. At its center they planned to leave a candle burning, the method employed in many of the suffragette arson attacks; the candle melted slowly, allowing the suffragette arsonist plenty of time to get away from the site of the fire. This not only reduced the risk to their lives, but also provided them with the time to find a strong alibi.

The candle Kitty and Clara had with them was supposed to give them an hour before the flame reached the oil-soaked base the candle was placed on and the fire started. But as they lit it, something went horribly wrong. The fire suddenly spread around them and, although they rushed for the exit, the choking smoke and flames would have made it impossible to see. Hampered by their heavy skirts, the hems of which would likely have now also soaked up the oil while they spread it around the pavilion, Kitty and Clara desperately searched for a way out. Breaking through the flames, singed but somehow alive, they raced back to the fence. The flames were already burning brightly against the gloom surrounding them, and as they struggled back over the fence, the sound of an alarm being raised drifted toward them. There wasn't much time to catch their breath; bruised and battered, but triumphant, they laughed as they picked themselves up and began the walk toward Kew, where a safe house had been arranged for them to hide in.

On the bridge near Hampton Court Palace, the fire brigade and police on motorbikes dashed past them. Their laughter at escaping this near-death experience must have faded as they realized just how much danger they were still in; it was a three-hour walk back to the safe house in Kew and somehow they had to avoid being seen by any policemen—policemen who might easily put two and two together at the sight of two lone women out in the early hours of the morning, whose clothes would have smelled of smoke and whose faces might have been marked with dust and grime. Reaching their destination at last, Kitty and Clara realized their attempt at escape had been in vain.

There was already a policeman watching the house. As soon as the police had identified suffragette literature at the scene, the motorbike-mounted constables had spread out in every direction to watch the houses that were known to shelter suffragettes. Weary and in need of rest, they felt they had no choice but to at least get a few hours' sleep in a comfortable bed.

Letting themselves in, Kitty and Clara must have felt the adrenaline leak out through the soles of their shoes. The high emotion of an arson attack, especially one that carried with it such meaning as a beacon for Emily Wilding Davison, then their own near-death experience and long walk back to supposed safety, had ended in disappointment. They were trapped. Kitty was well aware of what this meant. She would be arrested, found guilty, and forced to hunger strike and suffer the tortures that went with it, all in the name of the glorious cause. Those quiet hours as dawn broke were surely some of the most unbearable.

At eleven thirty in the morning, which had at least allowed for the women to have a decent breakfast, the doorbell rang. It was Detective Inspectors Pride and Pike, tasked with the specific investigation, prosecution, and retrieval of suffragettes. Reading the arrest warrant to Kitty and Clara in an upstairs bedroom, they charged the women with being "suspected persons found loitering in certain streets with intent to commit a felony." There was nothing to tie them to the attack at Hurst Park yet, but once under arrest their lodgings would be searched and their landladies questioned. Once bailed from Richmond Police Court, Kitty and Clara returned to the WSPU bazaar in Kensington, and perhaps it was here that they first heard of Emily's death. How did they feel, standing under that same statue of Joan of Arc, looking up at the martyr who had so inspired their close friend and ally to sacrifice her own life for their glorious cause?

The detectives found cans of kerosene, suffrage literature recording the previous fires, letters, notebooks, and petty cash accounts, all of which revealed that Clara and Kitty had planned and executed the Hurst Park attack. The original charge was dropped, and they were rearrested for "wilfully and maliciously setting fire to the Hurst Park Grand Stand," with a trial set for July 3 at the Surrey Assizes in Guildford. Kitty found herself with just enough time to attend the funeral procession for Emily. Her memories of that moment evoke a scene of heartfelt mourning, an outpouring of shock and surprise among those who had had no idea of the true risks the militants were willing to take. For those who had known Emily, who knew her resolution to risk death to save others from suffering, the pain must have been extreme. For Kitty, Emily had now achieved an almost religiously reverential position:

> The earthly remains of the Supreme Sacrifice were brought from Epsom to Victoria Station, where over 3000 women, representing all sections of the Suffrage movement awaited her, and paid their tribute to the memory of Emily Wilding Davison by escorting her through the streets of London lined by enormous, silent, sympathetic crowds, to St. George's Church, Bloomsbury where the memorial service was held, on to King's Cross Station from whence, with a guard of honour of militant comrades, the train carried her home to Morpeth near Newcastle.

Emily's funeral was a pantomime of epic proportions, orchestrated down to the smallest detail by Christabel Pankhurst, far away in France. Emmeline Pankhurst, dressed in full mourning, was arrested attempting to make her way to the church. Earlier, riding high on the passionate hysteria of her followers, she had issued a statement that included a pledge "to carry on our Holy War for the emancipation of our sex."[27] Just imagine the scene this would have created. The figurehead of the WSPU, the most notorious and dangerous organization operating in the United Kingdom at this time, terribly weakened from her most recent force-feeding and dressed head to toe in black to mourn one of her fallen soldiers, struggles from her sickbed only to be seized by the police and carted off back to prison. A year later, writing in *My Own Story*, Emmeline recalled, "The death of Miss Davison was a great shock to me and a very great grief as well, and although I was scarcely able to leave my bed I determined to risk everything to attend her funeral."[28]

Emmeline's arrest was a perfectly composed PR event, designed to inflame emotions on all sides of the debate. It had an instant effect. In the aftermath of Emily's funeral, the "whole country was seething with suffragette outrages," while Kitty and Clara awaited trial for their own actions.[29] Never one to miss an opportunity to maximize an emotional response to her campaign, Christabel suddenly rediscovered her copy of Emily's suicidal statement from 1912, the one she had refused to publish, and printed it in *The Suffragette* in full. Now, not only had she managed to distance herself and the leadership from Emily's actions, but she had proof that these actions were the choices of someone who had vocally proclaimed her own personal commitment to a suicidal attack on the government. Christabel managed to spin Emily's death not only to recommit and inflame her own supporters, but also to distance the movement from any direct responsibility for it. At the same time, she made the most of the impact it had on the general public. The procession that escorted Emily's body to St. George's Church was captured in detail by the *Illustrated Police News*:

> There were about 100 men, including Mr. E G Clayton, the chemist, who is on trial at the Old Bailey, and Ben Tillett. The rest were women, and among them Mrs. Sanders, Miss Kerr, Miss Barrett, Miss Lake, and Miss Lennox, who are also on trial. Miss Annie Kenney was not there. Thanks to the large escort of police, there was no interference on the part of the crowd. The Women's Social and Political Union ignored the suggestion of the police that the procession should be limited in numbers and should go by the side streets. It formed a striking spectacle, for it was marshalled in sections, each woman wore clothes of a particular hue, and carried flowers of a similar colour. It marched in ranks of four. It was led by a woman dressed in white who carried a gilt cross. Behind her were young girls in white, some carrying laurel wreaths and others a purple banner, with the device, "Fight on, and

God will give the victory." Then came some hundreds of London members of the WSPU, all in black and carrying purple irises. After these
were others in purple, each carrying a red peony. Next came women in
white, bearing white Madonna lilies. A small band of "hunger strikers"
followed, wearing medals, some with bars, and next marched a dozen
clergy in robes, including an archdeacon, with a banner borne behind
them with the words, "Greater love hath no man than this, that he lay
down his life for his friends."[30]

"Fight on, and God will give the Victory": the same motto as adorned
the statue of Joan of Arc, which Emily had visited the night before her
death. Christabel missed no opportunity to connect the death of one of
her fallen soldiers to the grander identity of a woman of mythological
status. It might feel less of a bitter pill if we didn't know how Christabel and the rest of the leadership had, before Emily's death, sought
to distance and ostracize her. Writing the official account of her life
in 1913—another way to capitalize on Emily's martyrdom—Gertrude
Colmore glossed over this, saying, "employment by the Union was not
compatible with the position of free lance which she had adopted."[31]
Sylvia Pankhurst was less inclined to ignore the hypocritical arrogance
with which those who had earlier hoped Emily would simply fade away
now made her into the sainted symbol of resistance. In her death, Sylvia
pointedly remembered, "All such criticism was now forever silenced;
she had risen to the supreme test of her faith. There remained only the
memory of her brave gallantry and gay comradeship, her tall, slight,
awkward figure and the green, elusive eyes in the small, jauntily poised
head."[32]

Within a month, Kitty found herself on trial. The occasion received
multiple column inches in the press, all of which Kitty cut and pasted
into her scrapbook. The crowd outside the courthouse grew each day,
as eager pro- and anti-suffragettes picked over every piece of evidence
displayed by the court. A favorite was a postcard found near the fire,
addressed to "The Sportsmanlike (?) Government" and continuing,

"The human race is more important than any other. Why handicap womanly disenfranchisement? Remove the handicap at once and give us the Vote." Another read, "I always go on till I am stopped, and I am never stopped."[33] It was a favorite motto of Kitty's, a calling card she left at several fires and a copy of which she also pasted into her own personal militant collection.

The trial was almost farcical, the evidence against Kitty and Clara was so overwhelming. When they were sentenced to three years' penal servitude, the court erupted, other suffragettes shouted "No surrender," and a chorus of the "Women's Marseillaise" rang out as the two defendants were dragged away.

Arriving at Holloway, Kitty immediately went on hunger strike. Determined to escape under the Cat and Mouse Act as soon as possible, she refused both food and drink, and after five days was released back into the care of the suffragette nurses. In the few days she had been inside, a number of attacks had been carried out, "which cheered me considerably. I gloried in others' keeping up the good work."[34] After four days of rest, Kitty felt well enough to return to attacking the government. "And so with printed, appropriate quotations pasted to a sheet of paper, wrapped round a small brick, a label tied to it, addressed to 'the Government' on one side, 'it's never too late to mend. Repeal the Cat and Mouse Act and give votes to women' on the other, I sallied forth after lunch on July 12th and made my protest through a window at the Home Office. Of course I was arrested, taken to Bow Street."[35] She lasted another four days on hunger strike before she was released again. Of her three-year prison sentence Kitty had managed to serve eight days, over a two-week period.

But the WSPU was not prepared to let one of its most valuable soldiers linger, being starved and tortured, while there was important work to be done. Taken in disguise from the suffragette nursing home, Kitty found herself reunited with Clara, also released after hunger striking, at a private home in the Surrey Hills. For the next two weeks, Kitty rested and prepared for travel. No longer was she a militant operating solely in

London; her methods, knowledge, and experience were needed across the country. In August, she had a stay with friends in Bristol, which resulted in the destruction of a mansion near Lynton. Then, leaving the south of England behind her, Kitty traveled up the country.

On September 23, she helped "communicate with the Government" by burning down Liverpool's Seafield House.[36] The huge property was being converted into a home for "imbeciles and harmless lunatics" and was guarded by a single caretaker, Mr. Thomas Wood Smith.[37] Woken by the sound of breaking glass, Wood had found the building ablaze and summoned the fire brigade, but little could be done to save what was left. Found in the grounds was the customary suffragette literature and a postcard bearing the words "Mene Mene Tekel Upharsin," words taken from the Old Testament with the meaning of "you have been weighed and found wanting."[38]

As Mary Richardson was carrying out her "Black Jenny" bomb attack on a Birmingham railway station, Kitty was planning her next two attacks, which resulted in one success and one failure. It was in Manchester on November 11 that we would have found her sneaking through the twilight, disguising her red hair under a mill-girl's shawl. Her target was the cactus house in Alexandra Park, and it would be reduced to rubble in the early hours of the morning by "a stout brass tube, about three inches in diameter, and strengthened at one end by a stout brass cap, which was screwed on to it." The bomb was a suitably unpleasant one, containing "a miscellaneous collection of pieces of metal, including such articles as a bed key, an iron chain, bolts, nuts and nails. . . ."[39]

On November 13, having returned to Liverpool, Kitty left another bomb in the porch of the Sefton Park palm house. Just as with Manchester, the glasshouse contained "a magnificent display of flowers and ferns."[40] The bomb had been made from an earthenware warming-pan, ten inches in length, and with a lit fuse that the wind had thankfully put an end to. The police recorded it as "formidable." Kitty remembered this as "a most interesting, busy time."[41]

After such an exciting few months, including an attempted attack on the grandstand at Aintree racecourse, Kitty unsurprisingly spent the Christmas of 1913 resting on the east coast, hidden by friends who she could trust not to willingly give up a well-known and hunted suffragette militant.

As the new year rolled in, she returned to London. It would be her undoing. Had she grown cocky, used as she was to the freedom and fast pace of her life on the run? Met at Charing Cross Station by a WSPU agent sent from headquarters, Kitty was just about to receive her latest orders when, as they waited for the call to come through at one of the phone booths, a well-known voice suddenly hailed her. Did she freeze, did the sound of that voice, the voice of the man she knew as her very own "shadow," make her blood run cold? Looking up, she found herself face-to-face with one of the many detectives who had been assigned to watch her. He had been lying in wait to catch the various women who used the platforms as a waypoint to transfer orders, luggage, and messages between the militants and their leadership. There was little point in protesting he had the wrong person; after so many years of violence and protest, the suffragettes and their policemen knew each other well. The months on the run had renewed Kitty's fighting spirit and she had little intention of walking back into the waiting arms of the doctors and the force-feeding tubes of Holloway Prison. Refusing to move and forcing him to call for backup, Kitty was half pulled, half dragged out of the station concourse, shouting "Votes for women!" at the top of her lungs. A taxicab was waiting for her and, as the policemen attempted to lift her in feet first, Kitty took aim at the opposite window, smashing her left foot through it with as much force as possible. The glass exploded, and in retaliation eight police officers were used to restrain her on the drive back to prison. The cabs were small, and it would have left very little room for any of them even to breathe.

Once back at Holloway, Kitty immediately went on hunger strike, but this time it would not result in her release. An old foe, Dr. Ahern, had been transferred to the prison from Birmingham, and his methods, and the callous disregard for the women he was using them against, saw Kitty force-fed 232 times in the four months she was held in Holloway. Recognizing the man who had instigated her force-feedings in previous years, Kitty reacted as anyone would if faced with torture:

> I became possessed of a most furious rage, like wanting to kill someone, so I got up, dressed and smashed every pane of glass in the window and everything else breakable in the cell, the glass over the gas, the wash basin and the jug containing hot water, which ran all over the floor. I found blessed relief to my feelings in screaming, exercising my lungs and throat after the frightful sensation of being held in a vice, chocking and suffocating. I had to scream or go mad.[42]

Writing "No Surrender" on the walls of her cell in soap must have felt like a small rebellion in the monotony of twice-daily, or even three-times-daily, force-feedings:

> No words can describe it. Resisting the gag was almost useless, since I had a back tooth missing, by the gap of which they could easily force my mouth open, but I resisted the tube with my throat, until my mouth was full of coiled tube and when swallowing, which happened involuntarily sooner or later, seemed to go down in lumps, uncoiling as it went. Sometimes when using the nasal tube it would come out of the mouth instead of going down, when they would quickly insert the gag and use the throat tube, which was thicker that the nasal. When, in my agony I managed to wrench a hand free from a wardress, I would snatch the tube out, which meant reprimand for her and repeated torture for me. Sometimes the doctor would even wait for me to regain my breath in my struggle to resist the tube, before continuing. I was always sick during and after feeding, so much so at times that the bed clothes as well as my dress had to be changed. The food was mostly milk and eggs, beef tea, sometimes cocoa and sometimes something of a peculiar salty taste which I later learned was bromide, though the

authorities denied it, since there was a great outcry against giving us sedative drugs. Vomiting would continue in small quantities for three hours, eventually tasting bitter. . . . I often felt distracted beyond endurance, like going stark, staring mad. At times when my chest and throat ached and I felt like bursting with the amount of food in me, I would throw myself about violently after feeding. Then they would hold me so that I should not hurt myself. Sometimes I seemed to have convulsions, and shake, shudder and tremble dreadfully. For several days at the beginning I felt a numbness all down my left side, as if it were contracting and smaller than my right, but it passed off. I often begged the doctor to put poison down the tube and finish me off.[43]

In the middle of March, Kitty learned Mary Richardson was in Holloway after her attack on the *Rokeby Venus* in the National Gallery. She had slashed the painting with a hatchet and been sentenced to six months. For the duration of their mutual imprisonment Kitty and Mary shouted "Votes for women" and "No surrender" out of their cell windows, under their doors, as they were being dragged along the corridor—anything to let the other know they were not alone, that the torture was shared. It provided Kitty with three weeks of companionship until Mary was released thanks to a complication with her appendix, and Kitty was left to endure the rest of her sentence alone. Finally, after four months of horrific torture at the hands of Dr. Ahern, Kitty was deemed so close to the point of death that she had to be released. She had lost thirty-six pounds and looked like a woman of seventy rather than forty-three.

Her first morning out of prison, under the care of a Nurse Pine at the rest home and reunited with Mary, Kitty opened her eyes to a sea of flowers and letters of support and commiseration. A flowering azalea from Mrs. Pankhurst, "with deep appreciation for your self-sacrificing work for the movement." A letter from Christabel in Paris: "My love and thanks to you for your magnificent fight and heroic endurance. You have had a great triumph and we are all proud of you, more proud than words can say. Think of getting well. There is so much rejoicing that you are free and out of the clutches of those terribly cruel enemies of our cause."[44] Annie Kenney, Constance Lytton, Constance Bryer, and Olive Walton had all sent thanks and declarations of love for her to read on her release from prison, welcoming a comrade-in-arms back to freedom. Among these letters, now held in the Museum of London, one in particular stands out:

Dear Old Kitty,

I see you are at least free, it is good news indeed. What a glorious fight you have made, and you've beaten them all by your indomitable courage and strength of mind ... I have been fairly busy while you have been in, I'll tell you all some day, as we shall probably meet again. ... I hope you'll get this letter, here's the best of luck to you and all good wishes for your speedy recovery.

Yours ever in the fight,
Hilda Burkitt

A battle-hardened solider in the suffragette fight, at thirty-one Hilda was well known in the militant movement. She had been held with Mary Leigh in Winson Green Prison in 1909 and was an early hunger striker.[45] In 1913, she had been held with Clara Giveen in Armley Jail, and by 1914 was suspected by the police of at least ten attacks that had occurred that year, from Bath to Birmingham. As Kitty was recovering, Hilda, alongside another suffragette, the twenty-six-year-old Florence Tunks, set fire to the Bath Hotel in Felixstowe. When she was arrested and her lodgings searched, a coded diary was found detailing her various attacks and misadventures.[46] The warmth of Hilda's letter to Kitty, and the hints held within it, show that a network of suffragette arsonists and bombers existed across the country and relied on the secrecy of sisterhood to keep its members safe. While Kitty was being held in Holloway, and during her recuperation, almost fifty attacks had been carried out, including an attempt to bomb Glasgow's Botanical Gardens in January; an arson attack on the Carnegie Library in Birmingham; gunshots were fired—albeit blanks—at the police attempting to arrest Emmeline Pankhurst at a rally in March; timber yards, chemical works, and churches, even Westminster Abbey, had all been damaged by bombs. And in July, the discovery of bombs at Robert Burns Cottage in Ayr and the fifteenth-century Rosslyn Chapel continued to threaten the cultural and social fabric of society.

A month after her release, and although Kitty was still terribly ill, it was decided she should be sent to Paris to show Christabel the results of force-feeding the suffragette prisoners. Escorted by Mary Leigh and Alice Green, as well as other high-ranking members of the WSPU, Kitty was secretly taken from Victoria Station to Paris on May 31. For such a momentous occasion she records little of it in her diary, virtually nothing other than the fact that she went. She returned within twenty-four hours and her meeting with the great revolutionary leader seems to have been less than impressive; for a woman so capable of recalling the important moments of her life, Kitty has nothing to say. Christabel had little interest in the damage her methods had wrecked on the bodies of her soldiers, unless of course they could be used to further the propaganda and press of the suffrage cause.

By July, Kitty was well enough to be sent by headquarters to Leicester, where she was to instruct the local branch of the WSPU in carrying out arson and bomb attacks. Alice Hawkins had written requesting advice as her members had so far managed only unsuccessful attacks, and Kitty was dispatched, as she was now considered to be one of the most prolific and dangerous members of the organization.[47] The result was the successful and almost total destruction of Blaby railway station. It was here, while on "danger duty," that Kitty received a telegram from headquarters ordering her to stop all activity. It was the first Sunday in August, 1914, and a new war had begun.

Looking at her actions, it seems now as though the scales were slowly falling from Kitty's eyes. "Though it had its humours, I hated the whole wretched business; we all did, and would much rather have had the vote than do this sort of thing to get it, but we did our 'duty' as we saw it, much like soldiers on the principle of, 'Theirs is not to reason why.'"[48]

During the WSPU's "Holy War," more than thirteen hundred people had been arrested and imprisoned for suffragette violence across the United Kingdom. But with the outbreak of a *world* war, the government offered amnesty to those who had broken the law in the name of women's suffrage—more than twelve hundred women and just over a hundred men, who were held in prisons, had fought, died, or, of course, were currently in hiding from the Cat and Mouse Act. Their names and arrest records have now been compiled in a book held in the National Archives, the "Suffragettes Index Names of Persons Arrested 1906–1914," which memorializes the actions of so many people who have been forgotten by us today.[49] There we see Kitty's ten entries, from Bow Street to Newcastle, 1909–1913; eleven for Emily Wilding Davison; nine apiece for Mary Leigh and Mary Richardson; six for Sylvia Pankhurst, and seven for Emmeline. For Christabel, of course, there are only two. But even an amnesty could not protect Kitty from what was coming next, as the home and sisterhood she had relied on for her security, her family, and her friends were now about to be brutally torn apart.

8

Betrayal Takes Many Forms

Betrayal is a consequence of war. For a long time Kitty had survived by her wits, and on the love and compassion of the women and friends she had made since her arrival in England more than twenty-eight years earlier. But now, as the suffragette war ended, a new one was beginning. On July 28, 1914, Archduke Franz Ferdinand, heir to the Austrian throne, and his wife, Sophie von Chotkova, had been assassinated in Sarajevo. His death was orchestrated by a secret Serbian military society, the Black Hand (also known as Unification or Death), who used a group of radicalized students and schoolteachers to carry out their plan. Much as the Young Hot Bloods were chosen to carry out some of the WSPU's most dangerous activities, the gang had been armed with pistols and bombs—live rounds, not the blanks favored by the suffragettes—and, after a failed bomb attempt on the archduke's motorcade, shot the duchess and the archduke as they left the Sarajevo town hall, fatally wounding them both. The political ripples from these brutal murders spread out across the continent of Europe, engulfing all its countries in what became devastating war within a single month. Britain joined on August 4, declaring war on Germany after it invaded Belgium.

* * *

Out in the English countryside, staying with friends in the small market town of Arnold, Nottinghamshire, and unsure of what to do now that there was no "danger duty" for her—and still uncertain of her status as a prisoner who had absconded from jail—Kitty felt little of the impact of events on the Continent. Apart from reports in the papers, there was little to touch her "perfect peace and harmony"—until the following year.[1] Visiting London in February 1915, bundled up against the cold and determined to test the government's claim that no suffragette prisoner at large would be rearrested, Kitty lost little time in visiting old friends. But a shock was waiting for her—the police had been making inquiries. Several of her old friends and suffrage companions had been visited and questioned on her whereabouts, "and did they know that I was a German Spy? 'Absurd,' they replied, and had not the slightest idea where I was."[2] What had happened to provoke such an odd line of questioning against one of England's most notorious suffragettes? Kitty had been a resident in Great Britain for almost thirty years, two thirds of her life. Her childhood in Germany was a distant memory, and she had had no contact with her family in decades. Was the government seizing any opportunity, and using the outbreak of war with the Germans, to finally rid itself of such a dangerous and militant woman?

Kitty went to call on an old neighbor of Ma Mac's, her much-beloved theatrical landlady who had recently died. If anyone would know what the police wanted, it would be her. Madame Louise Roger had been Ma Mac's closest friend; an immigrant like Kitty, she had adored her since they had first met. "Oh, my Katie, my Katie, be careful, the police are looking for you," she had exclaimed anxiously, "in her excited broken English," when Kitty appeared on her doorstep.[3] Calming Madame Louise's nerves and settling herself in by the fire, Kitty slowly drew out a complicated and confusing story.

Mr. Roger, Madame Louise's husband, was an Englishman to whom she had been married for more than fifty years. Recently, Madame

Louise had begun to suspect that he was "keeping" a woman some-where, a love affair that she was determined to put an end to. So she had hired a private detective to follow Mr. Roger, who had led the man to a house in Kensington Park Road. There, attempting to draw out further information on Mr. Roger's secretive affairs, the detective had fallen into conversation with the landlady's daughter, a middle-aged woman who used to be on the stage. After several discussions, she had revealed that she had previously been a member of the *Lady Slavery* company, the same one that had been Kitty's home for a number of years, and the detective, eager to form a connection to his new source, had enthused about his client's love and friendship with Kitty Marion, the well-known actress and music hall star. This had brought both a successful and disappointing result.

The woman revealed she had known Kitty well, "that she had been on the stage with me in the 'Lady Slavery' Company, that she had always thought me a 'nice girl' and liked me until I joined the Suffragettes, and that I was German."[4] These four pieces of informa-tion, of no use to Madame Louise, had somehow been fed back to the police—perhaps by the private detective hoping to make some cash on the side—and shortly after that, they had turned up on Madame Louise's doorstep, asking searching questions about the German suffragette. Determined to put them off, she had repeatedly insisted that Kitty was not German but English, and had spent every moment since hovering behind her curtains, waiting for something awful to occur. Kitty accepted this story without question, but contained within her Home Office file—which the government compiled for each of the dangerous militant suffragettes—is a vastly different story.

On February 2, 1915, the home secretary, Reginald McKenna, had received an unexpected letter from the London Variety Theatre's man-ager, Charles Thorburn. Sent on the headed notepaper of theatrical agent Hartley Milburn, Thorburn's letter was brusque:

Sir,

The enclosed cutting from a letter rec.d [received] from my sister, Mrs. E R Browne, Tryall Estate, Sandy Bay, Jamaica, may be of value to peruse.

Yours faithfully,
Charles Thorburn[5]

Mrs. E. R. Browne, Charles's sister, had previously been Marion Alice Thorburn, a little-known actress on the London stage. She had married Eugene Browne, a wealthy cane sugar and coconut plantation owner, in 1904, and soon found herself living far away from her London family, in Jamaica, mistress of the beautiful but brutal Tryall Estate in Sandy Bay.

Jamaica had recently established a direct shipping line with Bristol, but the journey often took two months, if not longer. Letters were far slower than telegrams, and yet surprisingly this is how she had chosen to communicate what appeared to be desperate information to her brother back in England. As news of the war filtered out of Europe and across the sea, a fear had taken over Alice Thorburn's mind. She knew something in her bones, something so terrible the home secretary must be told of it at once.

The somewhat incoherent letter, written in pencil on blue blotting paper in a looping and bold hand, reveals exactly what triggered the investigation into Kitty. It had been sent to another member of the Thorburn family, and Charles had cut out the relevant information from Alice's letter and enclosed it in the small envelope he had sent to the Home Office:

Be sure and ask to find out what has become of Kitty Marion. She is a German—born & bred—She can't speak a word of German—She has been in England since she was a child. She could, & would easily pass as an Englishwoman. You know her awful character—Suffragette—been in prison two or three times. She would be a fine person to "spy"— for she knows no German Language and her English is perfect—no German accent. Don't forget to ask Charlie to find out, she is a perfect brute—of a woman—& should be sent out of England—at once. Be sure and find out. Charlie may do his country a service. If she can help Germany, she will—that is sure as you are alive—I have been dreaming of the brute—so do be on the look out—I know Charlie will hoist her out if it is in his power.[6]

Fears of German spies were rife in the press since the outbreak of war. Stories of spy networks, disguises, betrayals, and seductions fed a growing fear of "enemy aliens," and the German immigrant population, located primarily in London, Essex, Lancashire, Middlesex, and Yorkshire, found itself under threat as the media manipulated the public's ignorance and self-interest.[7] Taking advantage of the growing culture of patriotic jingoism, fed by the music halls as well as the popular press, the government used any feelings of fear or resentment harbored by its populace—against the waiters, bakers, clerks, and sailors who walked the streets beside the native British population—to pass increasingly restrictive and dehumanizing measures against those it now considered a threat to the Crown. To make matters worse, Germany was also determined to win the war by any means possible, and had begun to utilize its network of secret agents the moment war had broken out.

The first spy to be executed after being discovered in England had been Carl Hans Lody, a German naval officer, killed on November 6, 1914. Lody had confessed that "when war broke out he came to this country with a mission, entrusted to him by the German naval authorities, to discover what he could of the movements of the British Navy."[8] He had been observed in England and Scotland, finally arrested in Ireland, and was shot by firing squad in the Tower of London. Was this the story that had worked its way into Alice Thorburn's mind? Her letter, given the time it took mail ships to cross between Jamaica and

England at that time, would certainly seem to date to being written in the immediate aftermath of Lody's death, as soon as the news of the German spy reached her. It would not have helped that there were rumors he had been seen with a mysterious and unidentified female companion.[9]

How did Reginald McKenna, the embattled home secretary, whose only respite from the threats and attacks of the suffragettes was the outbreak of a world war, feel when that pale blue letter floated across his desk? Kitty was hardly a stranger to him; they had been enemies in thought and deed for many years. Here, finally, was the evidence he needed to rid himself of one of the most violent and aggressive political agents ever to have operated in Britain. Although the WSPU had ceased militant activities at the outbreak of war, women still did not have the vote, and there was no telling what might happen when the war ended, how much worse things could get. He couldn't afford to miss the opportunity to remove a key agent in the organization if the situation had, in fact, presented itself. And how damaging would it be to the women's cause if he could expose a German spy hidden within their ranks?

The Home Office sent the letter to the assistant commissioner of the Criminal Investigation Department, and the police quickly opened an investigation. This was why the police had gone to Madame Louise— not because of her private detective, not because of a casual conversation between the landlady's daughter and the nice man who had come calling. It was a determined attack, a viciously direct campaign instigated from across the sea by a face from Kitty's past. She was never aware of this bitter betrayal, which could have resulted in her death.

Alice Thorburn was not someone who Kitty had unknowingly beaten to a part, who had carried a burning professional resentment and used the war to attack an old foe. In fact, Alice had been a friend, a confidante, and someone Kitty had deeply cared for.

They had met in Liverpool during the *Lady Slavery* tour and had lodged together. Once back in London in 1901, Kitty had become close

to Alice and her family, performing at the theater Charles was managing, the Duchess, in Balham on February 4.[10] The Thorburns were
strict Catholics, but they quickly decided Kitty was a good influence on
Alice, who was now allowed to accept "invitations to luncheons and
suppers 'if Miss Marion goes.'"[11] She was only a few years younger than
Kitty, "a pretty, dark, fluffy haired little thing" who reminded her "of a
fluffy 'chicken,' which I nicknamed her."[12] In Kitty's own autobiography
there is no hint of any discord between the two women, but instead a
clear affection, and then sadness at a correspondence ended by what
she assumed to be distance and marriage:

> She was "never going to marry" but a few years later a wealthy planter
> from Jamaica visited her family and fell in love with, married and took
> the "chicken" out with him. She threatened to find a rich husband out
> there for me. There evidently weren't any for she never wrote. Some
> years later, her brother whom I met in the Strand one day told me Alice,
> her husband and their three children were over on a visit, but they were
> all out when I called.[13]

So what on earth had caused such a rift in their friendship that Alice
had seen fit to send Kitty's name to the government as a potential foreign spy? It wasn't a professional falling-out, and it certainly wasn't
anything to do with a man, so what was the cause? Could it simply be
that Alice, raised in a prim and proper household that respected the
rules and social etiquette of the age, could not accept Kitty's actions
as a suffragette? Had her obvious disgust for her former friend come
from the fact Alice didn't believe, as a surprising number of women
agreed, that women wanted or needed a right to the vote? Or was it the
violence, the unwomanliness of Kitty's actions, the arson, the arrests,
that were not fitting for the wife of a plantation owner to be associated
with? We may never know what exactly caused Alice to send such a vit-
riolic letter to her brother, but it began a series of betrayals that would
test even Kitty's indomitable spirit.

The police investigation against her was continuing, and on her return to Arnold from London, Kitty found a note forwarded on to her Nottinghamshire landlady from the old WSPU headquarters. It was from another German girl, a music hall singer, who she had met in passing in various agents' offices over the years as they had both done the rounds attempting to find bookings. Kitty hadn't seen her for years, but the letter greeted her like an old friend: "Dear Kitty, I wonder if you will remember me, I should like to see you. Can you come for tea on Monday 5 PM, Leicester Square Tube. I want to ask you something. Best Wishes Flo."[14] Already suspicious that the police might try to catch her, Kitty dismissed the letter as a poor attempt at entrapment; she laughed at methods so transparently basic that had rarely worked when they had been tried during the suffragette campaign.

She replied, saying that she was still recuperating from the damage force-feeding had wreaked on her body, and was not able to meet at this present time. There was no response, and although she found the whole situation a humorous one, a nagging, fearful sensation began to gnaw at her subconscious. Kitty used a fake name, "Kathleen Meredith," for her return to the stage, an attempt to earn money now that the suffrage war was on hold, and to make sure her existence was undetectable. But as the war went on, anti-German feeling grew, and the world around Kitty became increasingly dangerous.

A wildly xenophobic novel by Walter Wood, *The Enemy in Our Midst*, had appeared. Written in 1906, it was focused on the plot by a German spymaster to bring about the successful invasion of Britain, and featured one of its leading characters, a stereotypical British working man, claiming that all of the economic and social problems he faced were "because we've given a welcome to every bit of foreign scum that's too filthy to be kept in its own country."[15] Now those sentiments had left the page, and the music halls, newspapers, songs, pubs, and parliamentary debates were all filled with vocal and passionate anti-German attitudes. Soon the government was being urged to arrest and deport all German nationals. At first Kitty ignored this new police state, but then, when everybody was ordered to register at their nearest police station:

> I felt as good as caught and wondered the best road to pursue. If I could
> have remained hidden without involving others I would have done so.
> And I did not care to risk complicating matters by registering under
> a false name etc. So I wrote to Christabel Pankhurst, putting my case
> before her. She advised me to go to Scotland Yard and make a clean
> breast of it to SuperIntendent Quinn, who knew me from the old Suf-
> frage fight and was quite a friendly enemy.[16]

It's not surprising that Kitty would return to her old commander for advice when faced with an impossible situation. Her closest friends were hopeful that, given the long time she had been living in the country, and the WSPU's support of the war, she would be granted an exemption from deportation and become a naturalized citizen of Great Britain. So Kitty packed her bags and returned again to London. It was a brave thing to do, for a former runaway career criminal—at least in the eyes of the law—to choose to step back over the threshold of a police station and ask for help.

But Kitty didn't get the reaction one might have expected. Instead, Superintendent Quinn seemed happy to see her—what a bit of luck to have the woman they were searching for appear on his doorstep! He took her to meet Mr. Bingham, a man Kitty understood to be a higher-ranking official in the Criminal Investigation Department, and one who might hold some sway at the Home Office. Both men seemed to listen "most courteously and sympathetically" to her story, and soon after that a policeman was dispatched to accompany her back to Chelsea, where she was staying, while she filled in a detailed report of all of her movements and life in the country since she had arrived as a child, and registered with the police.[17] There's no record of this meeting in her official file, but there is a copy of the form. Dated May 5, 1915, and filled in with Kitty's slanting, close italics, it contains fragments of information about her life that can be found nowhere else. For the first time, she names her place of birth: Rietberg. And on the back of the form, as the reason for her application not to be sent out of the country, Kitty wrote a perhaps unsuitably precocious defense of her right to stay:

> I prefer to remain in this country; and having always been perfectly loyal to it I see no reason why I should leave it. Though I am well known, and I may safely say loved and respected, as an actress, music hall artiste and Suffragette, imperatively few people know I am German, and none would wish me to leave on that account. My sympathies in the war are, as they have been in other fights, on the side of Justice and Right against Might.[18]

Few people may have known Kitty was German, but at least one of those she had trusted with the story of her birth, Alice Thorburn, had already used it against her. However, there is a gentle surprise on the form. There, in a looping grand hand, is Bernard Halford's signature. The young man Kitty had been supposed to marry, the young man whose father had rejected Kitty, causing her such pain, had not abandoned her at this vital hour. He was acting as one of her two sureties, the other being Mrs. Williams of 10 Grove Court, Drayton Gardens, southwest London. Friends from across the country rallied to support Kitty, writing letters of support and keeping up a continual bombardment in the hope that the government would be convinced to allow her to stay. "What a wretched, anxious, harassing time I had," Kitty remembered, "and I was only one of thousands during the war, going through similar hell through no fault of their own."[19]

Although hopeful of success, Kitty soon began to hear stories of British-born women married to German men who were now being deported. If that was how the British government treated its own women, why would they show her any mercy? On July 16, her application for exemption from repatriation back to Germany was refused.

Kitty now faced a terrible reality. Reginald McKenna had decided to send her back to the country of her birth, a place she hadn't set foot in for more than thirty years, to a family where her father had abused her and with whom she had had no contact since she marched out of Aunt Dora's home, a hot-tempered young woman determined never to return. It was an alien place to her, the situation a nightmare brought about by war. The country she thought of as home, the society she had spent her life fighting to change for the better, that she believed to be one of the greatest in the world, did not want her. Instead, they were choosing to send her into the hands of their enemy.

How lonely, even with the support of her friends, Kitty must have felt. Once again, she would feel like that young child on the deck of a boat, leaving the country she thought of as home for another life, another new beginning. But in the middle of such anguish, there was a small ray of hope. The police appear, on August 30, 1915, to have concluded their investigations. Their final report to the government cleared Kitty of any suspicions that had stemmed from Alice's accusation:

Sir,

With reference to your letter of the 31st ultimo, respecting the case of Kitty Marion, alias Katherine Marie Schafer, I have to acquaint you, for the information of the Secretary of State, that, so far as is known to the Police, this woman does not maintain any connection with Germany and is not suspected of any disloyal practice in this direction. Her sentiments appear to be pro-British, and she has recently been seen singing patriotic songs at recruiting meetings.

She is, however, a suffragette of dangerous character, and in June, 1913, she was charged, with Clara Giveen, with setting fire to the Grand Stand and other buildings at Hurst Park Race Course. She was sentenced to three years' penal servitude; but owing to the fact that she was released from Prison on several occasions under The Prisoners

(Temporary Discharge for Ill-Health) Act, there are still two years and 256 days of her sentence unexpired.

I am,

Sir,

Your Obedient Servant[20]

Five days later, someone wrote in the margins of Kitty's file, "This woman deserves to be in prison, but I agree that it is no use sending her back to Germany when she left the country at the age of 15 and has been here for 29 years. Such a hard measure might open up fresh trouble with the suffragettes who have behaved well since the war began."[21] Although Reginald McKenna was determined finally to get rid of one of the wildest of the "wild wreckers," he was also aware that to do so might cause him more harm in the long-term than he was willing to risk. But how could the home secretary allow such a violent woman, and self-proclaimed German, to stay in England while the country was in the middle of this devastating war? There had to be a compromise. It was, of course, the suffragettes themselves who thought of it. If Kitty was not allowed to stay in England, why not send her to America? There, at least, would be millions of like-minded individuals, and both Constance Lytton and Mrs. Pethick-Lawrence would be able to write her letters of introduction to friends and organizations that they had connections to. The following month, Kitty received a permit to leave for New York. She was to travel to Liverpool, the city she had wreaked such havoc in just over a year ago.

It is impossible to express my appreciation of the true, helpful comradeship of all who made life worth living during those last few weeks in London, by entertaining me and raising my fare to America, for which latter Mrs. Alice Green, Mrs. Pethick Lawrence, Lady Constance Lytton, Mrs. Rose Lamartine Yates, Mrs. Williams, Miss Ada Wright, Miss Lal Forsyth, Miss Peggie Fletcher, as far as known, were responsible.[22]

Although Kitty could no longer fight the reality that she was to leave, she was not going to be alone. Elsie McKenzie, another hunger-striking suffragette who was closely connected to the American suffrage movement, helped Kitty to book her passage, and with filling out the huge American questionnaire that all immigrants to the United States faced at that time. Cabin chosen, questionnaire filled in—with the triumphant answer to "Have you ever been to prison?" a ballsy "Yes, for Woman Suffrage"[23]—Kitty's final few weeks in her adopted home passed in a blur. Walking home one evening she witnessed the October 13 "Theatreland Raid" by a German zeppelin, "floating like a huge silvery electric blue cigar, at intervals dropping bombs. I felt a thrill of exultation at my countrymen having created this graceful, majestic thing, and deep revulsion at their prostituting it in the destruction of their fellow creatures."[24] The bombs fell on the Lyceum Theatre, killing seventeen people and wounding another twenty. The boom of the antiaircraft guns firing at the sky were the closest the people of London would get to the real horrors happening on the Continent.

On October 24, which happened to be a Sunday, the Emily Wilding Davison Club, which had kept so many of the secrets of the suffragettes, met at 144 High Holborn to say goodbye to one of its members. Not only the offices of the Women's Freedom League and the headquarters of the volunteer organization the Women's Police Service, this address was also home to the League's vegetarian restaurant, Minerva Café.[25] "Till the war is over, it can't last much longer, and then you'll come home," Kitty's closest friends proclaimed. "'Blood is thicker than water,' I heard quoted very extensively during the war, but always found the spirit of friendship, love, justice, truth, and so forth, 'thicker,' stronger and more sustaining than 'blood.'"[26]

The next Wednesday, waved off by a crowd of her old comrades and friends, Kitty left for Liverpool. As the train pulled into the station, she realized her past was not as willing to let go of her as some may have hoped, as a police escort was waiting to transfer her to the port. Checking through her paperwork, she was informed that they intended to "wash England's hands" of her the moment she was on board the *Cym-ric*. This must have been a cruel goodbye, but Kitty was bolstered by the company of Elsie McKenzie and her own sense of adventure. Even though she was being forced to leave behind those she loved and the life she had built, Kitty's innate wandering spirit had taken over.

Part of the White Star Line's fleet, the *Cymric* had been crossing the Atlantic between Liverpool and New York since 1898. As war broke out, she had transported troops to France, and a few months before Kitty stepped on board, the *Cymric* had carried one of the war's largest shipments of ammunition from America, a whopping 17,000 tons, to its British allies. It was a brave choice. On May 7, 1915, another British passenger ship traveling the same route, the RMS *Lusitania*, had been torpedoed by the German submarine U-20, killing 1,198 of the ship's 1,959 passengers. Almost exactly a year later, on May 8, 1916, the U-20 finally torpedoed the *Cymric* 140 miles off the coast of Ireland. Her wreck has never been found.

The risks would have weighed heavily on the minds of the *Cym-ric*'s passengers in 1915. The journey was not an easy one, and "during the first five days of which I was more dead than alive," Kitty recalled, overwhelmed by the emotions of both loss and anticipation. But on November 7, 1915, Kitty landed in New York.[27] She had little to say about her arrival; the outbreak of war had seen a significant reduction in the numbers of immigrants arriving at Ellis Island to be inspected before being allowed in to the United States. And to be surrounded by families searching for a new life, citizens returning home, and lovers reunited was not a new experience for Kitty, although this time she was not a child but a woman of forty-four years of age.

Producing her documentation, which raised a few eyebrows with her admittance to both a prison record and her life as a militant suffrag-ette, as well as the ever-questionable career as an actress in the music halls, Kitty left the island and quickly found a place to stay on East 10th Street. Boisterous and quick to recover, she was determined to seize whatever new opportunities America would present to her. After all, she had found such welcome and friendship after her arrival in England; surely it would be the same here? She had two letters with her, one from Constance Lytton to a Miss Madeleine Doty, then an assistant police commissioner, and one from Mrs. Pethick-Lawrence to Miss Lillian Wald of the Henry Street Settlement. Madeleine Doty was a lawyer, journalist, and suffrage activist who was well known in New York. At that time she was working on reforming prison conditions for women and children, and so you might think that the arrival of a militant suffragette, who knew firsthand what life in the prison system could be like for women, would be useful to her. But over tea, Madeleine found that "she could suggest nothing in the way of work" for Kitty, while Lillian Wald, eventually agreeing to a meeting at eleven o'clock one morning, suddenly found she had to attend an urgent Women's Peace Meeting, and was no longer home when Kitty called for her.[28]

> As I meandered about New York trying to find my bearings, admiring skyscrapers and other individual features of the city, I wished that all my friends in England could be here to share my new experiences . . . I was surprised and amused at the apparent stock question with which some people greeted me. "How do you like America; don't you like America better than England?" All in one breath. How could I, knowing and loving England as I did, and feeling wounded and sad at parting, "like" America better?[29]

Standing in Times Square, lost in thought and memory, Kitty suddenly found herself hailed by a familiar voice: Mr. Barry, an old acquaintance from her music hall days. He was overjoyed to see her, as two travelers with a shared homeland often are on discovering one another on a distant shore. Solving an immediate problem, Mr. Barry recommended a comfortable and well-priced theatrical lodging house on 42nd Street— now buried underneath the Times Square Theater—run by a lovely French and German couple, Mr. and Mrs. Mourey. Three meals a day, a clean, bright room, and the happy company of a rambunctious and eclectic mix of Australian and English vaudeville artists suited Kitty perfectly, especially at the cost of only eight dollars a week. Now all she needed was work. If the worthy ladies of New York weren't going to help, then it was time to return to the world she had loved since she was a little girl, and which had ultimately seen her become a suffragette. It was time to return to the stage.

But the stage wouldn't have her. Overrun by artists fleeing the war, many of the agents and managers didn't need or want another foreign artist on their books. Some were anti-suffragists "who were most facetiously afraid I might smash their windows or burn the theatre."[30] Others were simply anti-German, and none were interested in a forty-four-year-old ex-actress and "Notorious Character," whose once-fine singing voice had been irreparably damaged by the torture of force-feeding. In desperation, Kitty decided to try her luck with the film studios. As Charlie Chaplin was conquering Hollywood with *The Tramp*, Kitty's photo and résumé were falling on the desks of producers and directors on both the west and east coasts. She became a regular ghost, haunting the New York area studios in Englewood, New Jersey, yet was always rejected because of her lack of film experience.

With the money she had saved, and the little that had been raised by the Emily Wilding Davison Club to send her to and set her up in New York, Kitty decided to seek out the American suffrage movement, hoping to find herself welcomed by the WSPU's American cousins. Although America had not granted women the right to vote across the country, many states were deliberating on it; and in 1915 New York had voted on whether or not to amend the state's voting rights to allow women to participate in elections. The vote had failed a few days before Kitty arrived, with 553,348 for and 748,332 against. The tide was slowly turning, and suffragists in New York State could see that their dreams might one day be within reach. Kitty managed to secure a meeting with Alva Belmont, the twice-married millionairess and socialite who was a prominent leader in the New York suffrage movement. The sixty-three-year-old titan had presided over the disastrous marriage

of her eldest daughter, Consuelo Vanderbilt, to the 9th Duke of Marlborough, Charles Richard John Spencer, in 1895. The marriage had
made Consuelo cousin to Winston Churchill, and they had remained
close throughout their lives. Pictures of the pair sitting on the steps of
Blenheim Palace show two people utterly at ease in each other's company, even perhaps slightly annoyed at the camera's intrusion into their
private conversation. But Consuelo's marriage was deeply unhappy,
and many years later her mother admitted, "I forced my daughter to
marry the Duke. I have always had absolute power over my daughter.
When I issued an order nobody discussed it. I therefore did not beg,
but ordered her."[31] This was a woman Kitty was hoping to impress. It
was not to be:

> "Like a bit of dirt" is the best description of that lady's treatment of
> me. She thought she might find something for me to do, but "Forget
> that you have ever been militant, we don't want that kind of militancy
> here." Though I controlled my tongue and my temper, I heard nothing
> further from Mrs. Belmont.[32]

There was little Kitty could do to change the minds of those whose
experience of the militant movement came from the newspapers. The
WSPU's violent campaign had received widespread international cov-
erage, alienating many and exciting some; when Olive Hockin had
been charged with arson attacks on Roehampton Golf Club's pavilion and Kew Gardens' orchid house, the cutting of telegraph and telephone wires, and the destruction of letters in March 1913, her notoriety
reached as far as America, with the *Boston Herald* (reported secondhand
in the English papers) carrying a description of her trial, claiming her
home in Kensington was a "depot where people foregathered, armed
and prepared for any particular marauding outrage on hand."[33] In the
state of New York, the *Brooklyn Daily Eagle* throughout 1913 to 1914 had
carried numerous cartoons by Nelson Harding, under the title "Ruthless Rhymes for Martial Militants." Alongside images of the women

brandishing guns, bombs, and daggers, wrecking trains and blowing up buildings, were satirical rhymes like: "Mary had a little bomb, its fuse was trimmed and lighted; And everywhere that Mary went, The people fled, affrighted!"[34] Underneath a cartoon of three suffragettes gleefully emptying a machine gun, one of the most dangerous weapons of the age, into a cloud of smoke, ran the poem: "Few girls have ever had such fun, As these had with a Maxim gun, It quite convulsed the martial band, To see that weapon sweep the Strand."[35]

Even Germany was using images of the militant suffragettes in its war propaganda campaigns, printing postcards with pictures of the militants housed in cages, armed with bombs and guns, and being shipped to the front line, featuring captions like "Nachdem die englische Armee geschlagen, werden die Sufragetten mobililiert"—"After the English army is defeated, the suffragettes are mobilized." With this in mind, it is lucky that Kitty was not sent back to her homeland by McKenna, as the reaction there may have been far worse than the frosty reception she found in America.

But that did little to comfort her. Owing a number of weeks' rent at her lodging house, with no work to be found in the theaters or films and having received the brush-off from the worthy and powerful ladies of New York, Kitty felt utterly lost. By May 1916, she had fallen into painful memories and a deep sense of loss for her life in England: "Dear, dead days, beyond recall, and the future looking very black," she wrote.[36]

She found another rejection from the studios in Englewood, after she had walked from her lodgings across the city to get there, unbearable. "Oh, to get away from it all, to walk on until I dropped dead, fade out of existence, out of this futility, anywhere!"[37] She walked and walked until she could walk no further, and found herself in the middle of the woods as the sun was setting. Having not eaten since breakfast, and with no money to feed herself or find her way home, she sat down.

Utterly weary and discouraged, I fell asleep. Waking up in the dark, stiff and chilly, wondering for the moment where I was. No use trying to get out of the woods now, so I curled up on part of a newspaper I had, covering the rest over me, and tried to sleep again, feeling utterly crushed, wishing never to wake.[38]

Woken the next morning by birdsong and soft drizzle, Kitty couldn't face returning to either the kindness of Mr. and Mrs. Mourey, or to the debts she owed them. For such a proud woman, who had fought so hard throughout her life and had always managed fiercely to maintain and protect her independence, this new situation was intolerable. Throwing herself on the mercy of a Mrs. Lucy B. Carmody, whom she had met attending one of the New York suffrage meetings, Kitty put all her pride aside. She wanted work, any work; she could do anything, no matter how menial, whatever it was, she would do it. A little taken aback at first by the bedraggled and desperate woman who had appeared in her sitting room, a far cry from the indomitable suffragette most knew Kitty to be, Lucy soon rose to the occasion. Giving Kitty a bed for the night, and making some determined and practical calls, she quickly found her a situation on West 126th Street, in the boardinghouse of a Mr. and Mrs. George de Weerdt, who were looking for a maid of all work, at five dollars a week. It was perfect. Kitty found her way there, planning to call on the Moureys the moment she had earned enough to pay back the debts she had accrued. In the meantime, she settled into life at the de Weerdts', relishing the relative ease and simplicity of her life now.

Attempting to gloss over this difficult period of her life, Kitty mentions only in passing that her friends were concerned by her disappearance, although she had quickly gotten in touch with them and let them know she was all right and would return when she was ready. But the papers tell a different story. The *Brooklyn Daily Eagle* ran an article under the heading, "Suffrage Hunger Striker Missing From Hotel," complete with a large photograph of Kitty.

Women suffrage leaders in this city are worried over the absence of Miss Kitty Marion, the famous English militant suffragist, who disappeared from her hotel in Manhattan on Saturday. She took no baggage with her. It is known she was in a despondent frame of mind. Mrs. OHP Belmont, who is much interested in the English woman, would be glad to receive news that she is safe.[39]

The same Mrs. Belmont, Mrs. Alva Belmont, who had turned Kitty away not long before? Surely not. But it was one and the same. Yet even this outstretched hand was not enough to lure Kitty back from the comfort of her life as a maid. She wanted the peace, the removal from the world until she was ready to join it again. But the press interest had gotten under her skin. A reminder of the old days, and the old fights. As separate as she was now, was her life fighting for women's rights really over?

Of course not. Having made enough money to pay Mrs. Mourey back, and feeling that she must now resume "association with the outer-world," Kitty opened the newspaper one day in October 1916 and discovered her next cause.[40] Its leader was Margaret Sanger, and this was the dawn of the international birth control movement. A prominent nurse and campaigner, Margaret Sanger, much like Annie Besant in the 1870s, had been attempting to publish and politicize information on birth control and sex. This was illegal under Section 1142 of the Penal Code, which had been designed to prevent the dissemination of information about how to stop pregnancy. On October 16, alongside her sister Mrs. Ethel Byrne, also a trained nurse, and Miss Fania Mindell, an interpreter, she had opened a family planning clinic in Brownsville, Brooklyn, catering to the largely immigrant population. With leaflets printed in multiple languages, and at the cost of only twenty cents, women could access information on diaphragms, condoms, and other contraceptive aids, and also on sexual pleasure. It was a revolutionary project, and one Margaret Sanger was wholly committed to.

But almost as soon as the clinic had been opened, it was shut down, and Sanger was arrested, charged, and bailed. She reopened the clinic, which saw her rearrested, charged, and bailed—and she reopened the clinic again, only to be arrested for a third time. The clinic was shut down for good only about a month after it had been opened. "The whole question was 'Greek' to me," Kitty recalled, "beyond knowing that many women limited their family by abortions and some used methods of prevention. It was a very personal matter and not openly discussed in England, to my knowledge."[41] But here was a woman who wanted to discuss it, out in the open, without shame or fear. She followed the press reports surrounding Margaret Sanger into the new year, and when a Carnegie Hall mass meeting was announced for January 29, 1917, with Mrs. Sanger as the principal speaker, Kitty knew she had to go.

Deciding to book tickets for herself, Mrs. de Weerdt, and her daughter, Blanche, Kitty called the birth control headquarters at 104 Fifth Avenue. Gone were the early WSPU days and her hatred of the telephone, and the booking was easy, but when Kitty said her name, the voice on the end excitedly replied, "Kitty Marion? We've heard of you, won't you come and help us?"[42] At last, here, after two years of wilderness and confusion, despair and despondence, was not only an opportunity, but a call to arms. As soon as she was able to, Kitty left for headquarters, and a meeting with Dr. Frederick A. Blossom, business manager and managing editor of the forthcoming *Birth Control Review*, which was to be the mouthpiece of the campaign. The movement, she found, was not the well-oiled and slick machine the WSPU had been when she joined, but was in its infancy, struggling to figure out how to make its campaign a success. Just as with the magazines *Votes For Women* and *The Suffragette*, Kitty offered her help as a newspaper seller, but this time for the *Birth Control Review*.

The *Review* was not being sold on the streets, as had been such a success for the WSPU; at that time it was being sent through the mail in an attempt to flout the laws—the hope was that no one would open the packages until they reached their destination, from where they would then be passed around.

But when January 29 finally came, Kitty found herself in a role of honor: selling the *Review* inside the hall "in true suffragette style."[43]

> Margaret Sanger with her quiet, forceful, determined way of presenting her argument won my heart at once. "She ought to have been in the WSPU" I thought, than which I could not pay her a greater compliment. "Shall we break this law?" stared me in the face from the cover of the "Review." . . . It was a glorious evening, reminiscent of defiant WSPU meetings.[44]

It is easy to understand why Kitty felt so at home in the birth control movement; not only was it a way of recapturing the happiness and comradeship of the WSPU, but she had faced so much sexual abuse in life. To be part of an organization that sought to put sexual power and sexual knowledge back in the hands of women themselves must have felt like destiny.

While Margaret Sanger served one of her many jail terms for the dissemination of birth control literature, Kitty set about giving herself a highly liberal and radical education.

> I learned how the Society for the Suppression of Vice and the Catholic Church were opposed to Birth Control, and that there was a Neo-Malthusian movement, etc., in England . . . I had often read of prosecutions for abortions, which struck me as unjust since no-one was to blame, it seemed to me, but the woman who was seeking relief, which it should be her right to receive.[45]

On March 6, Kitty joined the crowd of birth control supporters heading to meet Margaret Sanger on her release from prison. They huddled against the biting wind, waiting for the doors of the Queens County jail on Long Island to open; Margaret Sanger was finally released at 10:15 a.m. Thirty-eight years old and estranged from her husband, she was a force to be reckoned with. In 1914, she had set up a small monthly newsletter to promote contraception called the *Woman Rebel*, which had taken a popular slogan "No Gods, No Masters" as its motto.[46] She was an ideal leader for Kitty, the middle-aged suffragette who now found herself outside a new set of prison gates, cheering for a new feminist leader, a new cause, and a new reason to fight. The press had a field day; not only did they have the birth control movement to talk about, but here too was the missing militant suffragette turning up suddenly to support her. One report in the *Brooklyn Eagle* ran:

> Miss Kitty Marion, English militant suffragette . . . enlivened the processing while Mrs. Sanger's release was awaited by singing the suffragist version of "La Marseillaise," underneath the jail windows. Miss Marion has a good mezzo soprano voice and the jail windows, especially on the upper floors where the women are confined, were thrown open. Applause was generous and hearty.[47]

Back at birth control headquarters, Kitty set out her plan to sell the *Review* on the streets, and this was widely supported; the organization also agreed that she could keep half of the profit on what she sold. Kitty took a room at 13 West 18th Street, just off Fifth Avenue, and "settled down to work in earnest."[48] Finding that the best time to sell the *Review* was in the afternoon and early evening, she was soon selling more than a hundred a day, at a profit to herself of ten cents of the twenty-cent price. Lost in her new campaign, when New York finally awarded women the vote in November, Kitty paid little attention. The vote was always only ever a means to an end for her, a way to give women back control and protection over their own bodies, freedom, and independence. The vote wouldn't change a woman's right to birth control, and this, the ability to give women ownership over the sexual culture around them, was where her priorities had always truly been. She had become a suffragette to combat the sexual abuses she had experienced in the music halls, but far from being a prudish conservative, determined to outlaw sex, it was those music halls that had also taught her the value and enjoyment many women placed on a sexual relationship. It was time for women to have it all.

Kitty's life settled into the traditions of a radical feminist activist; she was arrested for selling the *Review*, she was released, she wrote to the papers, she gave interviews, and she became a recognizable sight on the streets of New York, well known for her birth control activism, often identified as that "famous English militant suffragette." As the war on the Continent raged on, Kitty barely acknowledged it, her adventure as the German spy long forgotten—until one day in 1918.

Marching into the office of the *Birth Control Review*, two men who refused to identify themselves, but flashed badges to anyone who asked, requested Kitty leave at once and accompany them to "headquarters." Finding the whole thing laughable, but deciding to accompany them without too much argument, Kitty was in for a terrible shock. She was taken to a place she only describes as the Federal Headquarters, 14 Park Row. There she was introduced to a Mr. Finch and a stenographer, and Finch immediately requested that they return to Kitty's lodgings.

> There, with much bluster, which no official should be permitted to use even to a convicted criminal, Mr. Finch told me I was a German Spy and ordered me to pack every piece of printed and written matter to bring with me to headquarters. I owned to being German, but not to a spy, and I objected to his manner of speech. "These gentlemen," I told him, indicating the detectives who had arrested me, "have been perfectly courteous and treated me as a lady, and I expect you to do the same. I am not a spy, and have nothing to hide, and you are welcome to read every printed article and written word in my possession."[49]

Taken back to Federal Headquarters, Kitty soon found herself on the list to be interrogated:

> Mr. Finch, who I learned was a "special investigator" and Mr. Davis, his stenographer, much too nice a youth for that environment, were ready

to examine me: when and why I had come to America, what had been my activities since, did I know any radicals and anarchists like Emma Goldman, Elizabeth Curley Flynn . . . He refused to tell me the source of his information, that I was German, and I was mystified for I could not think of anyone who would betray me. My "grilling" lasted from about 3pm until nearly 11, excepting dinner, which was quite a friendly affair, cocktails and all, at which I talked very freely, having nothing to conceal. . . . Was there anything so cock-eyed? For over twenty years I had, according to German Law, ceased to be German, yet in America, Land of the Free, where I had my first papers, which should have entitled me to the mere courtesy of being looked upon as more American than German, they wanted me to register as a German Alien.[50]

What on earth had happened this time? Had Alice Thorburn seen the reports of Kitty's birth control activism in the news, and *again* written to government, this time the American administration, to warn them of the dangerous woman they were harboring in their midst? Could such a bitter enmity truly exist? Mr. Finch appeared satisfied with Kitty's answers and soon released her, but the precarious nature of her situation had, once again, been made all too clear to her.

A few months later, as she was selling the *Birth Control Review* on Fifth Avenue, Kitty spied Mr. Finch walking toward her. She had clearly made an impression—forthright and occasionally imperious as she was, it would be hard not to be at least a little curious about the woman who seemed to spend her life getting into trouble—and she and Mr. Finch fell into easy conversation. As they walked together, he revealed that he had found out Kitty was German quite by accident, in the middle of another investigation into a radical organization operating in New York. "You know your militant suffrage friends working in a certain Radical organisation here?" he said to Kitty. "'Yes,' I said, wondering for I knew she would not betray me. 'Well, the day after you were arrested for giving birth control information, she read it in the paper and remarked, "Oh, poor Kitty Marion, arrested again, and Emmeline Pankhurst in the country; if she sees this, she'll tell the authorities that Kitty is German." ' "[51] The entire conversation had been caught on a hidden dictation machine, and the recording of it was what had brought Mr. Finch to Kitty's door. To her, it seemed a ridiculous situation, but lurking within it was the final and greatest betrayal of Kitty's life.

Why on earth would Mrs. Pankhurst give up one of her most loyal and committed soldiers? Why would Kitty's German heritage, well known in the suffrage movement, be of any importance to her now? It would take some years until Kitty had the unpleasant answer she was looking for.

> Here's another strange experience. Mrs. Pankhurst was in New York and I pictured a joyous meeting, should she come along and see me selling the Birth Control Review. I felt sure that with her knowledge of the unspeakable poverty-stricken, overcrowded slum conditions in England she would be delighted with my present activities. One afternoon at Macy's corner she did appear with Miss Pine, dear old "Piney" who, in her Nursing Home had been such a good Ministering Angel to me and other hunger strikers. I saw them crossing Broadway and my heart beat high in anticipation of our mutual pleasure of a reunion. I stood ready to "pounce on them," like a cat on two mice, at the moment of recognition.[52]

Standing on that New York pavement watching Mrs. Pankhurst walk toward her must have released an instantaneous flood of memories. How often Kitty had stood on street corners selling *The Suffragette* in the Pankhurst name. And here Kitty was again, fighting for women's rights in an alien country, about to greet her mentor for the first time since she had fled from England after the outbreak of war. It must have felt like an overwhelming moment, full of triumph, familiarity, joy, and longing for the sisters and companions she had left behind.[53] Surely Mrs. Pankhurst must feel the same. After all, Kitty had been one of her most active soldiers, her most loyal warriors. She had faced countless jail sentences, been force-fed more than any other suffragette prisoner, all under the leadership of Mrs. Pankhurst and her daughters.

> But, oh, what a crashing of castles upon my unwary head when they did see me! Their faces hardened, their heads went up and they passed me, staring stonily in front of them. I felt stunned, hurt to the quick, but remembered Mrs. Pankhurst's anti-German attitude during the war. I felt sad at my shattered idol, but separated, preserved, and continued to revere the spirit of the great, wonderful Suffrage leader, from which subsequent events could detract nothing. I learned later that Mrs. Pankhurst developed a strong anti-German complex as a child in school in Paris during the Franco–Prussian war, 1870–1871. Another good reason why war should be abolished from the earth and the minds and emotions of future generations saved from its distorting, devastating influences.[54]

What a cold, callous dismissal this must have been. What justification, even after the horrors of the war, could there possibly be for such a public rejection of the woman who had fought so hard, and supported the Pankhursts, for so long? For Kitty, who held her suffragette experiences at the center of her own identity, the pain must have been acute. Equally, in her new American life, her connections, real and historical, to the leadership of the suffragette movement in the United Kingdom had been intensely valuable. With one gesture, one single action, Mrs. Pankhurst had swept aside Kitty's place not just in the eyes of her new compatriots, but also in suffrage history. She was no longer to be acknowledged.

9

Sex: A Woman's Choice

Clattering down the stone corridors of New York's "Tombs"—the municipal jail located at 125 White Street in Lower Manhattan—came Kitty Marion. Pail in hand, ready to scrub walls and floor, she would call out "Three cheers for birth control!" to prisoners and matrons alike, although it was only the prisoners who would return the cheer in kind.[1] Agnes Smedley, imprisoned due to her radical political work, wrote to Margaret Sanger to inform her that Kitty had turned the prison "into a regular forum for birth control agitation."[2] Working through a sentence of thirty days while lawyers for Margaret Sanger put together an acquittal defense using America's First Amendment (part of which protects the right to free speech), Kitty was surprisingly content. She was reliving old patterns in new movements. Although the suffragette leadership had abandoned her, her new cause, birth control, gave her exactly the same experiences, and a new sense of community and camaraderie. By 1921, Margaret Sanger's organization had grown at such a pace across the country that it was renamed the American Birth Control League (ABCL). It held its inaugural conference under this name on November 11 and 12 at the Plaza Hotel in New York. Twenty years later, it would take on a name most would still recognize today,

Planned Parenthood, or (in full) the Planned Parenthood Federation of America.

A year later, building on the growing success of her movement, Margaret Sanger decided to attend the fifth Neo-Malthusian and Birth Control Conference—or the International Birth Control Conference, as most people called it—to be held in London that summer. She decided to take her secretary, Anna Lifshitz, and Kitty as her companions, and as dedicated representatives of the League and its work. This may have seemed a canny political move, arriving with one of England's foremost suffragettes, but it also shows just how important a figure Kitty was to Sanger at this time for her work in America and overseas. Kitty was overjoyed. Procuring an emergency German passport and a visa to allow her entrance into Britain, Kitty began to prepare to return to the home and friends she had not seen in almost seven years. She was now fifty-one years old. The young music hall singer who fought against sexual harassment and marched with the suffragettes was a distant memory, and in her place was an older, tougher, more experienced activist. She knew what it was to be alone, in a way she had not experienced since childhood. America, while exciting, did not have the warm comfort and nostalgia of the country where she had spent most of her life. But now she could go home, even if it was only for a few short weeks.

Landing in Liverpool in early July, the same city she had been so unceremoniously bundled onto a boat and expelled from in 1915, Kitty felt a sense of joyful sanctuary: "What thrilling heartfelt joy to be on English soil once more, on a train going to London over a familiar old route!"[3] David Lloyd George, her old suffrage foe, was now prime minister, and the country was preoccupied with the looming establishment of the Irish Free State—the Republic of Ireland, as it is today. On June 22 the Irish Republican Army, the forefathers of the modern-day IRA, had assassinated Field Marshal Sir Henry Wilson, shooting him on the doorstep of his Belgravia home. Wilson had played a large part in the violence and terror on the British side during the Irish War of

Independence, and his assassination was retribution for much of the murder and bloodshed that had been caused at the hands of British troops. As Kitty arrived in England, the trial of the two men arrested for Wilson's murder, Reginald Dunne and Joseph O'Sullivan, had gripped the country.

Casting her eyes over the newspapers on her way to London, did Kitty allow herself to wonder how far the suffragettes would have gone if the war had not partially brought them the vote? Guns had slowly become an increasing feature in the violence of some of the militants. Arrested in July 1913 for blowing up an empty carriage on the Lancashire and Yorkshire Railway, Jennie Baines, alongside her husband and son, was discovered in possession of yet another prepared bomb, a large quantity of gunpowder, a revolver loaded in three chambers with ball cartridge, and an unloaded pistol.[4] This was not Jennie's first violent attack; she had been part of Mary Leigh's squad, attacking Asquith at the Theatre Royal and throwing a hatchet at Mr. John Redmond in Dublin in 1912. She was not alone in her use of guns. When Emmeline Pankhurst spoke to a crowded hall in Glasgow on March 10, 1914, the police had rushed the stage to try to seize her. Gertrude Harding, a dedicated suffragette, had reported that:

> to my amazement, Janie Allen, tall and handsome in a black velvet evening gown, arose from her seat and pointed a pistol straight at the man in the door! There was a loud explosion, and the policeman tried frantically to push back those behind him, thinking no doubt that he had been mortally wounded. But the pressure behind him was too great and soon the platform was filled with the policemen using their truncheons without mercy. Miss Allen's blank pistol shot had both startled and angered them.[5]

But now, for many, that war was in the past. Arriving in London, Kitty registered at an old and familiar haunt, Bow Street Police Station, and found that Mr. Harold Cox, the old Liberal MP for Preston, had been instrumental in convincing the Home Office to extend her visa for a further six weeks. He had been the principal speaker at the ABCL's inaugural conference in New York, and since April had been attempting to convince the Home Office to allow Kitty to return to the country. But although seven years may have passed since she had left, the government was not willing to forget one of its most notorious enemies. The reaction to her application to return, held in her Home Office file, was a vehement no. "This woman was German and a very aggressive suffragette," the 1922 entry reads. "There seem to be no reasons for allowing her to come on a visit . . . Request Refused."[6] Under section 10 (1) of the Aliens Restriction (Amendment) Act of 1919, which had enforced the serious penalties the wartime government had passed against "enemy aliens," Kitty had no right to return to England. But Harold Cox's determination and persistence had paid off. This was why she had had to travel on a passport from Germany, the country she spent the least amount of her life in and yet was never fully able to leave behind.

Walking the streets of London once more was a bittersweet homecoming for Kitty. The conference's four days of sessions were to be held at Kingsway Hall, almost exactly opposite the WSPU's old Lincoln's Inn headquarters. Kitty attended them all, and steadfastly believed that the conference was instrumental in providing solutions that "were most instructive, inspiring and suggestive of a speedy, universal practice of Birth Control."[7] Meeting with Margaret and Anna, Kitty "felt a great pride and satisfaction to be cooperating with such an indomitable little fighter as Margaret Sanger in doing something with such far-reaching results for the ultimate benefit of all humanity."[8]

> The social life of the Conference was delightful. A reception given by Mr. and Mrs. H. G. Wells at their home, overlooking the Thames Embankment, a ride in charabancs to historic Penshurst in Kent, luncheon at the local hotel, tea at Mr. Harold Cox's flower-surrounded cottage where Mrs. Cox received us on the return trip . . . Meeting

Havelock Ellis was an event to Anna and me. As he was not going to attend the Conference, Mrs. Sanger let us carry her gifts from China to him at his home in Brixton. As for myself, I felt much like a ghost haunting the scenes of my "life," but I revelled in meeting some of my old pals again.[9]

Perhaps Kitty was unaware, or perhaps simply too loyal to say, but both Ellis and Wells had been (or rather, were still) Margaret Sanger's lovers. Author of some of the most fantastical and exciting science fiction books of his age, H. G. Wells had long been a supporter of birth control. An early advocate of sterilization, he had quickly moved to support the freedom and independence contraception could offer to men and women alike, which had led him to become a vocal supporter of Sanger and her work. Havelock Ellis, one of the most influential writers on human sexuality in the last two centuries, was an idol to Sanger, who held a long and intimate correspondence with him until his death in 1939. The relationship between these three people, each so influential in their own world, had such a profound effect on Wells that he wrote a loosely based portrayal of them in his 1922 novel *The Secret Places of the Heart*.[10] In it, an English gentleman, Sir Richard Hardy, accompanied by his psychiatrist, Dr. Martineau, meets a young American woman, Miss Grammont, who confidently lectures them on the uses and benefits of birth control. The characters were, of course, Wells, Ellis, and Sanger respectively.

Leaving the joy and excitement of the birth control conference behind her, Kitty managed to attend a small gathering of the Emily Wilding Davison Club, organized by Alice Green, before she returned to America in August. She refused to divulge anything that happened there, perhaps finding it too painful after Emmeline Pankhurst's recent and callous dismissal of her on the streets of New York. Her visa finally running out, Kitty left from Southampton, on board the *Aquitania*, on August 12, arriving back in New York six days later. Determined never to be kept out of England again, she had decided to apply for American citizenship, to throw off the old German identity that had ruled her life for so long. The accusation of "enemy alien" would be left behind, and the memories of rejection and betrayal with it. On October 6, 1922, and giving her address as 333 West 22nd Street, Kitty appeared before County Clerk James A. Donegan at the Supreme Court. But there was a problem. Donegan was an avid opponent of the birth control movement, and refused point-blank to grant Kitty a certificate of naturalization unless she agreed to give up her work selling the *Birth Control Review* outside of Macy's department store, or in Times Square, as she was now so well known for doing. Never one to fear an appearance on the witness stand, Kitty pleaded her case fiercely, saying that what he was asking her to do was give up her livelihood, but that it would hardly prevent the doctrine of birth control from spreading. Forceful as ever, and always a passionate and convincing speaker (or perhaps Donegan was simply unable to withstand the onslaught any longer), Kitty argued her way into her citizenship; Donegan finally relented and allowed her to take the oath: "And so I left the Supreme Court, the proud possessor of a certificate of naturalisation."[11]

For the next eight years, Kitty would spend her time between England and New York, working for the League. Boarding the *Pittsburgh* in June 1925 for two months in London, Kitty knew she would finally be able to witness a truly unique moment in history: a female MP had taken her seat in Parliament. Nancy Astor had been elected MP for Plymouth Sutton in 1919. She was not the first female MP—that honor belonged to Constance Markievicz, the Irish MP elected in 1918, but as a member of Sinn Féin, Constance had refused to take her seat. But although not the first female MP per se, Nancy was the first woman to sit in the House of Commons, and Kitty could not contain her joy: "Looking down from the gallery on Lady Astor's hat, I felt a great thrill of pride to have been one of the women who had forced open the doors for her and others."[12]

Traveling across England dispensing birth control literature, Kitty found herself falling quickly back into her old militant methods: "I lost no opportunity spreading birth control propaganda wherever I went . . . and left them about in places where they were sure of being found, such as the tool boxes of workmen renovating some of the churches."[13] It wasn't a bomb, but for the workmen at Gloucester Cathedral, Kitty's pamphlet may have had a similarly explosive impact.

Back in America, Kitty watched from afar as the United Kingdom finally awarded women and men the equal right to vote in 1928. It was also a year that brought with it the end of the great leadership of the WSPU; on June 14, Emmeline Pankhurst died. At the end of her life, Emmeline's health had been thrown into rapid decline by the news of her daughter Sylvia's public refusal to marry the man she was living with. To compound what Emmeline viewed as a terrible scandal, Sylvia had proudly given birth to a boy, a story the Brooklyn Daily Eagle carried in 1928 under the heading "Sylvia Pankhurst an Unwed Mother Since Christmas Eve."[14] Defiant of convention, Sylvia had issued a widely reported statement: "My son is the child of a happy union of affection and long friendship of two people who care for each other."[15] In England, the Leeds Mercury carried a photograph of Sylvia lovingly cradling her baby boy, captioned by a quote saying that she had "long wanted a child without the ties of marriage."[16] In retaliation, Emmeline left her entire estate to Christabel, who, after failing to win a seat in the 1918 election, had found religion and moved to America to await the second coming of Christ.

At the end of 1929, Kitty received an invitation to the unveiling of a statue of Emmeline. It was due to take place in March 1930, which she thought would be well timed for her next vacation from selling the Birth Control Review and allow her to visit friends and reminisce about the old days of the suffragettes. "Having been through so much of the 'fight' I felt I was entitled to my part in this festive occasion and decided to go," she declared, obviously determined, if somewhat apprehensive, about returning publicly to the suffragettes after the bitter wound she had suffered so many years earlier.[17]

In the new year, though, just as she had reserved a cabin on the *Ascania* to sail on February 22, she received some unexpected news. The League had decided to stop selling the *Review* on the streets, and so they had no more need of Kitty Marion. "It fell upon me with a sickening thud . . . depriving me of a livelihood."[18] Lost, and without any time to find a job or formulate a plan for what to do next, Kitty left for England. The journey was rough, and heavy fog delayed the *Ascania* for two days, but on March 6, Kitty arrived back in the country she had so often found herself seeking sanctuary in.

> I reached London the day before the unveiling . . . The Unveiling, how can I describe it? Meeting the "Girls of the old brigade!!!," the changed attitude in the police who were most deferential to the "women voters." Even the weather was in harmony with the occasion, sunny and warm just for the day. The ceremony of unveiling Mrs. Pankhurst's Statue by Mr. Stanley Baldwin, who as Prime Minister had signed the Woman Suffrage Bill, was most impressive. At night there was a dinner given in honour of Mrs. E K Marshall through whose efforts and influence the Statue was made, and placed in the gardens near the House of Lords. When I arrived at the dinner, I was placed at the speakers' table at Mrs. Marshall's right. I had not anticipated such honour and felt proud as a peacock . . . especially when I caught sight of Miss Pine, "Piney," who with Mrs. Pankhurst had "cut me dead" in New York. She was at the other end of a long table placed at right angles to the speakers'. We had not met in the crowd at the Unveiling and she was the most surprised woman I ever saw when the Chairman, Mr. F L Pethick Lawrence, MP, announced me to say a few words. I felt thrilled and elated with the spirit of the occasion and while speaking, smilingly watched "Piney" as she gazed at me open-eyed, and referred to Mrs. Drummond at her right, who nodded and smiled, for we had met in the morning. I thoroughly enjoyed the little byplay of which the guests were unconscious, while I referred to Mrs. Pankhurst and the old days, lapsing into my work with Margaret Sanger, whom many people present knew and applauded.[19]

Although she does not explicitly say it, this last line in Kitty's account does seem to imply that she was well aware of the possibility that it was her public work and association with the birth control movement that resulted in Pine and Pankhurst's refusal to acknowledge her in New York.

Visiting London in early August, Margaret Sanger invited Kitty to come and see her before she left for a conference in Zurich. The politics of the American birth control movement were no place for a loyal and outspoken campaigner like Kitty, who survived by the hands-on application of her practical skills as an activist. She would be wasted in New York, and more likely to cause trouble—without meaning to—than to be of aid. Instead, Sanger had found a solution that solved many problems. She was currently president of London's Birth Control International Information Centre (BCIIC), based at 9 Parliament Mansions, which at that time had Edith How-Martyn as director. Edith had been an early member of the WSPU, but had left the suffragettes after the Pankhursts had committed to a campaign of violent militancy. She was a pacifist, and had disapproved of the bombing and arson campaign. She was also a founder of the Suffragette Fellowship, which sought to conserve and protect the legacy and memories of the suffrage movement.

Here were two women, Kitty and Edith, from opposing backgrounds in the women's suffrage movement, now both involved in the fight for women's right to birth control. Sanger thought this was ideal, and suggested that Kitty work as a birth control pamphleteer for the center, a job she would excel at, for three months, at three pounds a week. Kitty was delighted; here was work that allowed her to stay in England and also made her feel useful again. She found a room for rent near the BCIIC, and Edith quickly set her to work distributing leaflets across the city that contained the addresses of every birth control clinic in every part of London. "The surprise of most women when they heard of prevention instead of abortion, was an eye-opener," Kitty recalled.[20] It was here she was happiest. Retracing the routes and old pathways of her suffrage and music hall days, Kitty found herself continually aware of all of the different lives she had lived in London, each layer woven on top of the other. Not long after she had begun work at the BCIIC, Kitty paid a visit to 108 Whitfield Street, then the location of the clinic of the most well-known British birth control campaigner, and author of *Married Love*, Marie Stopes:

> I received a most flattering reception from one of her secretaries, Mrs. Elizabeth Bootle, to whom my appearance in the flesh was "like a wonderful dream come true." She remembered seeing me "on the halls" when she was quite a youngster and was a great admirer of mine. Then she followed me in the papers through the Suffrage movement, then I turned up in the Birth Control Review and at last here I was myself. It was "wonderful!" It was, and most stimulating to me.[21]

Standing at the threshold of what seemed to be a new sexual revolution, Kitty was reminded of the experiences that had set her on her path to becoming a suffragette and ended with her activism for the birth control movement. As she reflected on her past lives, the music hall's attitude to sex and how the industry had treated the women within it would have weighed heavily on her mind. The halls had had a long and complex relationship with the women who walked their stages, manipulating and objectifying them in equal measure. But fixation on the horrific experiences Kitty and her companions had suffered left no room for the possibility that there were also women who enjoyed and embraced consenting sexual experiences, and who did not conform to the prudish and anti-sex doctrines of the feminist movements. This was the group of women Kitty belonged to, and she and women like her were responsible for pushing the acceptance and acknowledgment of female sexuality to the forefront of the modern feminist movement.

As Mary Shelley was creating her monster, the song and supper clubs, the music hall's earliest incarnation, were full of songs with titles like

"He Did It Before My Face"—where the opening verse began "One day, as I was walking out / And crossing o'er the plain / I suddenly beheld, O dear / A very handsome swain; / And while I looked at him about / and viewed his manly grace / A certain member he pulled out / He did, before my face."—and "The Flea Shooter," featuring a thinly disguised metaphor for female masturbation; not to mention the far more explicit "The Ladies and the Candle," the language of which is clearly, overtly sexual.[22] When the music halls arrived, and while Kitty was taking her early steps on their stage, Marie Lloyd sang of winking "the other eye" and Marie Collins issued her passionate declaration that "Life was made for pleasure, so enjoy it without measure."[23]

Female sexual agency was not created solely by the enfranchisement of women in 1928; in fact, by the nineteenth century birth control was already widely available and continually discussed. From 1898 to 1900, the *Illustrated Police News* ran weekly advertisements for "French and American Letters," "Rubber Preventive Devices," and "Malthusian Appliances" alongside "Saucy Songs" and general news.[24] These early condoms were offered from numerous different agents, based variously in Holywell Street, Wych Street, King's Cross, and across north London.

Birth control was clearly, then, not a secret in the 1890s, but its rejection by the early suffrage societies created a world where respectable women, women who deserved the vote, were not supposed to know anything about sex. Kitty contradicted that belief passionately, but she was unaware of, or perhaps simply dismissed as ridiculous, the prudish notions of some suffrage activists that sex was something to be ashamed of or that sexual knowledge was something a respectable woman should not have. She knew from her life in the music halls that sex was something *everyone* had an interest in. Women were no different than men in that regard. In the decade before Annie Besant chose to publish *Fruits of Philosophy* came the story of Emma Devine, "a good-looking girl, only 13 years of age," who was accused of stealing from the St. John's Wood home of Mr. James Tipping, where she had been engaged as a nursemaid.[25] On her arrest, the girl was found to have "a song of the most infamous character" among her belongings.[26] When she was asked how she had obtained such a disgusting and immoral song, Emma had replied that she had been given it by another young girl in Lisson Grove.[27] A gentleman gave it to her and it was done up in an envelope. "That's how girls get them, sir," she informed the judge.[28]

So often we think that the desire of women for sexual knowledge and understanding is a luxury experienced only by modern Western women, but by looking more closely at our history it is clear that these attitudes have been part of much of human culture for a very, very long time. Women enjoy sex, they want to have sex, and they want to have sex as safely as possible, without the risk of getting pregnant. Perhaps surprisingly, the idea of mutual sexual fulfillment, albeit within the boundaries of married life, was highly influential during the Victorian era.[29] Although sex outside marriage was often seen in a negative light by the press, sex within marriage was hugely important.[30] Both *Etiquette of Marriage* (1857) and *The Lover's Guide to Courtship and Marriage* (1883) argue for the valuable impact married life would have on an individual, while texts such as *Dr. Teller's Pocket Companion, or Marriage Guide: being a popular treatise on the anatomy and physiology of the genital organs, in both sexes, with their uses and abuses; together with a complete history of secret diseases, their causes, symptoms and treatment, in plain language devoid of all technicalities* (1865), and *Fruits of Philosophy: An essay on the population question . . . Second new edition, with notes* (1877) went into practical details of the sex act, fertility, and contraception for their readers, albeit in varying detail, as they either attempted to flout the obscenity laws or refused to comply with them.

This was the sex education heritage Margaret Sanger intended to build on. Kitty served as a unifying symbol; she brought the practical, open sexual culture of the music halls, the reality of the world many people lived in offstage, into the feminist activism she had always fought for. But she was not going to find it easy. The suffragette leadership had a difficult relationship with sex, often seeing it as the main cause of women's subjugation in society. For women like Kitty, who had experienced violent abuse but were also able to see sex between consenting partners as something to be protected and celebrated, the suffragettes' black and white approach was never going to work.

When Kitty had telephoned the birth control headquarters at 104 Fifth Avenue, New York, to book tickets to Margaret Sanger's Carnegie Hall speech in 1917, she had professed her ignorance of "Malthus, Bradlaugh, and Mrs. Annie Besant, as pioneers in the movement."[31] This is somewhat surprising, given that Emmeline Pankhurst had previously enjoyed a close relationship with Annie Besant, and would have been well aware of her publication and promotion of birth control methods. Annie Besant had even become a frequent visitor to Mrs. Pankhurst's home in the 1880s while they fought against the horrific conditions suffered by working-class women in the East End match factories.[32] Although Pankhurst calls her the "celebrated Mrs. Annie Besant" in her 1914 autobiography *My Own Story*, there has never been any investigation into the relationship between these two women; one among the most important birth control campaigners of her time and the other the figurehead of the women's suffrage movement in England.[33] Annie Besant, much like Kitty Marion, has not been seen as worthy of serious investigation by feminist historians; and Annie's contemporaries wanted nothing to do with a woman who would advocate for sexual freedom at a time when they were insisting such independence only resulted in female disempowerment.

So why did early feminists struggle so much with the idea of safe sex? The rejection of the birth control movement by nineteenth-century feminists has colored our entire understanding of the history of women and sexual relationships. This rejection was due to the complex relationship between suffrage, respectability, and sexual permissiveness that has dominated feminist thought from the 1820s onward. This in turn has informed our view of women's agency and sexuality, as female sexual identities were co-opted by nineteenth-century feminists to form the basis of a narrative of victimhood. The rejection of birth control as a disreputable form of sex tied sexual permissiveness, and therefore sexual independence, to immoral female behavior.

When Francis Place, the father of the British birth control movement, was attempting to reconcile the views of Mary Wollstonecraft's husband, William Godwin, with Thomas Malthus, he published an early pamphlet in favor of birth control. This led to one of the earliest rejections of birth control by a prominent female figure, Mary Fields, in 1823.[34] Fields was a member of the Manchester Reform Society, and both she and her husband were forced to deny, publicly, that they supported Place's ideas after receiving a number of his pamphlets and a letter asking her to distribute them.[35] The implication that Fields would support birth control was too great a risk to her social standing and respectability to be ignored. As the nineteenth century progressed, the rise of the *demi-mondaines*, young, attractive, and increasingly adventurous women who did not conform to the respectable idea of sexual social identity, threatened the security and economic stability of the marital home.[36] If birth control became legitimized, it was possible that the arguments of the women's movement—led by Contagious Diseases Act–repealer Josephine Butler and founded on stories of female victimhood—could begin to lose power.

The suffrage movement of the 1860s–1890s divided women into two groups and set them against each other: those who were good, and those who were bad. And those who were bad were automatically classified as sex workers. Not only did feminists fear the possibility of disease being spread from a man who slept with a sex worker to his wife, and possibly his children, but if he kept a mistress, she would take a share of the financial security intended for his family.[37]

Opposition to birth control was not, then, based on a feminist reaction to radical or religious reasons, but on social fear. Legitimizing sexual freedom and the women who traded in sex or objectification— often conflated with the women of the music halls—would have a detrimental impact on those fighting for women's rights, who conversely suffered the most from their lack of sexual knowledge, as they were unable either to stop or to limit STD infections that might be passed to them by their promiscuous husbands. To combat and silence the women who did support birth control, the opposing feminist side focused on the implications of the actions or morals of a woman who "desired sexual intercourse without reproduction," invariably labeling them whores and specifically reducing their sexuality to an economic trade, rather than an erotic or romantic connection.[38]

Millicent Fawcett, a prominent member of the women's movement, had refused to testify during Annie Besant's trial, and another notable early feminist, Elizabeth Blackwell, denounced contraception as "a national danger."[39] These attitudes, either fear or fearmongering, have directed British feminist history for the last 150 years. All discussion or acknowledgment of birth control is historically placed after women have achieved the vote, with the rise of Marie Stopes—who some claim to have been a "one-time member of WSPU"—and her publication of *Married Love*.[40]

The rejection of birth control by the conservative feminist movement, until the legitimization of female enfranchisement, has created an assumption that female sexual agency could not have existed prior to 1918. But birth control was clearly a widely acknowledged topic in the nineteenth century, just as much as the women who engaged in the subject, promoted, and used it. Perhaps their absence from our current history has been due to an unwillingness by feminist historians to see challenges to their early history. Or has it been seen as a threat to the foundational history on which the women's rights movement is based?

Feminist attitudes to birth control did change with the campaigns of Margaret Sanger and Marie Stopes, both of whom can be linked to suffrage organizations; it was only with their influence that birth control became an accepted feminist issue. Before this point, birth control had been used by early feminist campaigners to denounce women, not to support them. Christabel Pankhurst in particular "chose to excite sex hatred . . . as a spur to revolutionary violence" by focusing on the sexual immorality of men and the damage it wreaked on women's lives.[41] So the message from one of the most important figures in the suffragette movement was that birth control would not help women, but rather only allow men to continue to abuse them—that they could seek sexual gratification from wives, or sexually available women, without risk of pregnancy but continuing the risk of infection and disease. This was Christabel Pankhurst's belief, and the publication of *The Great Scourge and How To End It* in 1913 played resoundingly on the sexual politics of chaste, innocent middle-class women against the victimized, destitute women of the working class and the threat of male sexual debauchery.[42]

Kitty Marion's entrance into the history of birth control is both surprising, given her involvement with the British suffrage movement, and unsurprising, given her personality. When *The Great Scourge* was published, Kitty wrote that it caused "a terrific sensation and discussion" by advocating a "warning against venereal diseases, white slavery, and insisting upon an absolute moral standard between the sexes."[43] But, loyal to the end, she does not mention her own feelings on this view after working for the birth control movement. For Kitty, there is a deep and continual connection between her life as a suffragette and her later work as a birth control activist; throughout her life, you cannot separate one from the other, each of her experiences feeding in to creating one determined and committed feminist solider.

It is unsurprising that Kitty, adrift in a new country for the second time in her life, gravitated toward the social organizations geared toward women's rights as a place in which to find security and acceptance. However, what will always be surprising are the types of organizations she chose to become involved with. She was a music hall actress, a militant suffragette, and finally a birth control activist. Throughout her life she maintained a deep and unwavering commitment to the concept of respectability, and yet she was connected to some of the most disreputable social and cultural identities of the nineteenth and early twentieth centuries. Although Kitty's music hall experience was beneficial to the suffrage movement before the war, and later to Margaret Sanger, she could never be—and refused to be—solely identified as a militant, but would always be connected in some way to the sexually active world of the music hall. Even though Kitty made clear her own belief in an actress's respectability, her connection to the birth control movement could have potentially brought to light any hidden fears the suffrage movement had toward her own sexual permissiveness. Kitty could not escape the prudish belief held by many that actresses were little better than whores, and her choice to promote birth control—something she believed would ultimately benefit humankind—had the potential to remove her from the respectable circles she had previously inhabited. Kitty was arrested nine times between 1918 and 1928 for selling the *Birth Control Review*[44] but, as these arrests were no longer in the noble name of "women's suffrage," instead now in the promotion of methods and social activism that her fellow suffragettes had historically rejected, it left her place in the remaining suffragette movement on shaky ground.[45] Kitty's life within the birth control movement, and her faith in it as a cause, were not guided by the idea of population control over physical pleasure, as Annie Besant might have protested; rather, it was informed by her lived experience. Although she suffered serious abuse and assault during her working life, Kitty also paid attention to and thought it was important to record the many happy and sexually fulfilled relationships that she encountered among her friends, as well as her own feelings of desire and attraction, although it seems she may have never fully acted on them.[46]

Almost a year after she left New York, rudely ousted from the organization she had helped build and promote for over a decade, on January 19, 1931, Kitty returned to America, bidding England a final goodbye from the port of Southampton. She was a naturalized citizen of the United States, a wanderer finally home, yet it appears she never truly felt she belonged to the country. She was sixty years old, but as determined as ever to support herself and earn her living. Calling on Margaret Sanger, Kitty felt sure that she would be able to find some way, any small way, to be of service to the movement she had spent so much of her later life serving. But there was nothing for her. The new leaders of the birth control movement, much like the old leaders of the suffrage movement, wanted nothing to do with the old warhorse on their doorstep, a reminder of battles fought and tactics past.

> I walked home in a trance, conscious of an aching, icy void in the regions of my heart and solar plexus. Was it possible? I, who had felt so sure of steady work with Margaret Sanger and Birth Control... who by my thirteen years' work had helped to build up the Birth Control movement in America, the two factions of which had now "ousted" me. Was it just, ethical? What a smashup of "clay gods"![47]

When the final copy of the *Birth Control Review* reached her in July 1933, Kitty, now surviving on handouts from old friends, felt a bitter pang at the loss of her employment and identity for one last time. The *Review* had been taken off the streets as a concession to the medical doctors, "scientists and 'Society' within and outside of the League, who considered that way of most effective advertising 'degrading.'"[48] Now, three and a half years after they had unceremoniously ousted Kitty and removed the *Review* from the streets, the publication was dead.

Kitty felt utterly betrayed. As far as she was concerned, the medical profession was the biggest enemy to freedom and validity of birth control, even with the support of the few who had been brave enough to join Margaret Sanger's cause. But even with the League's continual campaigning and international appeal, there had been no change to the laws; "millions of poor, American women [were] still at the mercy of blind, uncontrolled nature and the inhumanity of their selfish, arrogant, dictatorial, would-be 'saviours' who tolerate no method of help and assistance."[49]

The burning rage at the unfairness of the world and its treatment of women, that rage that had driven her to fight against her father, to go on the stage, to reject the status quo of abuse and join the suffragettes, and, finally, to join the birth control movement—that rage still burned passionately, decades later. Kitty's anger and frustration, as she sat down to write her autobiography, at a world that no longer felt she was worthy of the fight, is clear. After all her battles, all the fights and prison sentences, imprisonment and force-feeding, after all of that, what good was the vote if it did not change the reality of women's everyday lives? What good were these organizations if they had not forced laws that protect women to be put in place? She offered a final, brutal judgment:

> As for me, whatever the future holds, I thank God that when I shuffle off this mortal coil, I am leaving none of mine in this Frankenstein of a civilisation, to perpetuate, or be victims of, human inhumanity, which makes this otherwise beautiful world unfit to live in.[50]

But this was not the end of Kitty. Like those of many battle-scarred fighters, her final years would be spent in peace. She had, for some time, shared a close friendship with Annie Gray, the director of the Women's Peace Society, and, learning of Kitty's dire circumstances, Annie offered her the job of an office girl at the Society's headquarters, at ten dollars a week. Kitty would work for Annie until the Society's lack of funds forced it to close the office in 1934, and she felt she was undergoing a "Spiritual Metamorphosis."[51] For the first time in her life, she was part of a movement whose motto was pacifism, not aggression.

As Europe began to move toward its second horrifying world war, Annie became treasurer of the American League Against War and Fascism, an organization set up to combat the rising tide of fascism and Nazi ideology flowing from Germany. Having been raised in the freedom and combined cultures of Jewish and Christian Germans in her grandparents' village, Kitty did not find Germany's new ideology in any way acceptable. Although many of the records left by her in England stop after 1934, a letter from 1938 to an old suffrage friend survives and reports that: "Irene Harand, who wrote 'Sein Kampf,' an answer to Hitler, spoke at a luncheon of Judge Parris' Current Events discussion group . . . got quite a fine, enthusiastic group together."[52] Even approaching seventy, Kitty refused to fade away or ignore what threatened the world around her. Her life had been spent in pursuit of an equal society, a better place for everyone, man or woman, rich or poor, whoever they might be. Her faith in the human spirit, in the face of tragedy and brutal life experience, was resolute, surviving every blow and every betrayal. She believed, to her last, that a better world was just around the corner.

10

Kitty's Legacy—
One Hundred Years Later

Kitty Marion died on October 9, 1944, aged seventy-three. Her life ended in the New York borough of Manhattan, where she was a naturalized citizen of the last country to give her refuge. The remaining years of her life feel like a mystery; her autobiography ends in 1934, and there are very few records of her after that. However, just before Christmas 1938, as Europe was moving toward a new world war, she wrote to friends in England detailing her plans for her autobiography, which existed at the time in three manuscript copies. She sent one to Alice Green, the close confidante of Emily Wilding Davison, and one to Edith How-Martyn, who had set up the Suffragette Fellowship in 1926 to conserve and protect the memory of the WSPU. "You say in your letter how difficult it is to get money, hence no hope for my book," Kitty wrote to Edith, with her customary forthrightness. "I didn't ask for money, merely to have the script read by some of you and an opinion given as to if anything could be done with it, and make an effort to get it published."[1]

How did those distant comrades feel, reading a story that exposed some of the most intricate workings of the suffragettes, and detailed the reality of sex, activism, and what it meant to be a woman during some of the most exciting events in feminist history? Not everyone shared Kitty's belief in the truth. And, unknowingly, she may have actually sent a copy of her manuscript to the very people who would be determined to suppress it. Eight years earlier, while planning a potential memoir of Emily Wilding Davison, another close friend, Edith Mansell Moullin, had also written to Edith How-Martyn asking for her advice on a difficult issue. Should she, "(as I do) . . . leave out the bombs?"[2] Only two years after universal franchise had been awarded to men and women over the age of twenty-one, there was no need to remind people of the true actions of the suffragettes in the fight for the vote. A determined sanitization was already under way, as a creation of the perfect "Suffragette Spirit"—a noble heroine whose purity and morality were the reason men had come to their senses and awarded women the vote—became the idolized cultural memory of the fighters of the WSPU. After the horrors of the First World War, and with almost a generation having passed since the suffragettes' campaign, a careful misconstruction was taking place. Gathering together the memoirs, artifacts, and ephemera from hundreds of different activists, behind the scenes quiet, subversive decisions were being made about just what and who would become part of the public record of the suffragettes.

"By the way, when you get hold of that script you may keep it for your museum, instead of my sending a copy which is not so perfectly typed," Kitty had written, hopeful that, if publication was not an option, her record would at least be safe, preserved for future generations. She knew her story could not, and should not, be forgotten. Yet, although it was intensely detailed, Kitty's autobiography was also a carefully constructed and edited version of her life. Deciding to cut all ties with her family by her early twenties, she never named her parents, but a year before she sent her meticulously typed manuscripts to England, she had applied for the new Social Security program offered in New York. On her 1937 application, under Social Security Number 121016689, she named her parents, Gustav and Lena Schäfer. Clearly, their omission from her autobiography was not accidental, but purposeful. They exist as constructs and shadows, the abusive father and loving mother, who brought this activist and warrior into being. Leaving them unnamed removes the power they had over Kitty's life as a child, and in their absence our focus becomes the life of this incredible woman, as she wanted to be remembered.

In her own manuscript, Kitty included only enough information to support her memories; she provided a detailed account only for the attack for which she was arrested and imprisoned, the burning down of Hurst Park. Evidence of her responsibility for many of the WSPU's multiple arson and bomb attacks comes from subtle hints and wry comments left in her manuscript, alongside her detailed militant scrapbook, which she never mentions the existence of in any record. Without this unique document, conserved by history, we would have little knowledge of the life she led, and therefore, of the reality of her actions. She is the ultimate enigma, a woman who seems to tell you everything and yet holds back so much. In a final twist, on the New York census of 1940 she lists herself as married, but alone and the head of the household—clearly a fabrication. She is recorded as living at 230 West 22nd Street, the same apartment from which she sent the copies of her manuscript to the UK. This seems to simply be a last joke by a woman determined never to marry, and a suffragette about to enter her seventies, for whom censuses would always represent an opportunity for rebellion.

Four years later she died, having taken as many steps as possible to make sure her life and contribution to the suffragettes and the birth control movement would be preserved. Her death was reported by Reuters and appeared in various forms across the newspapers. Under the heading of "Former Suffragette Dead," on October 11, the *Liverpool Daily Post, Birmingham Daily Gazette, Daily Record*, and *Nottingham Journal* all carried a report of her death, although the details were muddy. It fell to the *Birmingham Gazette* to provide, barring her age, the most accurate account:

Miss Kitty Marion, a leading member of the Suffragette movement before the last war, has died in New York, aged 71. She was arrested seven times in Britain for her activities, which included setting fire to the stand at Hurst Park Racecourse in 1913. She went to America as a crusader for the birth control movement, and was last heard of living in poor circumstances at Greenwich Village, New York's Chelsea.[3]

It was far too mild an epitaph for one of the suffragette movement's "Wild Wreckers," not to mention for a woman who had fought against sexual harassment throughout her working life, and campaigned to provide women with access to birth control and sexual advice from the United States to the UK, until her final breath. But how would she react to the world around us now, exactly one hundred years after the women of England won the first round in the battle for the vote?

At the time of writing, we are in the midst of the Harvey Weinstein scandal, the latest in a long line of reports of sexual abuse in Hollywood. In almost every decade since the 1920s, women have come forward with their accounts of sexual assault and manipulation at the hands of famous stars, agents, and industry heavyweights, yet time and time again they have been dismissed and ignored, often facing serious professional and personal consequences simply for trying to obtain justice. These stories are clear examples that the culture of sexual manipulation and abuse Kitty spent her whole life fighting so hard against has changed little since her death.

On October 5, 2017, Jodi Kantor and Megan Twohey, journalists from *The New York Times*, published an in-depth investigation into the repeated payoffs made by powerful movie producer Harvey Weinstein to a multitude of actresses and female assistants who had accused him of sexual harassment. Working through emails, litigations, and interviews with his victims, Kantor and Twohey unearthed more than three decades of abuse, and revealed at least eight financial settlements, ranging from 1990 to 2015, between the women and Weinstein, to keep quiet about his assaults. Much like the women in Kitty's world, whose

only opportunity to seek justice or retribution for a man's sexual mis-
conduct was by suing him for breach of promise, the women who
accepted financial restitution from Weinstein did so because it was the
only option open to them—their sole chance for justice. The power he
wielded in the entertainment industry was known to make or break
careers, and women who refused him would soon find their promising careers stalled, with offers of movie roles or meetings with industry professionals suddenly vanishing. More than a hundred years later,
the experiences Kitty had at the hands of music hall agents were still
being repeated, as women seeking work found that some of those who
controlled the industry were only willing to offer them opportunities
in return for sex.

The *New York Times* article, along with a separate piece in *The New
Yorker* published on October 10, 2017, a searingly brutal exposé of
Weinstein's behavior by Ronan Farrow, brought the issue to crisis
point and, on October 15, the Academy of Motion Picture Arts and Sci-
ences stripped Weinstein of his membership. It issued a statement: "We
do so not simply to separate ourselves from someone who does not
merit the respect of his colleagues but also to send a message that the
era of willful ignorance and shameful complicity in sexually predatory
behavior and workplace harassment in our industry is over."[4] Strong
words, over a hundred years in the making.

The public ostracization of Harvey Weinstein, and the scale of alle-
gations, reaching both across decades and across continents, opened
the floodgates to further stories and reports of sexual abuse, assault,
and harassment throughout Hollywood. A viral hashtag campaign
called #MeToo saw women and men across the world tweet, post,
and blog about their own experiences of sexual harassment in their
workplace, homes, and daily lives.[5] It had a startling effect in the UK:
triggering the resignation of a cabinet minister and an investigation
into sexual harassment at the heart of the British government; while in
the United States, President Donald Trump remained dogged by accusations of sexual assault from multiple women, a number of whom

found #MeToo gave them the courage to step forward publicly with their accusations. What a stunning, and long-awaited, cultural shift. A century earlier, and throughout his battles with the suffragettes, the then prime minister Herbert Asquith, as he was approaching sixty, was well known to have a "little harem" made up of the young women in his daughter's circle. His behavior ran from "flirting, a kiss, an intimate touch," to letters signed "your lover always."[6] Asquith's position as prime minister, overseeing one of the greatest moments of social revolution and civil rebellion England has ever experienced, at the hands of the suffragettes, obviously made him the most powerful man in government at that time; yet, like so many men in public power, he made full use of the opportunity to behave badly in private.

Asquith's behavior and attitude toward women did not go unnoticed at the time. Clementine Hozier, then newly married to Winston Churchill, held an active disdain for "Mr. Asquith's predilection for peering down 'Pennsylvania Avenue' (the contemporary expression for a lady's cleavage) whenever he was seated next to a pretty woman."[7] But even though this was the time of the suffragettes, Asquith's behavior would never be revealed in public; there was no prospect of bringing down such a powerful man.

A Hollywood star of an earlier age, the legendary Marilyn Monroe, refused to disguise her contempt for the men, the "wolves," who used Hollywood as their hunting ground as Weinstein would decades later:

> I met them all. Phoniness and failure were all over them. Some were vicious and crooked. But they were as near to the movies as you could get. So you sat with them, listening to their lies and schemes. And you saw Hollywood with their eyes—an overcrowded brothel, a merry-go-round with beds for horses.[8]

Monroe's celebrated looks and body, and her sensual femininity, were continually used against her, part of a culture that, as well as privileging male power and turning a blind eye to sexual misdemeanor, refused to allow women any sense of independence in their own sexuality. This is key to why women like Kitty have been largely erased from our history. As conservative feminism took a viselike grip of our history and the suffragettes began to sanitize their own story, the women who saw sex, freedom, and independence as a universal right were ignored, as were the real lives and experiences of the women who had fought so hard and risked so much. The historian Laura E. Nym Mayhall identified the importance of "a small group of former suffragettes" in the 1920s and 1930s who "created a highly stylised story" of the WSPU and the history of suffrage in England, which emphasized "women's martyrdom and passivity."[9] It was this group that compiled the documents, memoirs, and memorabilia that now form the basis of the Suffragette Fellowship Collection held by the Museum of London.[10] Although this is an incredible collection, Nym Mayhall points out that it has "come to serve as a basis for much of the current scholarship on the women's suffrage movement"; the Fellowship decided what constituted appropriate suffrage history, and which stories should be reduced or left out, creating a "master narrative of the militant suffrage movement" and those it involved.[11] At its most extreme, the Fellowship "lobbied to have incorrect passages excised from forthcoming memoirs or removed from subsequent editions of accounts already published."[12]

Perhaps this is a reason for Kitty's absence from the historical record, and her fleeting, rare occurrences in the histories written by second- and third-wave feminists. Her autobiography holds one further clue as to why she has been continually excluded. After attending one of the early Suffragette Fellowship meetings, Kitty angrily recorded:

> To my utter amazement and disappointment I found that many of my old militant comrades were opposed to birth control, for all the same stupid "reasons" one usually meets. Most of them elderly, single women who have had a regular income all their lives without having to work for it in an overcrowded labour market.[13]

Here, the clear divide between Kitty's life experience and the experiences of the majority of the middle-class suffragettes becomes apparent. Although she was dedicated to "the cause," Kitty's working life in the music halls and her experience of female agency, freedom, and independence gave her a view of the world that other suffragettes could not, and would not, understand. What Kitty discovered when faced with the "stupid reasons" from "elderly, single women" was the dominant view British feminism had taken toward sex and female agency since the nineteenth century: that sex was bad and something women were only ever going to be the victims of.

It was Kitty's experiences as a suffragette, in combination with her experiences as a music hall actress, that pushed her not to reject birth control but to embrace it. She was one of the earliest sex-positive feminists; she understood how power could be abused, but she also acknowledged that not every sexual relationship or encounter was about a power imbalance. In a world so often concerned with black and white—men bad, women good—Kitty and others like her saw all the many shades of gray. Women's enjoyment of sex should never be a threat to their independence. It should never be something that resulted in their abuse or manipulation. But Kitty's connection to the birth control movement and her refusal to shy away from the actions she had carried out on the orders of the WSPU were clearly viewed by middle-class suffragettes as so damaging as to compel those who created the suffragette legacy to ignore or abandon her story.

But surely, even if the suffragettes were determined to ignore Kitty Marion at the time, historians would eventually find her? After all, her autobiography did exist, held in the archives and museums that so much suffrage history has been built from. Why is she so absent in our history? Is this absence perhaps evidence of a determined bias in how we remember our feminist history, ignoring or concealing suffragette violence? Ever since Edith Mansell Moullin wrote to the Suffrage Fellowship in 1930, seeking permission and advice on whether she should discuss the bombs, we have seen the slow removal of these women and their actions from our public cultural memory.

Leading social historian Brian Harrison, writing in the 1970s, fleetingly referred to Kitty's autobiography as ". . . little more than an unreflective catalogue of [music hall] engagements."[14] This offhand remark is a scathing review of a work dominated by Kitty's personal philosophy on women's rights, experiences of sexual assault, and suffrage activism, which was left as a record of her motivations and her life within the global women's movement. For future scholars of the women's movement, such a quick dismissal by a leading historian may well have led them to ignore or pass over this source, and so they may be unaware of the wealth of evidence contained within it on the suffragettes' arson and bombing campaign, birth control activism in the early twentieth century, and the sexual attitudes of men and women in the Victorian era.

What is particularly surprising about Kitty's absence from our history is the intense effort she undertook to see her history conserved— multiple copies of her autobiography are in existence in both London and New York; a copy is held by the New York Public Library, along with her original papers and notes, and two copies are held in the UK, one in the archive of the Museum of London and one in the holdings of the Women's Library, now conserved by the London School of Economics (LSE). At least two copies of the autobiography have been permanently on public access since Kitty wrote them, via either the Women's Library or the New York Public Library, and yet this remarkable woman has been ignored and forgotten by history and historians alike. She has been reduced to a sentence, a name in a list, in works on suffrage or birth control in Britain, even though she worked and appeared continually in both campaigns. It is clear now that, whatever the reason for her earlier exclusion, Kitty's voice is critical to our understanding of the suffragettes, violence, sex, and the complex history of birth control in both the United States and the UK.

* * *

In the last years of Kitty's life, as she made plans for her legacy, the two copies of her manuscript had reached England and she was hoping that a publisher might be found; or at least that one copy would be held in an archive, so that her story would not be lost. Little could she have foreseen that the safekeeping she hoped for would in fact lead to her story being silenced for ninety years. But now, in 2018, it can be told for the very first time.

Writing and researching this book, I have been overwhelmed by the impression of strength and power that comes from women speaking for themselves. So often we try to reinterpret someone's thoughts and feelings from a moment lost to history, but in Kitty's case, she recorded her reactions, her beliefs, and her experiences in such detail that there was very little left for me to do but dress the stage and let her walk out on it. I hope this goes some way to giving her one final curtain call, and places her incredible life in its rightful and prominent position in our history.

At times, the revelations made me extremely uncomfortable. Reading descriptions of bombs loaded with nails, timed to explode when their makers or setters were long gone and had little opportunity to ensure the building, train, street, or theater would, in fact, be empty, or of attacks that clearly endangered the lives of both the suffragettes and the innocent people around them, made me question both the morals of the women involved and the idea of venerating these soldier suffragettes.

So is it possible to accept our heroes as flawed? This is a question I have returned to over and over again while piecing together Kitty's life. On one hand, she was a woman whose choices, activism, and pursuit of justice to protect women—women just like me—from sexual harassment, abuse, and manipulation is something I can easily idolize. I can fall in love with a romanticized idea of bands of passionate women, running around the countryside in the dead of night with guns loaded with blanks, cans of gasoline and firelighters, breaking into the empty or abandoned home of The Man, and setting fire to it as a beacon of rebellion. I can hear the breathless laughter, I can almost feel the adrenaline, I can picture what it would have been like—frost crunching under your shoes in the twilight, the heavy bag, the intense, addictive relationship between doing something bad, something criminal, and the commitment to the holy cause of your shared sisterhood. How alive it would make you feel, how powerful.

But on the other hand, there is the brutal destruction of homes, places of worship, trains, communication networks, and the chemical and physical attacks on ministers, postmen—people going about their daily lives. Perhaps growing up with the constant threat of terror, and in a time when so many of our wars for equal rights have been fought and won—enables us to see what has so often been dismissed or sanitized before: that the suffragettes were truly dangerous. They wanted to terrorize and destroy the very fabric of British society, and they were committed to doing so with a violent and aggressive campaign. For all that the official line and leadership claimed to value human life, who knows how far the violence could have gone if the First World War hadn't stopped it?

I cannot reconcile these two halves of the same whole. I cannot excuse the actions of the suffragettes, but I will always support their reasons for fighting. So I have learned to accept one idea above all others: history is not supposed to be comfortable. It should always be questioned; it should always be held to account. False idols are the most dangerous gift history can give you. If we choose to ignore or sanitize the actions of those who founded our societies, who changed them and, in the long run, made them a better, fairer place to live, we choose a life of ignorance and lies. Heroes can be corrupted, leaders can make terrible choices, but each moment, each action—whether questionable or justified—has led us to where we are today.

Kitty's choices were shared by so many within the suffragette movement, and yet we know so little about them. They have been erased from the record, deleted by a process of PR and simplified storytelling. This has lost us so many opportunities to find out about the real lives, and the real cost, women experienced during the fight for the vote. A life like Kitty's acts as a telescope, and as we change focus each era of her life comes into view, each one intimately connected to the other. They are all held together by the same force of will, the same strength of character that saw an abused runaway flee across the sea to England, pursue her dreams, find them shattered, and fight back, not only for herself, but for all the women around her; through sexual abuse to the suffragettes, from bombs to birth control, her life spans the end of the Victorian era, two world wars, multiple prisons, countries, and continents, and sets the stage for almost every battle modern feminism has fought in the last hundred years. She was a true revolutionary, never frightened to stand up for what she believed was right, for what she knew to be true. Her incredible life cannot remain in the dark any longer—like a true star, Kitty Marion must always shine.

With Thanks

This book has been a dream of mine since 2012. Researching for my PhD, I first met Kitty Marion on paper in the archives of the Museum of London. I will be forever indebted to Beverly Cook for that introduction, as well as her awe-inspiring expertise and support of a young researcher who became so quickly obsessed with her subject. Historians are nothing without the support and knowledge of archivists, and over the last few years, as I have pieced together Kitty's story, I have been overwhelmingly grateful for their expertise and guidance many times. The generosity of Victoria Iglikowski, at the National Archives, in answering both my wailing emails and frantic phone calls pursing wild theories and missing records, led to some of my favorite discoveries regarding the suffragettes' bomb-making activities. Kitty's papers lie scattered across two continents, multiple archives, and personal records, and bringing them all together for the first time has been an adventure.

My faith that this story needed to be told received a generous shot in the arm thanks to the encouragement of Matthew Sweet and Brad Beaven, whose comments on my PhD shaped and informed many of the arguments within this book. I also owe a debt of thanks to Lyndsey Jenkins, Kate Wiles, and David Andress, who refused to let me give up on bringing Kitty's story to life. This has only been possible thanks to the determination of my fantastic agent, Kirsty McLachlan, and my incredible editor, Maddy Price.

Finally, my love and thanks to my long-suffering and intensely supportive family, who have challenged and argued with me throughout my writing. I am a better historian because of you.

Notes

Manchester, 1913

1. *Leeds Mercury*, November 12, 1913.

To Begin

1. *Daily Record*, April 17, 1914; see also HO 144/599/184276 for other force-feedings Marion was subjected to.

2. *Dundee Courier*, April 7 and 10, 1913.

3. HO 144/1721/221874 (investigation into Marion, including the letter and subsequent findings).

Chapter 1

1. Barbara Caine (1997) "Victorian feminism and the ghost of Mary Wollstonecraft," *Women's Writing*, 4:2, pp. 261–75, p. 261; Jessie Bouchert (1858) "Maria Edgeworth," *English Woman's Journal*, 2, p. 11.

2. Janet Todd, *Mary Wollstonecraft: A Revolutionary Life* (Weidenfeld & Nicholson, 2000), p. 11.

3. Mary Wollstonecraft, *A Vindication of the Rights of Woman: with Strictures on Political and Moral Subjects* (J. Johnson, 1792; reprint New York, 1833), p. 46.

4. William Godwin, *Memoirs of the Author of a Vindication of the Rights of Woman* (J. Johnson, 1798; 2001 edition), p. 95.

5. William Godwin, *Enquiry concerning political justice, and its influence on morals and happiness*, Vol. 2 (London, 1793; reprint 1842), p. 243.

6. "The Literature of the Social Evil," *Saturday Review*, October 6, 1860, and Lynda Nead, *Myths of Sexuality: Representations of Women in Victorian Britain* (Wiley-Blackwell, 1988), p. 1.

7. Judith R. Walkowitz and Daniel J. Walkowitz, "'We Are Not Beasts of the Field': Prostitution and the Poor in Plymouth and Southampton under the Contagious Diseases Acts," *Feminist Studies* (1973), pp. 73–106; Glen Petrie, *A Singular Iniquity: The Campaigns of Josephine Butler* (Macmillan, 1971); Philip Howell, "A private Contagious Diseases Act: prostitution and public space in Victorian Cambridge," *Journal of Historical Geography* 26.3 (2000), pp. 376–402.

8. "The Contagious Diseases Acts," *Daily News*, December 28, 1869.

9. Margaret Hamilton, "Opposition to the Contagious Diseases Acts, 1864–1886," *Albion*, 10.01 (1978), pp. 14–27; Jeremy Waldron, "Mill on Liberty and on the Contagious Diseases Acts," in Nadia Urbinati and Alex Zakaras (eds.), *J.S. Mill's Political Thought: A Bicentennial Reassessment* (Cambridge University Press, 2007), pp. 19–20.

10. Derek Johns, *Censorship: A World Encyclopaedia* (Routledge, 2001), p. 241.

11. *The Boston Medical and Surgical Journal*, September 10, Vol. XLV, No.6 (1851), p. 112. Taken from "The Late Charles Knowlton, M.D," an obituary written by Stephen J. W. Tabor after Knowlton's sudden death at the age of fifty. Tabor included the preface of Knowlton's unpublished Preface to his Case Book from November 26, 1840.

12. Charles Knowlton, *Fruits of Philosophy: or The Private Companion of Young Married People*, 3rd ed. (J. Watson, 1841).

13. Fern Riddell, *The Victorian Guide to Sex: Desire & Deviance in the 19th Century* (Pen & Sword, 2014), p. 134, Rosalind Mitchison, *British population change since 1860* (Macmillan, 1977), p. 28, and Annie Besant, Chap. IX "The Knowlton Pamphlet," in *An Autobiography* (T. Fisher Unwin, 1893).

14. Besant, Chap. IX, *An Autobiography*.

15. Ibid.

16. *United States Practical Receipt Book, or Complete book of reference, for the manufacturer, tradesman, agriculturalist or housekeeper; containing many thousand valuable recipes, in all the useful and domestic arts*, 1844.

17. Ibid. Also *Illustrated Police News*, weekly from January 15, 1898, to November 17, 1900.

18. Kitty Marion, Unpublished Autobiography, p. 286.

19. George Drysdale, *Physical, Sexual and Natural Religion*, (1854), p. 330; Hera Cook, *The Long Sexual Revolution: English Women, Sex and Contraception, 1800–1975* (Oxford University Press, 2004), p. 60.

20. Ibid.

21. *Dr. Teller's Pocket Companion, or Marriage Guide: being a popular treatise on the anatomy and physiology of the genital organs, in both sexes, with their uses and*

abuses; together with a complete history of secret diseases, their causes symptoms and treatment, in plain language devoid of all technicalities (1865).

22. I am most grateful to Professor David Andress, of the University of Portsmouth, for bringing this earlier work to my attention.

23. George Sebastian Rousseau and Roy Porter (eds.), *Sexual Underworlds of the Enlightenment* (Manchester University Press, 1987) p. 48; Thomas Walter Laqueur, *Making Sex: Body and Gender from the Greeks to Freud* (Harvard University Press, 1990), p. 102.

24. Besant, *An Autobiography*, p. 209.

Chapter 2

1. *Reynold's Newspaper*, July 15, 1888.

2. *Huddersfield Chronicle*, October 3, 1888.

3. Kitty Marion, Unpublished Autobiography, p. 1.

4. Ibid., p. 4.

5. Ibid., p. 2.

6. Ibid., p. 20.

7. Ibid., pp. 5–6.

8. Ibid., p. 6.

9. Ibid.

10. Ibid., p. 8.

11. Ibid., p. 9.

12. Ibid., p. 11.

13. Ibid., p. 15.

14. Ibid., p. 17.

15. Ibid., p. 18.

16. Ibid.

17. Ibid., pp. 25–6.

18. Ibid., p. 22.

19. Ibid., p. 30.

20. Ibid., p. 31.

21. Ibid., p. 32.

22. Henry Vigar-Harris, *London at Midnight* (General Publishing Company, 1885).

23. Ibid.

24. Kitty Marion, Unpublished Autobiography, p. 35.

25. Ibid.

26. Ibid., p. 39.

27. Charles Douglas Stuart and A. J. Park, *The Variety Stage* (T. Fisher Unwin, 1895), p. 53.

28. W. H. Morton and H. Chance Newton, *Sixty Years' Stage Service* (Gale & Polden, 1905), p. 32; Stuart and Park, *The Variety Stage*, p. 53; for relative economic worth in 2015, see: http://www.measuringworth.com/ ukcompare/relativevalue.php

29. Stuart and Park, *The Variety Stage*, p. 54.

30. Brad Beaven, *Leisure, Citizenship and Working-Class Men in Britain 1850–1945* (Manchester University Press, 2005), p. 51; S. D. Pennybacker, *A Vision of London 1889–1914: Labour, Everyday Life and the LCC Experiment* (Routledge, 1995), p. 211.

31. "A Music Hall Agent," *The Era*, May 28, 1892.

32. Algar Thorold, *The Life of Henry Labouchère* (Constable & Co., 1913).

33. Jane W. Stedman, *W. S. Gilbert: A Classic Victorian and His Theatre* (Oxford University Press, 1996), p. 147.

34. Ibid.

35. Ibid.

36. Ibid.

37. Ibid.

38. Ibid.

39. Ibid.

40. "A Music Hall Agent," *The Era*, June 25, 1892.

41. Ibid.

42. Ibid.

43. Sarah Annie Frost, *The Book of Tableaux* (Dick & Fitzgerald, 1869); Nicole Anae, "Poses Plastiques: The Art and Style of 'Statuary' in Victorian Visual Theatre," *Australasian Drama Studies*, 52 (April 2000), p. 123.

44. Edith Wharton, *The House of Mirth* (Charles Scribner's Sons, 1905) and *The Age of Innocence* (D. Appleton & Co, 1921); Charles Dickens, *The Lazy Tour of Two Idle Apprentices*, in *Household Words* (1866). Both of these are referenced in Anae, "Poses Plastiques: The Art and Style of 'Statuary' in Victorian Visual Theatre," p. 120, alongside Emile Zola's *Nana* (T. B. Peterson & Bros, 1880).

45. Wharton, *The House of Mirth*, p. 211.

46. *Western Mail*, April 21, 1874; *My Secret Life* (Amsterdam, 1888), *Index Librorum Prohibitum*, 1877, p. xixn.

47. Munby's diaries, dating from the 1850s to 1907, along with those of his wife, Hannah Cullwick, are held in the Trinity College Library, Cambridge, GBR/0016/MUNB. See also: Jerry White, *London in the Nineteenth Century: "A Human Awful Wonder of God"* (Jonathan Cape, 2008), p. 319; D. Hudson and A. J. Munby, *Munby, man of two worlds: The life and diaries of Arthur J. Munby, 1828–1910* (J. Murray, 1972), pp. 117–18; Diane Atkinson, *Love and Dirt* (Macmillan, 2003), pp. 96–7.

48. Alison Smith, *The Victorian Nude: Sexuality, Morality and Art* (Manchester University Press, 1996), p. 57, believed to be from A. J. Munby's diary, June 11, 1870, quoted in Michael Hiley and A. J. Munby, *Victorian Working Women: Portraits from Life* (Gordon Fraser, 1979), p. 116.

49. Kitty Marion, Unpublished Autobiography, p. 38.

Chapter 3

1. Kitty Marion, Unpublished Autobiography

2. Ibid.

3. Ibid., p. 39.

4. Ibid.

5. Ibid., p. 40.

6. Ibid.

7. Ibid., p. 42.

8. Ibid., p. 41.

9. Ibid., p. 42.

10. Ibid., p. 44.

11. Ibid., p. 45.

12. Ibid.

13. Ibid., pp. 44–6.

14. Ibid.

15. Ibid., pp. 48–9.

16. *St. James Gazette*, April 21, 1892.

17. *Nottingham Evening Post*, November 23, 1899.

18. *South Wales Daily News*, July 22, 1892.

19. *Western Times*, July 17, 1889.

20. *Northern Echo*, July 31, 1890; *Hull Daily Mail*, January 1, 1907; *Lancashire Evening Post*, January 1, 1907.

21. *Northern Echo*, July 24, 1890; *Lancashire Evening Post*, January 1, 1907; *Dundee Courier*, February 18, 1929.

22. *Western Times*, July 17, 1889; *Lancashire Evening Post*, January 1, 1907; *Northern Echo*, July 24, 1890.

23. John Hollingshead, *Plain English* (Chatto & Windus, 1880), p. 185.

24. *Western Times*, July 17, 1889.

25. Ibid.; *Hull Daily Mail*, January 1, 1907.

26. *Western Times*, July 17, 1889; *Northern Echo*, July 24, 1890.

27. *Dundee Courier*, July 16, 1889.

28. *Western Times*, July 17, 1889.

29. *Hull Daily Mail*, January 1, 1907; *Northern Echo*, July 24, 1890; *Northern Echo*, July 25, 1890.

30. Ibid.

31. *Hull Daily Mail*, January 1, 1907; *Gloucestershire Echo*, July 24, 1890.

32. Kitty Marion, Unpublished Autobiography, p. 95.

33. *Northern Echo*, July 31, 1890.

34. Ibid.

35. *Northampton Mercury*, August 1, 1890.

36. Ibid.; *Reynolds's Newspaper*, July 27, 1890.

37. *Northern Echo*, July 24, 1890.

38. *Leeds Times*, July 26, 1890.

39. Ibid.

40. *Leeds Times*, July 26, 1890; *Northern Echo*, July 26, 1890.

41. *Northern Echo*, July 26, 1890.

42. *Leeds Times*, July 26, 1890.

43. Ibid.

44. Ibid.

45. *Hull Daily Mail*, January 1, 1907.

46. *Yorkshire Evening Post*, January 1, 1907.

47. Ibid.

48. *Northern Echo*, July 24, 1890.

49. *Reynolds's Newspaper*, July 27, 1890.

50. *Vanity Fair*, April 21, 1888; *Northern Echo*, July 31, 1890.

51. Anne Humphreys, "Coming Apart: The British Newspaper Press and the Divorce Court," in L. Brake et al., *Nineteenth Century Media and the Construction of Identities* (Palgrave Macmillan, 2000), p. 227.

52. *Hull Daily Mail*, January 1, 1907.

53. *Cardiff Times*, August 2, 1890.

54. Ibid.

55. Ibid.

56. Ibid.

57. *Lancashire Evening Post*, January 1, 1907; *Yorkshire Evening Post*, January 1, 1907.

58. *Hull Daily Mail*, January 1, 1907.

Chapter 4

1. Kitty Marion, Unpublished Autobiography, p. 46.

2. Ibid.

3. Ibid., p. 55.

4. Ibid.

5. Ibid.

6. Ibid., pp. 55–6.

7. Ibid., p. 56.

8. Ibid.

9. Ibid., p. 57.

10. Ibid.

11. Ibid., p. 60.

12. Ibid., p. 67.

13. Ibid., pp. 77–8.

14. Ibid., p. 82.

15. Ibid., p. 83.

16. Ibid., p. 86.

17. Ibid.

18. Ibid., p. 94.

19. Ibid.

20. Ibid.

21. Ibid., p. 95.

22. "Breach of Promise," *Sunderland Daily Echo and Shipping Gazette*, July 30, 1898.

23. *Western Mail*, July 31, 1895.

24. "An Actress's Revenge," *Daily Gazette for Middlesbrough*, October 30, 1896.

25. "Catherine Kempshall Case," *Bath Chronicle and Weekly Gazette*, April 1, 1897.

26. "Catherine Kempshall Reprieved," *Northampton Mercury*, April 2, 1897.

27. Kitty Marion, Unpublished Autobiography, p. 96.

28. Ibid., p. 97.

29. Ibid., p. 101.

30. Ibid., p. 143.

31. Ibid., p. 107.

32. Ibid.

33. Ibid., p. 126–7.

34. Ibid., p. 144.

35. Ibid., p. 147.

36. Ibid., p. 144.

37. Ibid., pp. 147–8.

38. Ibid., p. 148.

39. Ibid., pp. 151–2.

40. *Lincolnshire Echo*, May 15, 1895.

41. *Driffield Times*, December 30, 1882.

42. *The Era*, April 29, 1882.

43. "Duke of Manchester Dead," *New York Times*, August 19, 1892.

44. Andrew Cook, *Prince Eddy: The King Britain Never Had* (The History Press, 2011), p. 139; Guy Deghy, *Paradise in the Strand: The Story of Romano's* (The Richards Press, 1958), p. 58.

45. *The Era*, June 25, 1892.

46. Kitty Marion, Unpublished Autobiography, p. 152.

47. Ibid.

48. Ibid., pp. 152–3.

49. Ibid., p. 153.

50. Ibid., p. 161.

Chapter 5

1. *Denbighshire Free Press*, July 4, 1908.

2. Hansard, August 3, 1832, Vol. 14 c1086.

3. Elizabeth Crawford, *The Women's Suffrage Movement: A Reference Guide 1866–1928* (Routledge, 2003), p. 452.

4. Kenneth Florey, *Women's Suffrage Memorabilia: An Illustrated Historical Study* (McFarland & Co., 2013), p. 80.

5. Kitty Marion, Unpublished Autobiography, p. 172.

6. *Kalgoorlie Miner*, March 11, 1907.

7. *Denbighshire Free Press*, July 4, 1908.

8. Kitty Marion, Unpublished Autobiography, p. 169.

9. Jane Marcus, *Suffrage and the Pankhursts* (Routledge, 1987), p. 52, transcript of Frederick Pethick-Lawrence's 1908 pamphlet "The Trial of The Suffragette Leaders."

10. *Western Gazette*, October 16, 1908.

11. Kitty Marion, Unpublished Autobiography, p. 172.

12. Ibid.

13. Ibid., p. 174.

14. Ibid., p. 177.

15. Ibid., p. 182.

16. *Lincolnshire Echo*, June 30, 1909.

17. HO 45/10418/183577.

18. Kitty Marion, Unpublished Autobiography, p. 183.

19. Ibid., p. 184.

20. Ibid.

21. Ibid., p. 185.

22. For Churchill's whipping, see "Suffragette Hits Churchill," *Dundee Courier*, November 15, 1909, and "Suffragette Outrage," *Morpeth Herald*, November 20, 1909.

23. *Manchester Courier and Lancashire General Advertiser*, December 28 and 31, 1909.

24. Kitty Marion, Unpublished Autobiography, p. 191.

25. Ibid., p. 192.

26. Ibid., p. 194.

27. "Suffragettes Meet Again," British Pathé, February 10, 1955.

28. Kitty Marion, Unpublished Autobiography, p. 197.

29. Ibid.

30. Ibid., p. 198.

31. *Nottingham Evening Post*, November 19, 1910.

32. *Votes For Women*, December 11, 1911.

33. Ibid.

34. Kitty Marion, Unpublished Autobiography, p. 212.

35. Jane Chapman, "The Argument of the Broken Pane," *Media History*, 21:3 (2015), pp. 238–51.

36. Kitty Marion, Unpublished Autobiography, p. 216.

37. Ibid., pp. 219–20.

38. "Gunpowder and Oil," *Hull Daily Mail*, July 19, 1912; "Prime Minister in Dublin," *Derby Daily Telegraph*, July 20, 1912; "Suffragette Outrages," *Western Times*, July 20, 1912; "Sensational Evidence Is Given," *Dundee Courier*, July 20, 1912.

39. Ibid. For Jennie Baines, see Elizabeth Crawford, *The Women's Suffrage Movement: A Reference Guide 1866–1928* (Routledge, 2003), p. 25.

40. "Gunpowder and Oil," *Hull Daily Mail*, July 19, 1912; "Prime Minister in Dublin," *Derby Daily Telegraph*, July 20, 1912; "Suffragette Outrages," *Western Times*, July 20, 1912; "Sensational Evidence Is Given," *Dundee Courier*, July 20, 1912.

41. "Suffragette Outrages," *Western Times*, July 20, 1912; "Sensational Evidence Is Given," *Dundee Courier*, July 20, 1912; "Suffragist Outrages," *Evening Telegraph*, July 20, 1912.

42. Ibid.

43. "Foolish Art Gallery Outrage," *Hull Daily Mail*, August 6, 1912; "Suffragette Outrage in Glasgow Art Gallery," *Western Times*, August 10, 1912. For the *Telegraph* cutting, see "The Latest Suffragette Outrage," *Derby Daily Telegraph*, September 4, 1912.

44. Kitty Marion, Unpublished Autobiography, p. 223.

45. *Votes For Women*, September 13, 1912.

46. Kitty Marion, Unpublished Autobiography, p. 225.

47. "Suffragette Outrage," *Hull Daily Mail*, November 2, 1912; "Pillar Box on Fire," *Evening Telegraph*, November 11, 1912; "Hundreds of Letters Are Damaged," *Dundee Courier*, November 29, 1912; "Suffragette Outrages," *North Devon Journal*, December 5, 1912.

48. "To-day's Parliament," *Derby Daily Telegraph*, January 28, 1913.

49. During 1913, the *Gloucester Journal* ran a column called "The Militant Suf-fragists," and the *Liverpool Echo* dedicated a space entitled "The Wreckers" or "Wreckers" to reporting all attacks and trials linked to the suffrage movement.

Chapter 6

1. 1913, HO 45/10695/231366.

2. *Hampshire Telegraph*, May 9, 1913.

3. *The Suffragette*, April 11, 1913.

4. Kitty Marion, Unpublished Autobiography, p. 229.

5. Emmeline Pankhurst, *My Own Story* (Hearst's International Library Co., 1914; Hesperus Press, 2015), p. 237.

6. Ibid., p. 244.

7. Kitty Marion, Unpublished Autobiography, p. 225.

8. "The Wreckers," *Liverpool Echo*, March 29, 1913; "Hoaxcd in thc Hills," *Manchester Courier and Lancashire General Advertiser*, May 20, 1913; "The Wild Women: More Suffragette Freaks," *Coventry Evening Telegraph*, August 27, 1914.

9. *Suffragette*, February 7, 1913; February 21, 1913; April 11, 1913.

10. Sylvia Pankhurst, *The Suffragette Movement—An Intimate Account of Persons and Ideals* (Longmans & Co., 1931), pp. 481–2.

11. *Globe*, January 13, 1913.

12. Sylvia Pankhurst, *The Suffragette Movement*, pp. 482–3.

13. *Pall Mall Gazette*, February 19, 1913.

14. Sylvia Pankhurst, *The Suffragette Movement*, pp. 481–2.

15. *The Scotsman*, April 5, 1913.

16. *Surrey Mirror*, April 11, 1913.

17. *Gloucestershire Echo*, April 11, 1913.

18. *Diss Express*, April 11, 1913.

19. *Cambridge Independent Press*, April 18, 1913.

20. Reported in multiple newspapers across the country.

21. "Bomb Found At Taunton," *Taunton Courier and Western Advertiser*, July 30, 1913.

22. *Taunton Courier and Western Advertiser*, April 23, 1913.

23. Bodleian Library, Papers of Lewis Harcourt, 1st Viscount Harcourt, 1884–1922, *Political Journal*, January 1–March 26, 1907, MS. Eng. d. 4174.

24. *Morning Post*, July 2, 1908.

25. *Belfast Weekly News*, September 23, 1909.

26. *London Evening Standard*, November 16, 1909.

27. National Archives, reported in the press http://www.telegraph.co.uk/news/uknews/1530065/Suffragette-plot-to-assassinate-Asquith.html, HO 144/1038/181250/MEPO 2/1310.

28. Ibid.; "Dhingra Shows No Fear," *Evening Telegraph*, August 17, 1909.

29. *Yorkshire Evening Post*, May 8, 1913.

30. *Nottingham Evening Post*, May 8, 1913.

31. Sylvia Pankhurst, *The Suffragette Movement*, pp. 446–7.

32. Syndicated to *Sheffield Evening Telegraph*, May 16, 1913.

33. HO 45/10642/207007.

34. Mary Richardson, *Laugh, A Defiance* (G. Weidenfeld & Nicholson, 1953), pp. 142–4.

35. Ibid.

36. *Sheffield Evening Telegraph*, May 16, 1913.

37. *Nottingham Evening Post*, May 8, 1913.

38. Kitty Marion, Unpublished Autobiography, p. 225.

39. Quoted in Kitty Marion, Unpublished Autobiography, p. 226.

40. Emmeline Pankhurst, *My Own Story*, p. 255.

41. The nineteenth century had no equivalent of the Terrorism Act, and suffragettes were most commonly charged under the Malicious Injuries to Property Act, 1861.

42. Emmeline Pankhurst, *My Own Story*, p. 280.

43. *Illustrated Police News*, July 10, 1913.

44. *Sheffield Evening Telegraph*, May 16, 1913.

45. Sylvia Pankhurst, *The Suffragette Movement*, p. 483.

46. Marsha L. Richmond, "'A Lab of One's Own': The Balfour Biological Laboratory for Women at Cambridge University, 1884–1914." *Isis* 88, no. 3 (1997), pp. 422–55.

47. *Cambridge Independent Press*, May 23, 1913.

48. Ibid.

49. Ibid.

50. Ibid.

51. *Cambridge Independent Press*, October 17, 1913.

52. Ibid.

53. *The Suffragette*, October 24, 1913.

54. *Cambridge Independent Press*, October 31, 1913.

55. Sylvia Pankhurst, *The Suffragette Movement*, pp. 446–7.

56. "Women's War," *Evening Telegraph*, March 10, 1913; "Suffragette Outrages," *Aberdeen Journal*, April 12, 1913.

57. "Suffragettes Accept Responsibility For Burning Of Railway Station," *Evening Telegraph*, March 11, 1912.

58. Sir A. Markham, "Vote To Account," *Commons*, March 18, 1913.

59. "Our London Letter," *Exeter and Plymouth Gazette*, February 24, 1913, although the report in the *Manchester Courier and Lancashire General Advertiser*, February 22, 1913, claims the targets to be Herbert Asquith and Lewis Harcourt.

60. "Wreckers," *Liverpool Echo*, April 26, 1913.

61. Now held in the Museum of London.

62. "Wreckers," *Liverpool Echo*, April 26, 1913.

63. "Malignant Suffragists," *Western Gazette*, May 23, 1913.

64. "The Militant Suffragists," *Gloucester Journal*, May 17, 1913.

65. "Suffragette Is Charged," *Evening Telegraph*, July 10, 1913.

66. "Miss Pankhurst Defends The Bombs," *Evening Telegraph*, February 21, 1913.

67. "Suffragette Army Is Inaugurated," *Dundee Courier*, November 13, 1913. "Sidney Street" refers to the "Siege of Sidney Street," a gun battle that took place on January 3, 1911, in the East End, between two supposedly foreign revolutionaries and the police.

68. "Suffragist Procession In London," *Aberdeen Journal*, June 20, 1910.

69. "Suffragette Is Charged," *Evening Telegraph*, July 10, 1913; "Suffragette Threatens Something Desperate," *Dundee Courier*, December 19, 1912.

70. *Yorkshire Post and Leeds Intelligencer*, May 15, 1913.

71. *Folkestone, Hythe, Sandgate & Cheriton Herald*, May 17, 1913.

72. Ibid.

73. Ibid.

74. *Manchester Courier and Lancashire General Advertiser*, May 16, 1913.

75. Ibid.

Chapter 7

1. Hierax is well known for his belief that only the celibate would enter the kingdom of God, so he was clearly trouble from the start.

2. "Transcript of the Church Trial and Excommunication of Ann Hibbins," Nancy F. Cott et al. (eds.), *Root of Bitterness: Documents of the Social History of American Women* (UPNE, 1996), p. 12.

3. John Mills Whitham, *Men and Women of the French Revolution* (Books for Libraries Press, 1933, 1968), pp. 154–5.

4. Simon Schama, *Citizens: A Chronicle of the French Revolution* (Random House, 2005), p. 736.

5. Richard Cobb, *The French Revolution. Voices From A Momentous Epoch* (Simon & Schuster, 1988), p. 192.

6. Chantal Thomas, "Heroism in the Feminine: The Examples of Charlotte Corday and Madame Roland," *The Eighteenth Century*, Vol. 30, No. 2; *The French Revolution 1789–1989: Two Hundred Years of Rethinking* (Texas Tech University Press, 1989), pp. 67–82.

7. *Lichfield Mercury*, July 19, 1912.

8. http://blogs.bl.uk/untoldlives/2013/07/the-davisons-of-northumberland-and-bengal.html; IOR/L/AG/34/29/37 Will of John Hay of Calcutta proved 1825; IOR/L/AG/34/29/52 Will of George Chisholm of Calcutta proved 1833.

9. *The Scotsman*, May 22, 1897.

10. *Edinburgh Evening News*, May 22, 1897.

11. Kitty Marion, Unpublished Autobiography, p. 235.

12. *Daily Herald*, July 4, 1912.

13. Sylvia Pankhurst, *The Suffragette Movement—An Intimate Account of Persons and Ideals* (Longmans & Co., 1931), pp. 518–19.

14. *Pall Mall Gazette*, September 19, 1912.

15. Gertrude Colmore, *The Life of Emily Davison* (1913), in Ann Morley and Liz Stanley, *The Life and Death of Emily Wilding Davison* (Women's Press, 1988), p. 56.

16. Sylvia Pankhurst, *The Suffragette Movement—An Intimate Account of Persons and Ideals* (Longmans & Co., 1931), pp. 518–19.

17. Kitty Marion, Unpublished Autobiography, p. 234.

18. Mary Richardson, *Laugh A Defiance* (G. Weidenfeld & Nicholson, 1953), p. 18.

19. Ibid., pp. 19–20.

20. HO 144/1150/210696, *Morning Post*, June 5, 1913.

21. Richardson, *Laugh A Defiance*, p. 21.

22. Ibid., p. 22.

23. Kitty Marion, Unpublished Autobiography, p. 239.

24. Ibid., pp. 230, 235.

25. Ibid., p. 232.

26. Ibid., p. 230.

27. As quoted in Andrew Rosen, *Rise Up, Women!: The Militant Campaign of the Women's Social and Political Union 1903–1914* (Routledge, 2012), p. 200.

28. Emmeline Pankhurst, *My Own Story* (Hearst's International Library Co., 1914; Hesperus Press, 2015), p. 287.

29. Kitty Marion, Unpublished Autobiography, p. 242.

30. *Illustrated Police News*, June 19, 1913.

31. Colmore, *The Life of Emily Davison*, in Morley and Stanley, *The Life and Death of Emily Wilding Davison*, p. 52.

32. Sylvia Pankhurst, *The Suffragette Movement*, pp. 518–19.

33. Kitty Marion, Unpublished Autobiography, p. 244.

34. Ibid., p. 246.

35. Ibid., p. 248.

36. Ibid., p. 251.

37. *The Scotsman*, September 24, 1913.

38. Ibid.

39. *Leeds Mercury*, November 12, 1913.

40. *Yorkshire Post and Leeds Intelligencer*, November 17, 1913.

41. Kitty Marion, Unpublished Autobiography, p. 251.

42. Ibid., pp. 255–6.

43. Ibid., pp. 257–8.

44. Ibid., pp. 264.

45. HO 45/10417/183577.

46. HO 144/1205/222030.

47. Richard Whitmore, *Alice Hawkins and the Suffragette Movement in Edwardian Leicester* (Breedon Books, 2007), pp. 149–50.

48. Kitty Marion, Unpublished Autobiography, p. 232.

49. HO 45/24665.

Chapter 8

1. Kitty Marion, Unpublished Autobiography, p. 273.

2. Ibid.

3. Ibid.

4. Ibid.

5. HO 144/1721/221874.

6. Ibid.

7. Panikos Panayi, *German Immigrants in Britain during the 19th Century, 1815–1914* (Berg, 1995), p. 91.

8. *Manchester Courier and Lancashire General Advertiser*, November 11, 1914.

9. *Sunday Post*, January 26, 1919.

10. Kitty Marion, Unpublished Autobiography, p. 112.

11. Ibid., p. 111.

12. Ibid.

13. Ibid.

14. Ibid., p. 274.

15. Panayi, *German Immigrants in Britain*, p. 241.

16. Kitty Marion, Unpublished Autobiography, p. 274.

17. Ibid.

18. HO 144/1721/221874.

19. Kitty Marion, Unpublished Autobiography, p. 275.

20. HO 144/1721/221874.

21. Ibid.

22. Kitty Marion, Unpublished Autobiography, p. 275.

23. Ibid., p. 276.

24. Ibid.

25. Angela Woollacott, *To Try Her Fortune in London: Australian Women, Colonialism, and Modernity* (Oxford University Press, 2001), p. 168.

26. Kitty Marion, Unpublished Autobiography, p. 277.

27. Ibid.

28. Ibid., p. 278.

29. Ibid.

30. Ibid., p. 279.

31. "Mrs. Balsan Dies," *New York Times*, December 7, 1964.

32. Kitty Marion, Unpublished Autobiography, p. 280.

33. "The Wreckers," *Liverpool Echo*, March 29, 1913.

34. *Brooklyn Daily Eagle*, August 29, 1913.

35. *Brooklyn Daily Eagle*, June 1, 1913.

36. Kitty Marion, Unpublished Autobiography, p. 280.

37. Ibid.

38. Ibid., p. 281.

39. *Brooklyn Daily Eagle*, May 11, 1916.

40. Kitty Marion, Unpublished Autobiography, p. 283.

41. Ibid.

42. Ibid., p. 284.

43. Ibid., p. 285.

44. Ibid.

45. Ibid., p. 286.

46. Margaret Sanger, "No Masters," *The Woman Rebel*, Vol. 1, No. 6, August 1914.

47. *Brooklyn Daily Eagle*, March 6, 1917.

48. Kitty Marion, Unpublished Autobiography, p. 289.

49. Ibid., pp. 299–302.

50. Ibid.

51. Ibid., p. 315.

52. Ibid., pp. 316–17.

53. Andrew Rosen, *Rise Up, Women! The Militant Campaign of the Women's Social and Political Union 1903–1914* (Routledge, 1974), p. 164.

54. Kitty Marion, Unpublished Autobiography, pp. 316–17.

Chapter 9

1. Ellen Chesler, *Woman of Valor: Margaret Sanger and the Birth Control Movement in America* (Simon & Schuster, 2007), p. 170.

2. Ibid.

3. Kitty Marion, Unpublished Autobiography, p. 320.

4. *Leicester Chronicle*, July 12, 1913.

5. Antonia Raeburn, *The Militant Suffragettes* (New English Library, 1973), pp. 224–5.

6. HO 144/1721/221874.

7. Kitty Marion, Unpublished Autobiography, p. 321.

8. Ibid.

9. Ibid., pp. 321–2.

10. "The Passionate Friends: H. G. Wells and Margaret Sanger," *The Margaret Sanger Papers*, Newsletter no. 12 (Spring 1996).

11. Ibid., p. 325.

12. Ibid., p. 327.

13. Ibid., p. 328.

14. *Brooklyn Daily Eagle*, April 5, 1928.

15. Ibid.

16. *Leeds Mercury*, April 10, 1928.

17. Kitty Marion, Unpublished Autobiography, p. 336.

18. Ibid., p. 337.

19. Ibid., pp. 339–40.

20. Ibid., p. 345.

21. Ibid., p. 345.

22. George Speaight, *Bawdy Songs of the Early Music Hall* (David & Charles, 1975), pp. 27, 45, 56.

23. Marie Collins, "Take it On, Boys!" (1893); Marie Lloyd, "Wink The Other Eye" (1890).

24. *Illustrated Police News*, weekly from January 15, 1898, to November 17, 1900.

25. "London Police," *Cork Examiner*, February 4, 1864.

26. Ibid.

27. Ibid.

28. Ibid.

29. Fern Riddell, *The Victorian Guide to Sex: Desire and Deviance in the 19th Century* (Pen & Sword, 2014), pp. 80–4.

30. "The Prevention of Prostitution," *North & South Shields Gazette and Northumberland and Durham Advertiser*, May 24, 1850.

31. Kitty Marion, Unpublished Autobiography, p. 284.

32. June Purvis, *Emmeline Pankhurst: A Biography* (Routledge, 2002), p. 26.

33. Emmeline Pankhurst, *My Own Story* (Hearst's International Library Co., 1914; Hesperus Press, 2015).

34. Hera Cook, *The Long Sexual Revolution* (Oxford University Press, 2005), p. 71; M. L. Bush, *What Is Love? Richard Carlile's Philosophy of Sex* (Verso, 1998), pp. 41, 72.

35. Cook, *The Long Sexual Revolution*, p. 71.

36. Peter T. Cominos, "Late-Victorian Sexual Respectability and the Social System," *International Review of Social History*, 8:1 (1963), p. 233.

37. Cook, *The Long Sexual Revolution*, p. 72.

38. Ibid., p. 73; *The Lancet*, April 10, 1869, pp. 499–500; E. P. Thompson, *The Making of the English Working Class* (Victor Gollancz, 1963), p. 803; Peter Fryer, *The Birth Controllers* (Seker & Warberg, 1965), pp. 184–5.

39. Susan Kingsley Kent, *Sex and Suffrage in Britain, 1860–1914* (Routledge, 1990), p. 105.

40. Purvis, *Emmeline Pankhurst*, p. 316. Although Purvis makes this claim in her biography of Pankhurst, Stephanie Green, in *The Public Lives of Charlotte and Marie Stopes* (Routledge, 2016; p. 145)—which deals with the life of Marie Stopes in depth—makes much of Marie's dislike and rejection of the Pankhurst and WSPU rhetoric.

41. Jane Marcus, *Suffrage and the Pankhursts* (Routledge, 2010), p. 14.

42. Ibid.

43. Kitty Marion, Unpublished Autobiography, p. 2.

44. Ibid., p. 335.

45. Ibid., p. 345.

46. Ibid., pp. 57–60, 76–7, 80, 82–3, 94–6, 100–101, 126–9, 132–3, 151–2, 154.

47. Ibid., p. 346.

48. Ibid., p. 349.

49. Ibid., p. 350.

50. Ibid.

51. Ibid., p. 354.

52. Museum of London holdings.

Chapter 10

1. Letter to Edith, December 10, 1938, Museum of London holdings.

2. Quoted in Ann Morley and Liz Stanley, *The Life and Death of Emily Wilding Davison* (Women's Press, 1988), p. 160.

3. *Birmingham Gazette*, October 11, 1944.

4. http://www.telegraph.co.uk/news/2017/10/14/harvey-weinstein-expelled-academy/

5. "How 'MeToo' is exposing the scale of sexual abuse," BBC News, http://www.bbc.co.uk/news/blogs-trending-41633857

6. Naomi Levine, *Politics, Religion, and Love: The Story of H. H. Asquith, Venetia Stanley and Edwin Montague, Based on the Life and Letters of Edwin Samuel Montague* (NYU Press, 1991), p. 112; H. H. Asquith, *Letters to Venetia Stanley*, edited by Michael Brock (Oxford University Press, 1982), p. 573.

7. Levine, *Politics, Religion, and Love*, p. 112.

8. Marilyn Monroe, *My Story* (W. H. Allen, 1975; Taylor Trading Publishing, 2006), p. 43.

9. Laura E. Nym Mayhall, "Creating the 'suffragette spirit': British Feminism and the historical imagination," *Women's History Review*, 4:3 (1995), p. 319.

10. Ibid., p. 321.

11. Ibid., pp. 321, 331–2.

12. Ibid., p. 332.

13. Kitty Marion, Unpublished Autobiography, p. 345.

14. Harrison, Brian, "Review of Antonia Raeburn's *The Militant Suffragettes*," in *Oral History*, 2:1 (Spring 1974), pp. 73–6.

Index

age of consent 20, 44
agency of women 30, 132, 213, 215,
  217, 230; *see also* empowerment of
  women
Ahern, Dr. 112, 168, 170
Alexandra of Denmark 69
Aliens Restriction (Amendment) Act
  (1919) 206
Allen, Janie 205
American Birth Control League
  (ABCL) 203, 206
Anderson, Millicent 45
*Apology for a Latin Verse in Commenda-
  tion of Mr. Marten's Gonosologium
  Novum, An* (Paré) 28
Argus, Conny 54, 69
arson attacks, WSPU *see* bomb and
  arson attacks, WSPU
Art of Begetting Handsome Children, The
  (anon.) 28
Asquith, Herbert 101, 228
assassinations 125, 149, 205
Astor, Nancy 208
Autobiography, An (Besant) 26

Baines, Jennie 113, 205
Baldwin, Stanley 210
ballet 46, 47, 50, 51, 53, 72
Barrett, Rachel 126, 141
Barry, Mr. 189

Bartels, Olive 135
Barwell, Ellen 102
Bearman, C. J. 139
Bellwood, Bessie 89, 90, 109
Belmont, Alva 190, 194
Besant, Annie 24–26, 33, 194, 213, 215,
  217, 219
Besant, Frank 24
Bilton, Belle 61–69, 75, 82, 90, 109
Bingham, Mr. 183
Birmingham
  Winson Green Prison 102, 112, 171
  WSPU attacks 102, 128, 167, 172
Birmingham Daily Gazette 225
birth control, common practices of
  5, 10, 22, 24–27, 29–30, 33, 196–
  199, 203–204, 207–209, 211–213
Birth Control International Informa-
  tion Centre (BCIIC), London 211
birth control movement
  in America 11, 27, 203, 211; *see also*
    Sanger, Margaret
  in Britain 24, 25, 27
  rejection by suffrage societies/
    feminists 10, 93, 203
Birth Control Review 195, 198, 199, 208,
  209, 219, 220
"Black Friday" 110
Blackwell, Elizabeth 217
Blossom, Dr. Frederick A. 195

bomb and arson attacks, WSPU
    American views on 147
    Bristol 104
    Essex 179
    forgotten by history 7, 8, 173
    Hertfordshire 151
    impact on perpetrators 121, 138
    justifications 19, 149, 159, 201
    Kent 142, 206
    Liverpool 11, 41, 58, 82, 104, 138,
        167, 186–188, 204
    London 9, 17, 24, 25, 34, 50, 54, 94,
        118, 122, 127
    Manchester 5, 167
    methods 113
    nationwide campaign 3, 8, 118, 130
    Oxfordshire 123
    police responses 1, 3, 11, 34, 50,
        69, 92, 98, 101, 110, 114, 127–129,
        131–136
    Surrey 121, 163, 166
Bootle, Elizabeth 212
Boston Herald 191
Bradlaugh, Charles 24–27, 29
breach of promise actions 80–83,
    227
"Breach of Promise Case, The"
    (Dryden) 82
Briggs, Annie 4
Bristol
    Kitty with theater 50, 54, 70, 74,
        76, 79, 84, 91, 107, 108
    WSPU attacks 70–72
Brooklyn Daily Eagle 191, 193, 209
Browne, Mrs. E. R. 178; *see also* Thor-
    burn, Marion Alice
Brownsville family planning clinic,
    Brooklyn 194
Bryant and May match girls strike
    33, 34
Bryer, Constance 171
Burke, Edmund 16
Burkitt, Hilda 102, 171

Bury, Sam 87, 88
Butler, Josephine 22–23, 30, 72, 216
Byrne, Ethel 92, 194

Cambridge University 133–135, 152
Campbell-Bannerman, Sir Henry
    95, 101
Canterbury Music Hall, London 47
Capper, Mabel 102, 113
Cardiff Times 67, 68
Carmody, Lucy B. 193
Carson, Sir Edward 130
Catholic Church 27, 196
Chang, Vivian Ernest 54
Chapman, Annie 9, 34
chemical attacks, WSPU 4, 118, 120,
    121, 131
Churchill, Clementine Hozier 228
Churchill, Winston 104, 110, 128, 191,
    228
Clayton, Edwy Godwin 126, 141
Colmore, Gertrude 165
communication systems, WSPU
    attacks on 118, 121, 233
Conciliation Bill 111, 123
Conciliation Committee 110, 111
condoms 22, 27, 194, 213
Contagious Diseases Acts 21, 22, 29,
    31, 72, 74, 216
Cooper Key, Major 128
Corday, Charlotte 148, 150
Cowell, Sam 43
Cox, Maude 45
Cox, Mr. and Mrs. Harold 205, 206
Craggs, Helen 121, 123, 150
Criminal Law Amendment Act 44
Cunningham, Marianne 129
Cymric, SS 188
Cyril of Alexandria 146

Daily Herald 153, 154
Daily Mail 94
Daily Record 225

Davison, Charles 151
Davison, Emily Wilding
  background 151
  bomb attacks 121
  death 158, 162
  Epsom Derby 13
  force-feedings 11, 13, 153
  funeral 163–164
  hunger strikes in prison 104, 141
  Marion's view of 163
  militancy 130
  night before Epsom Derby 155
  suicide attempt in Holloway
    Prison 154, 155
  university degree, barred from
    152
  WSPU, joining 11
Davison, Margaret Caisley 151
De Weerdt, Mr. and Mrs. George 193,
  195
death threats, WSPU 138
Devine, Emma 213
Dhingra, Madan Lal 125
Dickinson, W. H. 94
Donegan, James A. 208
Dora, Aunt 40, 41, 45, 49, 54, 64, 69,
  72, 185
Doty, Madeleine 189
Dr. Teller's Pocket Companion 214
Drummond, Flora 100, 126, 140, 141,
  210
Dryden, Leo 82
Drysdale, George 27, 28
Du Cros, Arthur 118–119, 142
Dublin, WSPU attacks in 113, 124,
  138, 205
"Duck Island Magazine" bomb dis-
  posal unit 127
Dundee Courier 11
Dunlo Divorce Case 66
Dunlop, Marion Wallace 101

Eddowes, Catherine 9, 34, 81

Edinburgh, WSPU attacks 78, 118,
  121, 138
education, women's 16, 19, 24, 71, 133,
  148, 152; see also sex education
Edwards, Mary 102
Ellis, Havelock 207
empowerment of women 11, 30, 140;
  see also agency of women
Enemy in Our Midst, The (Wood) 182
Epsom Derby (1913) 13, 153, 155
Era, The 44, 92
Etiquette of Marriage 214
Euphemia, Saint 146–147
Evans, Gladys 113

Farrow, Ronan 227
fascism 221
Fawcett, Millicent 217
feminism
  birth control, rejection of 215–217
  fear of sex 10
  history, manipulation of 9, 12, 19,
    46, 91, 226, 230, 232
  victimhood narrative 30, 47, 215,
    216
  see also suffragette movement
Fields, Mary 216
Finch, Mr. 198–200
First World War
  amnesty to suffragettes 173
  fear of German spies 179
  German propaganda 192
  German submarine threat 188
  registration of German nationals
    182
  start 4
  Theatreland zeppelin raid 187
"The Flea Shooter" 213
Fletcher, Peggy 186
force-feedings 10, 11, 13, 102, 107, 112,
  113, 117, 120, 130, 136, 137, 151, 153,
  155, 163, 168–169, 172, 182, 190, 221
Forrester, Edith 45

Forrester, Lillian 4
Forsyth, Lal 186
Frankenstein (Shelley) 19, 31
Franz Ferdinand of Austria, Archduke 175
French Reign of Terror 96
French Revolution 17, 120, 148
Freud, Sigmund 29, 30
Frost, Sarah Annie 46
Fruits of Philosophy (Knowlton) 26, 29, 213
Fry, Mr. 81

Gardiner, John James 43
Garnett, Theresa 104
Gilbert, W. S. 44
Giveen, Clara "Betty" 126, 159, 171, 185
Gladstone, Herbert 125
Glasgow
    Kitty with theater 50, 51, 54, 70, 76, 79, 84, 107
    WSPU attacks 118, 121, 172
    WSPU meeting 205
Gloucester Journal 115
Godwin, Charles 18
Godwin, Claire 18
Godwin, Mary see Wollstonecraft, Mary
Godwin, Mary Jane Clairmont 18
Godwin, William 17–18, 25, 216
Goldstein, Louis Leon 43
Goure, Matilda Rosalie 45
government responses to WSPU 10, 11, 21, 22, 94, 95, 97, 101, 102
Gray, Annie 221
Great Scourge and How To End It, The (C. Pankhurst) 218
Green, Alice 156, 172, 186, 207, 223
gun violence 103, 113, 117, 122, 172, 192, 205

Halford, Bernard 85–86, 92, 184
Halford, Robert 84
Hall, Leslie 102, 104

Hannen, Sir James 67
Harcourt, Lewis 121, 123, 150
Harding, Gertrude 205
Harding, Nelson 191
Harrison, Brian 231
Hawkins, Alice 172
Hayler, Henry 46
"He Did It Before My Face" 213
Hibbins, Ann 147
Hierax of Alexandria 146
historians, role of 7
history, manipulation of
    desexualization 21
    gendered treatment 131
    sanitization 224
    truth 7, 16, 44, 187, 224
Hobbes, Geraldine Mary 81
Hockin, Olive 126, 191
Hodson, Henrietta 44
Holland, Edgar 81–82
Hollingshead, John 62
Holton, Lily 43, 45
House of Mirth, The (Wharton) 46
How-Martyn, Edith 211, 223, 224
hunger strikes 101, 104, 107, 112, 117, 130, 136, 140, 141, 158, 162, 165, 166, 168, 171, 187, 193, 200
Hunt, Henry 93
Hypatia of Alexandria 145, 146
hysteria 12, 29, 163

Illustrated Police News 27, 131, 164, 213
Illustrations and Proofs of the Principle of Population (Place) 25
Imlay, Fanny 17, 18
Imlay, Gilbert 17
Indian independence fighters 125
International Birth Control Conference (1922) 204
Irish Free State 204
Irish independence fighters 125

Jack the Ripper 9, 34, 49
Joan of Arc 120, 156, 162, 165

J.P.C. (in Huddersfield) 80–81, 84

Kantor, Jodi 226
Kelly, Mary Jane 9, 34
Kempshall, Catherine 81–82
Kenney, Annie 125, 126, 141, 151, 164, 171
Kenney, Jessie 125
Kent, WSPU attacks in 142
"kept" women 89
Kerr, Harriet 18, 126, 141
Kerr, Ruby 72–74
kidnap plots 137
Knowlton, Dr. Charles 26, 29

Labouchère, Henry 44
"Ladies and the Candle, The" 213
Ladies National Association for
    The Repeal of the Contagious
    Diseases Acts, The 22
Lake, Agnes 126, 141
Lancashire Evening Post 68
Lancet, The 22
language, militant 139
Last Watch of Hero, The (Leighton) 4
Leeds Mercury 3, 209
Leigh, Mary 101, 102, 113, 123, 153, 155,
    171–173, 205
Lennox, Laura 126, 141, 164
Lenton, Lilian 121, 126
Lifshitz, Anna 204
Liverpool
    Kempshall v Holland case 81–82
    WSPU attacks 104
Liverpool Daily Post 225
Liverpool Echo 115
Lloyd George, David 4, 104, 111, 114,
    121, 139, 141, 143, 156, 204
Lloyd, Marie 83, 213
Lock Hospitals 22, 74
Locke, Joyce 121, 126
Lody, Carl Hans 179
London
    Birth Control International Infor-
        mation Centre (BCIIC) 211, 212

Bryant and May match girls strike
    33, 34
International Birth Control Con-
    ference (1922) 204
Jack the Ripper 9, 34, 49
Kitty with theater 50, 54, 70, 74,
    76, 79, 84, 91, 107, 108
Kitty's arrival 41
music halls 43, 44, 45, 61, 62
WSPU attacks 3, 4, 99, 101, 104,
    115, 117, 119, 121, 171
London County Council 100, 108
London Telegraph 127
Longshore-Potts, Dr. Mary 77
Lover's Guide to Courtship and Marriage,
    The 214
Lusitania, RMS 188
Lytton, Lady Constance 104, 106, 107,
    110, 171; 186, 189

Ma Mac 160, 176
mailbox attacks 4, 115, 118, 121, 140,
    153
Malthus, Thomas 25, 216
Manchester, WSPU attacks in 3–5, 10,
    24, 76, 89, 90, 93, 107, 122, 167
Manesta, Evelyn 4
Mansell Moullin, Edith 224, 230
Marat, Jean-Paul 149
Maria (Wollstonecraft) 18
Marion, Kitty
    CHARACTER
        anger at injustice 58, 97, 118
        courage 11, 35, 51, 55, 56, 92
        desire to be actress 9, 39, 40,
            43, 75, 79, 92, 95, 109, 177,
            218, 219, 230
        determination 47, 52, 55, 64,
            70, 71, 78, 85, 87, 99, 166,
            193, 230
        independence 24, 45, 49, 81,
            87, 230
        Jack's assessment 78
        loyalty to WSPU 96, 150

Marion, Kitty (*continued*)
    militancy 98, 110, 132, 139, 140, 211
    respectability 53, 219
  LEGACY 25, 211, 223–234
  LIFE IN GERMANY 36, 41, 53, 176, 186, 221
  LIFE IN BRITAIN OUTSIDE WSPU
    with Aunt Dora and family 64, 69, 72
    birth control pamphleteer 211
    with Conny Argus 54, 69
    dance school 49
    Halfords 84–86, 90–92
    immigration to England 38, 49, 176
    leaving Aunt Dora's 69
    music hall work 3, 10, 45, 54, 55, 61, 62, 64, 70, 87, 89, 188, 212, 213, 214
    romances and admirers 66, 212
    sex education 11, 214
    sexual harassment 10, 79, 81, 101, 132, 204
    stage name 74
    VAF meeting 99, 108
  LIFE IN WSPU
    decision to join 195
    Emily and Epsom Derby 13, 153, 155
    Emily's funeral 39, 163, 164
    imprisonments and force-feedings 10, 11, 137, 140, 170
    letters to Asquith 101
    post-prison recuperation 114, 171
    Royal Albert Hall meeting 107
    selling *Votes for Women* 98, 105
    training women in Leicester 172
    violence and vandalism 88, 98
    Aintree 168
    Coolinge 142
    Hurst Park 162–163

    Liverpool 41, 58, 167, 187
    London 9, 16, 40, 49, 55, 59–60
    Lynton 167
    Manchester 5, 24, 107, 167
    Newcastle 88, 91, 104, 153, 173
    St. Leonards-on-Sea 118
    Wrexham 114, 115
    visit to Christabel Pankhurst in France 150
    "Woman's Sunday" march 93
  LIFE IN WARTIME BRITAIN
    deportation 183
    music hall work 43
    police investigation 182
    registration at police station 183
  LIFE IN AMERICA
    American citizenship 207–208
    arrests 98, 101
    arrival and hunt for work 58
    birth control work/activism 5, 10, 27, 195–199, 203, 207, 208, 211, 212, 215, 218
    death 11, 37
    German spy allegations 11, 176, 179, 198
    rejected by birth control movement 213, 215
    trips to Britain 206
    Women's Peace Society 221
  MEMORIES
    autobiography 5, 59, 78, 159, 181, 221, 223, 224, 225, 229, 230, 231
    diary 123
    scrapbooks 28, 137, 142, 165
  OPINIONS/VIEWS
    Davison, Emily Wilding 104, 156, 162, 173, 207, 224
    education 17
    justification for violence 201
    marriage 66, 79
    Sanger, Margaret 11
    sex 9, 10, 15, 20, 25, 47
    sex education 11

sexual harassment 10, 12, 79, 81, 100, 101, 132, 204, 226, 232
the stage 47, 53
women's rights 9
WSPU 3
RELATIONSHIPS
  Argus, Conny 54
  aunts 38, 60
  dance school pupils 50
  father 16, 34–39, 41, 47, 75, 84, 91
  friends in theater groups 212
  grandparents 36, 221
  Halford, Bernard 85
  Halford, Robert 43, 45, 84
  male admirers 24, 25, 212
  Roger, Louise 176
  Sanger, Margaret 11, 20
  stepmother 18, 35–37
  suffragettes 3, 5, 10–11, 20, 95–99, 101, 106, 108, 112, 115
  Thorburn, Marion Alice 178–180, 184, 199
  Uncle Heinrich 38, 40
Markievicz, Constance 208
Marlborough, Charles Spencer, 9th Duke 191
Marlborough, Duchess Consuelo Vanderbilt 191
Married Love (Stopes) 212, 217
Married of Both Sexes of the Working People, The (Place) 25
Married of Both Sexes, The (Place) 25
Marsh, Charlotte 102
Marshall, E. K. 210
Marsham, Mr. 124
Martin, Selina 104
martyrdom
  female examples
    Corday, Charlotte 148, 150
    Davison, Emily Wilding 151, 158, 165
    Hibbins, Ann 147
    Hypatia of Alexandria 145, 146
    Joan of Arc 120, 156, 162, 165
    Saint Euphemia 146
  pointlessness 145, 152
  power 145
match girls strike 33, 34
McGuirk, Marcella Gertrude 138
McKenna, Reginald 137, 142, 150, 177, 180, 185, 186, 192
McKenzie, Elsie 187, 188
#MeToo campaign 227, 228
Mill, John Stuart 25, 26, 93
Mindell, Fania 194
Monroe, Marilyn 228
Moore, Mrs. 125
Morning Post 158
Morpeth Herald 104
Mourey, Mr. and Mrs. 189, 193, 194
Mrs. Pankhurst's Army 139
Munby, A. J. 46
Munro, Jack 87
music halls
  desire for work in 10
  public opinion of female performers 153
  sexual freedom 25, 46, 215, 216
  sexual harassment/assault 10, 12, 79, 81, 100, 101, 108, 132, 204, 226, 227, 232
  star earning power 43, 55
  success 43
My Own Story (E. Pankhurst) 163, 215

National Union of Women's Suffrage Societies 10
Nazi Germany 221
Nelson, Emily 45
Neo-Malthusian and Birth Control Conference (1922) 204
New, Miss 124
New York Times, The 226, 227
New Yorker, The 227
Newcastle upon Tyne
  prison 102
  WSPU attacks in 102

Nichols, Mary Ann 9, 34
Norris, Fanny 45
Northern Echo 65
Norwich Evening News 134
Nottingham Evening Post 61
Nottingham Journal 225
Nottingham Theatre Company 84
Nym Mayhall, Laura E. 229

Orestes of Alexandria 146
Oxford University 152
Oxfordshire, WSPU attacks in 123

Pall Mall Gazette 121, 155
Pankhurst, Adela 125
Pankhurst, Christabel
    advice to Kitty before war 183
    arrogance 155
    birth control 200
    Emily Wilding Davison, aban-
        donment of 80
    Emily Wilding Davison's death
        156, 164, 165
    Emily Wilding Davison's funeral
        163
    emigration to America 207
    France, living in 119
    French revolutionary spirit 70
    indifference to suffering of activ-
        ists 110, 125, 213, 224
    Joan of Arc 120, 156, 162, 165
    Kitty's meeting with 206
    letter to Kitty 182
    media, use of 179
    sacrifice and loyalty, demand for
        96, 150
    Suffragette, The (newspaper) 119,
        120, 122, 126, 136, 137, 154, 157,
        158, 164, 195, 200
    violence and vandalism 103–104,
        110–113, 115, 117–120
    Young Hot Bloods 141
Pankhurst, Emmeline
    arrests 141, 163–164, 172

death 163
dismissal of Kitty 207
Emily Wilding Davison's funeral
    164
force-feeding 163
friendship with Annie Besant 215
Glasgow meeting 205
militancy 98, 110, 132, 139, 140, 211
Royal Albert Hall meeting 107
WSPU, founding of 195
Pankhurst family 10
Pankhurst, Sylvia
    arrests 120
    Emily Wilding Davison 121, 139,
        141, 156, 173
    refusal to marry 209
    violence's impact on WSPU
        members 103, 126
    WSPU violence 132
    Young Hot Bloods 141
Paradise Lost (Milton) 19
Paré, Ambroise 28
Pathé 118, 119, 159
Performer 109
Pethick, Dorothy 102–103
Pethick-Lawrence, Emmeline 93, 94,
    132, 164, 173, 209
Pethick-Lawrence, Frederick 93
Physical, Sexual and Natural Religion
    (Drysdale) 27
Pine, Mrs. ("Piney") 200, 210
Place, Francis 25, 216
Planned Parenthood 35, 204
police
    attack on WSPU leadership 98
    bomb disposal 128
    brutality 13, 130
    playing down WSPU violence 96,
        101, 110
    raids on WSPU 129
    records 128
pornography 28, 46
power of men 70
Pratt, Miriam 132, 135, 136

Prisoners (Temporary Discharge for Ill Health) Act (1913) 130, 186
prostitution 21, 23

Quinn, Police Superintendent 183

railways, WSPU attacks on 4, 104, 118, 120, 121, 122, 128, 136, 141, 167, 172
Redmond, John Edward 113
Reflections on the Revolution in France (Burke) 16
Richardson, Mary 107, 126, 128, 156–158, 167, 170, 173
Rigby, Mrs. 138
Robespierre, Maximilien 148
Roger, Louise 176–177
Rosslyn Chapel, WSPU attack on 172

Sanders, Beatrice 126, 141, 164
Sanger, Margaret
    abandonment of Kitty 20
    Brownsville family planning clinic 194
    Carnegie Hall Mass Meeting 195
    International Birth Control Conference (1922) 204
    Kitty to work in London 40–41
    Kitty's admiration 18
    Kitty's release from jail 196
    lovers 207
    Woman Rebel 197
Saturday Review 21
Schäfer, Gustav (Kitty's father) 35–40, 224
Schäfer, Heinrich (Kitty's uncle) 38, 40
Schäfer, Katherine Marie *see* Marion, Kitty
Schäfer, Lena (Kitty's mother) 224
Secret Places of the Heart, The (Wells) 207
sex
    age of consent 20, 44

    false Victorian history 9, 12, 18, 19, 28
    female enjoyment 9, 11, 198, 214, 230
    feminism's fear of 10, 216
    male irresponsibility, accepted 79, 132
    pornography 28, 46
    respectability 20, 64
sex education
    Art of Begetting Handsome Children, The (anon.) 28
    Dr. Teller's Pocket Companion 214
    Etiquette of Marriage 214
    Fruits of Philosophy (Knowlton) 26, 29, 213, 214
    Longshore-Potts's lectures 77
    Lover's Guide to Courtship and Marriage, The 214
    Physical, Sexual and Natural Religion (Drysdale) 27
    Place's handbills 25–26
    Sanger's work 214
    see also birth control movement
sexual agency, female 30, 213, 217
sexual harassment/assault
    "Black Friday" 110
    continuing problem 15
    Gardiner and Goldstein case 43–44
    in Hollywood 226, 227
    Kitty's experiences 9–10, 66, 75, 81, 90, 100
    London Country Council's refusal to investigate 100, 108
    #MeToo campaign 227–228
    in music halls 43, 45, 47, 64, 67
    in Parliament 101, 110
    right to work without 58, 86, 132
sexually transmitted diseases (STDs) 21, 22, 74, 217
Shelley, Harriet 18
Shelley, Mary Godwin 18
Shelley, Percy Bysshe 18

Sibylla Delphica (Burne-Jones) 4

Smedley, Agnes 203

Smith, Mary 93

Smith, Thomas Wood 167

Smyth, Ethel 121

Society for the Suppression of Vice
    27, 46, 196

Somerset, WSPU attacks in 65, 71

Sophie, Duchess of Hohenberg 175

South Wales Daily News 61

spies, German 179

St. James Gazette 61

Stage, The 70

Stopes, Marie 27, 212, 217

Stride, Elizabeth 9, 34

subjugation, female 16, 24, 215

Suffragette Fellowship Collection 229

suffragette movement
    in America 187, 190
    birth control, rejection of 218, 219
    Conciliation Bill "torpedoed" 111,
        123
    "Deeds, Not Words" campaign
        10, 102
    early pioneers 215
    growth 201, 218
    National Union of Women's Suf-
        frage Societies 10
    sanitized history 118, 223
    views on sex 140
    violence *see* violence and vandal-
        ism by WSPU
    women as survivors and fighters
        140
    Women's Social and Political
        Union (WSPU) *see* Women's
        Social and Political Union
        (WSPU)
    see also feminism

Suffragette Movement, The (S.
    Pankhurst) 132

Suffragette, The (newspaper) 119, 120,
    122, 126, 136, 137, 154, 157, 158, 164,
    195, 200

"suffragette outrages" 4, 104, 120, 137,
    164

Surrey
    Kitty with theater 166
    WSPU attacks in 121, 163, 166

Tableaux Vivants 46, 47

terrorism 7, 127, 131, 139; *see also*
    bomb and arson attacks, WSPU;
    violence and vandalism by WSPU

Thorburn, Charles 177

Thorburn, Marion Alice 178–180,
    184, 199

Tunks, Florence 171

Twohey, Megan 226

university degree gender bar 152

Vigar-Harris, Henry 41

Vindication of the Rights of Men (Woll-
    stonecraft) 16

Vindication of the Rights of Woman, A
    (Wollstonecraft) 15, 17, 96, 148

violence and vandalism by WSPU
    American views on 98
    bomb and arson attacks *see* bomb
        and arson attacks, WSPU
    causing schism 119
    chemical attacks 1, 118, 120
    communication systems,
        destruction of 118, 121, 233
    cost to women involved 18, 99,
        111, 132, 150, 155, 159, 190, 194,
        234
    death threats to British public
        138
    escalation 115, 121, 141
    forgotten by history 7, 8, 173
    Germany's use 34
    glass smashing 4, 169
    guns 103, 117, 122, 172, 187, 192, 205
    justification 19, 149, 159, 201
    letter attacks 11
    media coverage and reaction 179

physical harm caused 98
police responses 1, 3, 11, 34, 50,
    69, 92, 98, 101, 110, 114, 127–129,
    131–136
public reaction 131
railway attacks 4, 104, 118, 120, 121,
    122, 128, 136, 141, 167, 172
response to police raids and
    arrests 138
on specific ministers 114, 137, 227
support for 103
threat to public 123
Young Hot Bloods 125–127, 129,
    141, 153, 159, 175
violence by other women's groups
    130, 216
Votes for Women newspaper 98, 114,
    119, 195

Wald, Lillian 189
Walton-Evans, Edith 95
Walton, Olive 171
Ward, William 134
Weinstein, Harvey 226–228
Wells, H. G. 206, 207
Werthcimer, Mr. 63, 65, 67
West, Margaret 135
Western Gazette 138
Western Mail, The 82
Wharton, Edith 46
White, Corporal Billie 76
Williams, Mrs. 184, 186
Wilson, Field Marshal Sir Henry
    204
"Wink the Other Eye" (Lloyd) 83
Wollstonecraft, Mary 15–18, 20, 24,
    30, 31, 96, 148, 216
Women's Peace Society 221
"Woman's Sunday" march (1908) 93
Women's Freedom League 125, 187
"Women's Marseillaise" 96, 108, 140,
    166
Women's Social and Political Union
    (WSPU) 3, 10, 93, 164

1908 Royal Albert Hall meeting
    107
administration 199
anthem 96
attraction 129
"Black Friday" 110
colors 94, 99, 100, 107, 120, 143
death threats 139, 140, 150, 153,
    158, 159
"Deeds, Not Words" motto 10, 102
Emily Wilding Davison, aban-
    donment of 80
Emily Wilding Davison's funeral
    39, 163, 164
force-feedings in prison 11, 117,
    163, 172
Hampstead Town Hall meeting
    117
House of Commons rush 98, 101
Hunger Strike medals 165
hunger strikes in prison 107, 117,
    141, 165, 166
militancy 98, 110, 132, 139, 140,
    211
Mrs. Pankhurst's Army 139
Raid on Parliament (1909) 101
reaction to end of Conciliation
    Bill 111, 123
schism 119
suffragette identity 94
"Suffragettes Index Names of
    Persons Arrested 1906–1914,"
    173
violence and vandalism *see*
    violence and vandalism by
    WSPU
Votes for Women newspaper 98, 114,
    119, 195
window-smashing campaign 112,
    113, 117, 119, 153
"Woman's Sunday" march (1908)
    93
Young Hot Bloods 125–127, 129,
    141, 153, 159, 175

Wood, Marmaduke 65
Wood, Walter 182
Woodlock, Patricia 102
working conditions 24, 25, 33
Wright, Ada 186
Wyllie, Sir William Curzon
   125

Yates, Rose Lamartine 186
Yorkshire
   Kitty with theater 205
   WSPU attacks 205
Yorkshire Evening Post 126
Young Hot Bloods 125–127, 129, 141,
   153, 159, 175

Picture Acknowledgments